...LIAMENT:
M... ...COUNTABLE

Report of the Hansard Society Commission
on parliamentary scrutiny

The Hansard Society

Recent publications

Race and Representation:
Ethnic Pluralism and Candidate Selection in British Political Parties
Dr Shamit Saggar

Dr Saggar examines the issues surrounding race and representation in UK politics, the impact of work by groups such as Operation Black Vote and makes a series of recommendations for change.

The People have Spoken: Who votes and who doesn't
Virginia Gibbons (editor)

A range of experts explore what 'voter apathy' means for politics, representation and election results.

New Media and Social Inclusion
Dr Stephen Coleman and Emilie Normann

In March 2000 the Hansard Society initiated an 'online consultation' for survivors of domestic violence. This report examines the innovative use of new communication technologies to link citizens to the parliamentary process and provides a guide to running web-based consultations.

Women at the Top 2000: Cracking the public sector glass ceiling
Dr Karen Ross

The Hansard Society's *Women at the Top*, published in 1990, looked at the position of women in public life. This new publication re-assesses the situation a decade on.

Making the Law:
The report of the Commission on the Legislative Process

First published in 1993 this highly influential report addressed concerns about the way in which legislation is made in Britain. A number of its recommendations have since been implemented and it continues to influence the process of reform.

The Hansard Society

In addition to its publications, the Society organises seminars and conferences for politicians, academics and opinion-formers, as well as anyone with an interest in democracy, to discuss the key issues of parliament and government.

For further information or to receive a regular briefing on the Society's work please contact us at:

The Hansard Society,
St Philips Building North,
Sheffield Street, London WC2A 2EX
e-mail: hansard@hansard.lse.ac.uk
Website: www.hansardsociety.org.uk

HANSARD
SOCIETY

PROMOTING EFFECTIVE PARLIAMENTARY DEMOCRACY

THE CHALLENGE FOR PARLIAMENT: MAKING GOVERNMENT ACCOUNTABLE

Report of the Hansard Society Commission on parliamentary scrutiny

Chaired by Rt Hon Lord Newton of Braintree

Vacher Dod Publishing Limited

Published by Vacher Dod Publishing Limited
1 Douglas Street
London SW1P 4PA

Tel: 020 7828 7256
Fax: 020 7828 7269
E-mail: politics@vacherdod.co.uk
Website: www.politicallinks.co.uk

Hansard Society
St Philips Building North
Sheffield Street
London WC2A 2EX

Tel: 020 7955 7459
Fax: 020 7955 7492
E-mail: hansard@hansard.lse.ac.uk
Website: www.hansardsociety.org.uk

ISBN 0 905702 31 X

Database typesetting by Vacher Dod Publishing Limited

Printed in Great Britain by The Cromwell Press, Trowbridge, Wiltshire

Contents

Introduction   vii

Executive summary   x

1. The changing role of Parliament: New forms of accountability   1

2. Building a culture of scrutiny in the Commons   14

3. Reforming the select committees   29

4. Restoring the centrality of the Commons chamber   46

5. Parliament and financial scrutiny   60

6. Scrutiny, accountability and the second chamber   70

7. Two-way communication: Parliament and the outside world   78

8. Parliament at the apex   89

Conclusions and recommendations   107

Appendices   114

    Appendix 1 – The theory and practice of parliamentary accountability   114

    Appendix 2 – Written evidence submitted to the Commission   123

    Appendix 3 – Meetings of the Commission   125

    Appendix 4 – Survey of MPs: The effectiveness of Parliament, parliamentary roles and workloads   128

    Appendix 5 – Survey of the subject-matter of House of Commons Select Committee Reports; Sessions 1997–98 and 1998–99   156

    Appendix 6 – Financial Procedures   174

Bibliography   179

Index   187

Introduction

The Commission on Parliamentary Scrutiny was established by the Hansard Society in September 1999. It was given an eighteen month brief to examine "how Parliament carries out its role as scrutineer of the words and actions of the Executive and assess whether the structure and processes are in need of change." The Hansard Society has set up a number of similar Commissions in recent years, to examine issues such as the electoral system, party funding and the regulation of privatised utilities.[1] In 1993 the Commission led by Lord Rippon of Hexham published its report on Parliament and the legislative process, *Making the Law.*[2] *The Challenge for Parliament* examines Parliament's non-legislative functions and how effectively Parliament holds Government to account.

The Challenge for Parliament highlights some of the problems with the way in which Parliament currently performs its scrutiny and accountability functions. The report makes a series of recommendations designed to place Parliament at the apex of a range of scrutiny mechanisms, enabling it to draw more effectively on the technical expertise of outside bodies and engage more fully with issues of public concern. The Commission firmly believes that Parliament must adapt quickly if it is to retain its centrality to British politics and be effective in holding Government to account.

Method of inquiry and research

The Committee's research was conducted through a series of private meetings and seminars as well as written evidence. It was decided at an early stage that the Commission would not take oral evidence in public. Given the sensitive nature of the subject and the fact that the most useful evidence would come from MPs, ministers, whips and civil servants the Commission believed that hearings would be more productive if they were held in private, on a 'Chatham House rule' basis.

During the eighteen months of investigation the Commission held meetings with the Leader of the House of Commons, Rt Hon Margaret Beckett MP, her then shadow, Rt Hon Sir George Young MP, and the Liberal Democrat spokesperson on constitutional matters, Robert Maclennan MP. The Commission had private sessions with the Liaison Committee, former ministers, the clerks of both Houses, senior civil servants and experts on European matters. The Commission also met individually backbench MPs, committee members, whips and ministers. The Commission published a consultation paper which was distributed to every MP and peer, as well as to around 800 individuals and organisations. The full list of contributors and participants is included in appendices 2 and 3.

The Commission met in plenary at least every two months for the duration of the Commission's work. However, at an early stage the Commission was split into three sub-groups, responsible for investigating the role of the chamber, the role of select committees and financial accountability. These sub-groups met once a month and took evidence for the first six months of 2000.

[1] Hansard Society, (1976, republished and updated 1998), *The Report of the Hansard Society Commission on Electoral Reform*, Hansard Society, London. Hansard Society, (1981), *Paying for Politics, Report of the Commission on the Financing of Political Parties*, Hansard Society, London. Hansard Society, (1996), *The Report of the Commission on the Regulation of Privatised Utilities*, Chaired by John Flemming FBA, Hansard Society/European Policy Forum, London
[2] Hansard Society, (1992), *Making the Law: Report of the Hansard Society Commission on the Legislative Process*, Hansard Society, London

The Commission was keen that the work should include a comparative dimension and not focus solely on Westminster. The Commission visited the Scottish Parliament early in its investigations and received valuable advice from officials from the Scottish Parliament and the Executive as well as from MSPs and ministers. We are also grateful to the Commonwealth Parliamentary Association and the Inter-Parliamentary Union for their help and advice.

The Commission published three discussion papers during its lifetime which reflected some of the interim conclusions of the sub-groups. These papers were *Systematic Scrutiny: Reforming the Select Committees*, *Creating a working Parliament: Reforming the Commons Chamber*, and *Parliament and the Public Purse: Improving Financial Scrutiny*.

The Commission conducted a survey of MPs' attitudes to Parliament during the summer of 2000. Every MP was sent a questionnaire asking them about their activity in the Commons and the effectiveness of the different methods of scrutiny. We received responses from 179 MPs and the results provide an internal perspective on the working of Parliament and inform many of the Commission's recommendations. The full findings are contained in appendix 4. The questionnaire was sent to Members with a covering letter from the then Speaker, Rt Hon Betty Boothroyd MP. The Commission is grateful to the former Speaker and her staff for their help.

The Commission is indebted to many of the staff of the Houses of Parliament. The report contains a detailed analysis of select committee activity during the 1997–8 and 1998–9 sessions. This work was compiled by a House of Commons clerk. His work provided a useful overview of the work of the select committees which would not otherwise have been available and we are very grateful to him. We would also like to thank the staff who kindly counted the number of MPs in the Commons chamber at set times.

The Commission secretariat would especially like to thank the Parliament and Constitution section of the House of Commons Library, in particular Barry Winetrobe, Oonagh Gay, Aileen Walker and Pat Strickland. Each of these provided valuable advice and support during the Commission's work for which we are very grateful. We would also like to thank Professor John McEldowney of Warwick University, for his contribution to the Commission's work.

Acknowledgements

The report was drafted by Greg Power, the Commission's secretary, and Alex Brazier, clerk to the Commission. They were ably supported by the research work of Angela Smith-Hughes. In addition, the Commission was assisted throughout their investigations by four clerks from Parliament. The Commission would like to thank them for their invaluable technical advice and support.

The Hansard Society is very grateful to the Nuffield Foundation who funded the Commission's work.

Membership of the Commission

Chair: Rt Hon Lord Newton of Braintree

Zeinab Badawi
Rt Hon Alan Beith MP
Professor Alice Brown
Lord Burns, GCB
Anna Coote
Professor Robert Hazell (vice-chair)
Robert Jackson MP
Kate Jenkins
Margaret Moran MP
Greg Power (secretary)
Steve Richards
Peter Riddell (vice-chair)
Dr Ann Robinson
Jill Rutter
Professor Colin Seymour-Ure
Lord Sawyer

Clerk to the Commission: Alex Brazier

Executive Summary

Parliament has been left behind by far-reaching changes to the constitution, government and society in the past two decades. Despite recent innovations, particularly in the handling of legislation, the central question of Westminster's scrutiny of the executive has not been addressed. Parliament performs a unique role in any representative democracy. It is the principal means for holding Government to account between general elections on behalf of the public. Parliament should provide a permanent monitor of the work of Government, regularly call ministers to explain their actions and, where necessary, seek remedial action.

The Commission examined the strengths and weaknesses of the various ways in which the Commons and Lords pursue accountability – through debates, ministerial statements, questions, select committee inquiries and the work of the Parliamentary Commissioner for Administration (the Ombudsman) and the National Audit Office. The Commission also examined the many non-parliamentary ways by which Government is scrutinised – through the courts, judicial inquiries, regulators and inspectors.

Serious gaps and weaknesses in the working of accountability were found. Scrutiny of Government by MPs and peers is neither systematic nor rigorous. The quality of information provided to Parliament is variable. Parliamentary inquiries have a poor record in locating responsibility for failures by the Executive, ensuring that the Government acts upon them and in following up recommendations for improvement. A survey of MPs' views carried out especially for the Commission[3] showed that Members themselves are sceptical about Parliament's ability to hold Government to account.

The Challenge for Parliament sets out a vision of how a reformed Parliament might work. Its central theme is that Parliament should be at the apex of a system of accountability – drawing more effectively on the investigations of outside regulators and commissions, enhancing the status of select committees and clarifying the role of Parliament and its politicians. The various activities of MPs and peers in the committees and chambers of both Houses should be better co-ordinated so that they complement each other in the pursuit of accountability. But, crucially, Parliament must reflect and articulate issues of public concern. Making Government accountable is a task undertaken by Parliament on behalf of the electorate with the aim of improving the quality of government. Parliament must respond to, and highlight, the most pressing political issues in a manner that the public understands.

The Commission's seven principles for reform

Our report sets out seven principles designed to achieve these objectives, which are supplemented by a series of detailed recommendations. The recommendations appear at the end of each chapter. The entire list of recommendations is included at the end of the report. The Commission's seven central principles for improving scrutiny are:

---

[3] See Appendix 4

Parliament at the apex

Parliament alone cannot guarantee accountability. Politicians do not have the time, resources or expertise to keep a close watch on anything as large, fragmented or complicated as modern government. However an array of independent regulators, commissions and inspectors responsible for monitoring the delivery of government services now exists outside Parliament. Parliament should be at the apex of this system of scrutiny. It should provide a framework for their activity and use their investigations as the basis on which to hold ministers to account. This is the central theme of the report, outlined in chapter one and more fully developed in the report's final chapter. Our recommendations aim to create a more formal and organised relationship between those outside bodies and Parliament, to promote more systematic scrutiny by both the Commons and the Lords.

Parliament must develop a culture of scrutiny

The Commission believes that MPs are unclear about their duties and, in particular, about how they can and should hold the executive to account. Vigorous scrutiny depends on politicians using the tools already available. That requires them to understand the unique role and potential of Parliament. *The Challenge for Parliament* is based on the belief that changes in the attitudes and behaviour of politicians themselves are as important as changes in the working of Parliament.

Parliament lacks a corporate ethos which promotes collective functions such as accountability. Members of the Commons have to balance a number of competing roles of varying significance – representing the interests of their political party and constituency as well as performing their parliamentary duties. Parliament should provide the means and opportunity for MPs to reconcile these diverse and conflicting roles. Party loyalties and demands need to be balanced with scrutinising the executive and holding government to account. Scrutiny should be an integral part of the work of every MP.

Committees should play a more influential role within Parliament

The Commission regards the system of select committees as the principal vehicle for promoting this culture of scrutiny and improving parliamentary effectiveness. The introduction of the departmental select committees in 1979 enhanced the ability of Parliament to scrutinise and hold ministers to account. The committees provide a means for monitoring and keeping a permanent eye on the work of government departments and agencies. Select committees can filter, and highlight, the work of other, external scrutiny bodies. The system should now be extended and developed so that they make a more significant contribution to parliamentary business and to the work of every MP.

The role of the committees needs to be more closely defined, so that each has a set of core responsibilities and a set of certain pre-agreed and public goals. Their reach should be extended to provide regular scrutiny of regulators, executive agencies, quangos and the like. Committee structures should adapt to new methods of work through sub-committees and perhaps the use of rapporteurs. In return, committee service should provide rewards for MPs – chairing a select committee needs to be recognised as a political position comparable to being a minister, and be paid accordingly. In addition, the committees should be given the staffing and resources needed to oversee the areas for which they are responsible.

The chamber should remain central to accountability

The chamber should remain the forum where ministers are held to account for the most important and pressing issues of the day. The chamber is the public face of the House of Commons and therefore the main means of informing and persuading the wider electorate. The structure and content of business in the chamber should reflect this important role. Reforms should aim to improve public interest, attendance and the influence of the floor of the Commons. The Commission believes that the scrutiny value of many lengthy debates is questionable. There should be more short debates and more opportunities for questions in the chamber. MPs should have the opportunity to question ministers on recent select committee reports. The Opposition and backbench MPs should have more opportunities to call ministers to account through ministerial statements or Private Notice Questions. There should be an opportunity for short cross-party 'public interest debates'. In short, the chamber should be more responsive to issues of public concern.

Financial scrutiny should be central to accountability

The Commons has a unique legal role in the authorisation of tax and spending proposals and therefore a special responsibility to scrutinise them. MPs have a responsibility to the public to ensure that the Government provides value for money in what it spends and that the money is spent wisely. At present, the Commons fails to perform this role in either a systematic or an effective manner. Financial scrutiny should be central to the work of the Commons since it underpins all other forms of accountability. The procedures of the Commons need to be adapted to ensure that all committees, and hence all MPs, have the scope and resources to ensure proper financial accountability.

The House of Lords should complement the Commons

For the most part *The Challenge for Parliament* concentrates on improving the efficacy of the House of Commons. At the time of writing, the future composition and role of the Lords is still uncertain and future changes to its structure and composition will inevitably affect what the House does. But whatever happens to the Lords, the Commission believes that it has an important role to play in holding the Government to account. The primary focus, particularly on financial matters, should still be the Commons. But the Lords plays a valuable role in complementing the scrutiny work of the Commons.

All the political parties are committed to a second chamber where no single party has an overall majority. Because of this, the second chamber provides a different perspective on accountability. It is likely to have a less adversarial approach and take a longer view of policy and administration. The Commission also believes that the Lords has a significant role to play in the scrutiny of issues which cross departmental boundaries. Where the Commons committees are tied to departments and ministries the Lords has proved itself effective in examining broader issues, for example, Europe or science and technology. It should have specific responsibility for ethical, constitutional and social issues for which the Commons has insufficient time. This though will require closer co-operation and co-ordination between the two Houses.

Parliament must communicate more effectively with the public

Parliament is at its strongest when it articulates and mobilises public opinion – both Houses need to improve their communication with, and responsiveness to, the public. Whereas Government, the political parties and individual MPs are attuned to media requirements, Parliament is not. Reforms are required at a number of levels. Parliament needs to adapt its procedures and hours to improve media coverage and make parliamentary business more comprehensible to voters. A designated press office should maintain media interest and co-ordinate select committee publicity. Committees themselves could improve their public profile and the range of their consultations by making greater use of the internet. A Petitions Committee would provide another channel for communication and might alert MPs earlier to issues of public concern. Overall, Parliament must improve its ability to respond.

The report is designed as a challenge to MPs and peers at the start of a new Parliament, at a stage when they are looking ahead and starting afresh on the work of scrutiny. The Commission recognises what the Select Committees – and, in particular, the Liaison Committee – have done in recent years. The report seeks to take forward some of the new ideas for change. But the Commission can only make suggestions. It is up to MPs and peers to give Parliament a more central role.

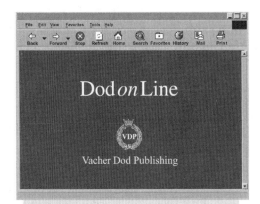

Chapter One

The changing role of Parliament:
New forms of accountability

1.1 Parliament performs a unique role in any parliamentary democracy. It provides the principal means by which the Government is held to account for its activities. However, the role of Parliament is changing. The size and complexity of modern government means that it is no longer possible for Parliament alone to ensure accountability across the wide range of activities of central departments, let alone the myriad of other public sector bodies. If it is to be effective in performing its core functions, Parliament must adapt.

1.2 The expansion of government since the early twentieth century has resulted in new mechanisms for the delivery of services. The bulk of government activity is now carried out through arms-length executive agencies, quangos and the like. Powers have been ceded by Westminster to other political institutions – in Brussels, Edinburgh, Cardiff, and Belfast. At the same time there has been a greater concentration of power within Whitehall around the office of the Prime Minister.

1.3 As Parliament's ability to achieve accountability has been called into question, there has been an increased use of the mechanisms of direct democracy, such as citizens' juries and focus groups. The expansion in the scope of regulators of privatised utilities, inspectors, commissions, ombudsmen, and even the Citizen's Charter have changed the public's understanding of what accountability means.

1.4 Government decisions are also increasingly being challenged outside Parliament – in the courts for example. Meanwhile, pressure groups and non-governmental organisations regularly question Government policy. But the biggest change has been the much greater role and influence of the mass media on the conduct and communication of politics.

1.5 These developments have provided opportunities as well as challenges for Parliament. MPs and peers now have a much greater and more diverse range of information available on which to question Government. However, Parliament has failed to adapt sufficiently and is, in many respects, the least reformed part of the British constitution. The role of Parliament needs to be clarified in the light of these changes. There are certain functions that Parliament alone can perform.

Defining accountability

1.6 The House of Commons is the main means by which the Government is held to account between general elections – ensuring that departments are run efficiently and effectively by providing oversight and calling ministers to account. However, there is no agreement, or clear definition, about how Parliament should perform this role or what it should achieve. In practice, accountability has been confused with the ill-defined and often muddled doctrine of ministerial responsibility. The goals of efficient and effective government have often been lost in the party battle over whether a minister should resign. Attempts to clarify Parliament's role have challenged the widespread view that accountability is tied up with ministerial resignation[4]. Following lengthy inquiries, both Houses of Parliament passed resolutions on a code of conduct for ministerial accountability just before the 1997 election. These have placed much greater emphasis on information and explanation, but there is little evidence since then that Parliament's ability to secure accountability has been strengthened.

1.7   Accountability requires Parliament not only to secure explanations from ministers but also to influence Government decisions. This might take a variety of forms, ranging from a ministerial commitment to review an administrative error or direct remedial action. The Commission believes that ministerial accountability in its many forms relies on MPs' ability to enforce both the spirit and the letter of the 1997 parliamentary resolution.

1.8   It will always be difficult to pin down responsibility and there will always be loopholes which can never be guaranteed by a parliamentary resolution or a ministerial code. Effective scrutiny is achieved when the activity of ministers and civil servants is conditioned by the knowledge of a vigilant Parliament, willing and able to use the powers at its disposal. The Commission believes that if Parliament is to perform its core function of holding Government to account, MPs have to be more effective, and seen to be more effective, in scrutinising the executive.

The changing structure of Government

The 'agencification' of Government

1.9   The use of arms-length agencies to either advise or deliver government services has been a feature of government for the last 30 years. However, the most significant change to the delivery of government services was the introduction of *Next Steps* in the 1980s and 1990s. The programme involved hiving off civil service functions to new agencies, created "to carry out the executive functions of Government within a policy and resources framework set up by a department."[5] Although they were to be given greater autonomy than while they were part of the Government department they remained responsible to the minister. The introduction of the agencies was designed in part to give a greater managerial freedom to agency chief executives. The *Next Steps* Agencies now account for three quarters of central government activity.[6]

1.10   It was envisaged that this drive for more efficient service delivery would make the task of identifying responsibility much easier than would have been the case within a Government department. Then Prime Minister Margaret Thatcher assured the Commons that there would be,

> ". . . no change in the arrangements for accountability. Ministers will continue to account to Parliament for all the work of their departments, including the work of the agencies. Departmental select committees will be able to examine departmental agencies' activities and agency staff in the same way as they examine departments now."[7]

---

[4] See Appendix 1
[5] Cabinet Office, (1988), *Improving Management in Government*, HMSO, para 19
[6] Weir, S. & Beetham, D., (1999), *Political Power and Democratic Control in Britain*, Routledge: London, p. 193
[7] HC Debs 28 Feb 1988, vol.127, col.1149–51

1.11 This quasi-government is both a challenge and an opportunity for Parliament. Ministers no longer answer directly to Parliament for the activities of their department's various bodies, but this does not mean that they should escape scrutiny by the Commons. However, rigorous scrutiny of the agencies relies on the willingness of the departmental select committees to pursue accountability from the agencies and their chief executives where once they would have questioned the minister. In practice, Parliament has been slow to adapt to the existence of the agencies. In the 1997–8 session of Parliament only 15 of the 117 select committee reports published dealt with the work of executive agencies, in the following session the number was 19 of a total 141.[8] Evidently the growth of the agencies has not been matched by a concomitant growth in parliamentary scrutiny.

Constitutional reform

1.12 Whilst the use of agencies by Government has had an impact on structures of accountability the programme of constitutional reform enacted by the Labour Government after 1997 sought to alter fundamentally the country's democratic processes. In their first Parliament the Government devolved power to Scotland, Wales and Northern Ireland, established the Greater London Authority, incorporated the European Convention on Human Rights into UK Law and enacted Freedom of Information legislation, not to mention the first stage in reforming the House of Lords.

Figure 1A – Constitutional legislation 1997–2000

Referendums (Scotland and Wales) Act 1997
Northern Ireland (Elections Act) 1997
Regional Development Agencies Act 1998
Government of Wales Act 1998
Scotland Act 1998
Northern Ireland Act 1998
Human Rights Act 1998
Greater London Authority Referendum Act 1998
Registration of Political Parties Act 1998
European Parliamentary Elections Act 1999
Greater London Authority Act 1999
House of Lords Act 1999
Freedom of Information Act 2000
Political Parties, Elections and Referendums Act 2000
Representation of the People Act 2000

---

[8] Research for the Commission on Parliamentary Scrutiny, 'Survey of the subject-matter of select committee reports, 1997–8 & 1998–9'. Appendix 5

1.13 Parliament has been slow to adapt its own procedures in the face of these sizeable constitutional reforms. Devolution, for example, means that the new bodies, and specifically the Scottish Parliament, remove responsibility from Westminster for a range of functions, and as the Procedure Committee noted in its report on the *Procedural Consequences of Devolution*[9] there is a degree of confusion as to what can and cannot be discussed in London. Since devolution certain matters are now ruled as inadmissible by the Speaker if they relate to devolved matters. Yet defining the specific ministerial responsibilities of the Scotland Office or Wales Office is not straightforward. There are many issues which overlap, where responsibility is not clear. The fear of some who gave evidence to the Procedure Committee was that this ambiguity would allow ministers in the Westminster Parliament to define those areas where they are willing to answer questions.

1.14 The model for incorporation of the European Convention on Human Rights (ECHR) into British law also has far-reaching effects on the activity of MPs and ministers at Westminster. The model means that Parliament can, if necessary, override judicial concerns that a law is not in keeping with the requirements of the ECHR. Where the judges declare the law to be incompatible with the ECHR, the defective provisions will be referred to a committee of both Houses which will decide whether legislation needs to be amended. The Bill became law in 1999 and came into force in October 2000. However, the joint committee was not established until February 2001 and, at the time of writing, it is not clear how the system will operate in practice.

1.15 As is often the case in such areas it appears that the House of Lords is adapting more quickly to events than the Commons. In February 2001, and following a recommendation of the Royal Commission chaired by Lord Wakeham into reform of the Lords,[10] the House established a new committee to examine issues of constitutional significance. Chaired by Professor the Lord Norton of Louth the committee's remit is to "examine the constitutional implications of all public bills coming before the House; and to keep under review the operation of the constitution."[11] However, given the scale of constitutional reform and its likely impact on Westminster, Parliament's overall response has been limited.

Europe

1.16 British membership of the European Union has undoubtedly blurred the line of accountability from Government to Parliament. The activity of Ministers in the Council of Ministers, for example, is largely beyond the scrutiny of Westminster. The Council of Ministers is the forum in which representatives of all the member-states meet to hammer out European policy. Because of the often sensitive nature of these negotiations the Council meets in private and only a small proportion of what is discussed ever reaches the light of day. Although Ministers are often obliged to report back to the House on their meetings, this only provides an attenuated form of accountability. The greater use of qualified majority voting in the Council (meaning that no single country has a veto) has increased the emphasis on horse-trading and made it even more difficult for Parliament to achieve clarity.

---

[9] Procedure Committee, (1998–9), *The Procedural Consequences of Devolution*, HC 185
[10] Royal Commission on the reform of the House of Lords, (2000), *A House for the Future*, Cm 4534. TSO: London
[11] 'Lords to probe constitution', Press release, 8 February 2001

1.17 This is of course not just a problem for the United Kingdom. Membership of the EU has an effect on all member-states' internal procedures for decision-making and accountability. There have been improvements in the way in which the Commons deals with European matters, for example, by increasing from two to three the number of standing committees dealing with European legislation, extending the scope of scrutiny to cover the second and third 'pillar' issues and allowing Parliament to conduct scrutiny before and after meetings of the Council of Ministers.

1.18 However, there is a sense that MPs, and in particular select committees have not adapted sufficiently to membership of the European Union. Evidence submitted to the Commission by David Millar a former Commons clerk and former director of research at the secretariat of the European Parliament suggested that,

> "With laudable exceptions, select committees have failed the electors by not pointing up the extent to which EU proposals, policies and activities make an impact on a widening range of national policies. . . . committees owe it to the public to illustrate and to comment, clearly and succinctly, on what has been, and is, happening in this regard in the course of scrutinising national policies."[12]

1.19 Although the House of Lords has taken an increasingly important role in monitoring developments within the EU and their impact on the UK, the changes in the Commons have been less dramatic. By comparison with other member-states, notably the Nordic countries, who have overhauled their internal mechanisms for scrutinising ministers more effectively[13] the provisions at Westminster are less comprehensive.

Centre of Government

1.20 The final trend which has characterised the operation of Government over the last thirty years is the centralisation of power within Whitehall and around the Prime Minister's office. Although the developments predate the Labour administration there have been significant changes since 1997. The Performance and Innovation Unit, the Social Exclusion Unit and the Centre for Management and Policy Studies were all established following the 1997 election with a view to providing a more strategic approach to policy making. Inside 10 Downing Street the staff and resources serving the Prime Minister have grown from 71 during Edward Heath's office in June 1970 to 148 in December 1998[14]. Much has also been made of the growing use of political appointees across government, and in particular, the enhanced influence of the policy unit based at 10 Downing Street. Giving evidence to a hearing of the Committee on Public Administration Professor Peter Hennessy commented that we have a Prime Minister's department 'in all but name'.[15]

---

[12] Appendix 2, Evidence 19
[13] See for example the special issue of the *Journal of Legislative Studies*, 'Delegation and Accountability in European Integration' edited by T. Bergman and E. Damgaard, Vol. 6, No. 1, Spring 2000; also, Hayward, J., Ed., (1995), *The Crisis of Representation in Europe*, Frank Cass: London
[14] Kavanagh, D., & Seldon, A., (1999), *The Powers Behind the Prime Minister*, Harper Collins: London, p. 300
[15] 24 May 2000

1.21 The growing influence of the Prime Minister and the Cabinet Office have not been matched by increased parliamentary scrutiny. Research by Burnham and Jones identifies a number of factors which have undermined the accountability of the Prime Minister in the chamber of the Commons.[16] In the first place, Prime Ministerial activity and attendance has declined. There was a marked decline under Major, who made fewer statements or speeches in debates than Wilson or Heath, and answered half the number of questions, including supplementaries, per session as Heath. Apart from Prime Minister's Questions (PMQs) Tony Blair rarely visits the Commons. He led the government in debate on only three occasions in the first two Parliamentary sessions and has attended fewer divisions than any other post-war Prime Minister.

1.22 Burnham and Jones also note John Major's tendency to use a question from a supporter to make what opposition backbenchers suspected was a substitute for a statement, "in a format which denied them the greater chances of questioning the Prime Minister offered by a formal statement to the House."[17] This practice has been continued by Blair, although the number of formal statements to the House has increased.

1.23 Parliament's ability to scrutinise the work of the Prime Minister relies almost entirely on PMQs. However, the accountability value of PMQs is minimal and serves more as a vehicle for the differentiation of the policies of the main political parties. Although the Committee on Public Administration is responsible for examining the work of the Cabinet Office, concerns about the inadequacy of current arrangements for interrogating and securing accountability from the Prime Minister led them to argue that he should appear once or twice a year before a select committee. The rejection by the Prime Minister's office to all such requests suggests that this is unlikely to occur in the near future.

1.24 The effective oversight of Government relies on Parliament keeping pace with changes to the structure and operation of Government. Parliament should provide a shadow for Government activity. However, its response to developments has been inadequate. It has failed to adapt sufficiently and remains, in many ways, the last unreformed part of the constitution. As a result Parliament is not effectively performing its core tasks of scrutinising and holding Government to account.

New forms of accountability and redress

1.25 At the same time as Parliament's effectiveness has increasingly been called into question, a host of complementary mechanisms have evolved which seek to scrutinise the activity of government, its delivery of services, and most recently the public utilities. The extent to which these are the result of parliamentary inadequacy or its cause is debatable, but they do provide an alternative means by which individuals and organisations can seek accountability and redress. However, their effectiveness relies on the effectiveness of Parliament. Their strength lies in supplementing parliamentary activity, not replacing it, so that their technical scrutiny is used as the basis for holding ministers to account. It appears that Parliament has, once again, failed to adapt sufficiently to capitalise on their expertise.

---

[16] Burnham, J., & Jones, G., (2000), *Accounting to Parliament by British Prime Ministers: Trends and Discontinuities; Illusions and Realities*, Paper presented to the PSA 50th Annual Conference, 10–13 April 2000
[17] *Ibid.*, p. 17

1.26 The most obvious new forms of scrutiny and regulation emerged during the 1980s and 1990s with the creation of regulators to oversee the work of the privatised utilities. The whole point of privatisation was to remove these industries from day to day interference by ministers, but since they remained in the main monopolies, continuing regulation was deemed necessary to encourage competition and protect consumers. Although these regulators are formally accountable by statute through ministers to Parliament – via the publication of annual reports and appearances before select committees – the relationship is indirect.

1.27 Other regulators have a similar relationship with Parliament. Ofsted, for example, responsible for maintaining educational standards in state schools is an independent 'non-ministerial government department' responsible for providing advice to the secretary of state for Education and Employment. The Chief Inspector is appointed by the Prime Minister. In 1999 the Education and Employment Committee raised its concerns, arguing for greater parliamentary scrutiny of its work.[18] Yet there are few formal links, scrutiny is still variable and there is no annual debate of Ofsted's work within Parliament.

1.28 Such concerns are shared by the regulators themselves. In evidence to the Commission Sir Ian Byatt, Director General of Ofwat, explained his concerns that Parliament was not making maximum use of the tools available.

> "The complexity and sophistication of the modern society, the economy and technology may make it increasingly difficult for Parliament to fully grasp the impact and outcome of the work of Government. We have been keen to brief and educate MPs on the role of Ofwat and the major issues affecting the water industry. We have, however, been disappointed by the results. Over the past year Ofwat delivered its price review of the industry, which included £15 billion of capital expenditure on treatment works and the infrastructure. The environmental and water quality guidance set by Ministers was subject to limited scrutiny by Parliament"[19]

1.29 Elizabeth France, the Data Protection Commissioner[20], raised similar concerns about the extent to which select committees were drawing on the work of bodies such as the DPC,

> "there appears to be no effective mechanism in place to ensure that all relevant and interested parties are invited to contribute to the deliberations of select committees. . . . Further there does not appear to be a clear mechanism for publicising the future work of select committees. The overall effect of this situation is likely to be that select committees are not taking advantage of a large amount of outside expert advice."[21]

1.30 The content of select committee reports between 1997 and 1999 reflects the low priority given to the work of external regulators with only 21 of the total 258 mentioning their activity.[22]

---

[18] Education and Employment Select Committee, (1998–9), Fourth Report, *The Work of Ofsted*, HC 62-I
[19] Appendix 2, Evidence 25
[20] Since 30 January 2001, the post has become the Information Commissioner to reflect its responsibilities relating to freedom of information
[21] Appendix 2, Evidence 23
[22] Appendix 5

1.31 The situation was summed up by David Edmonds, the Director General of Oftel who stated that although the process of parliamentary scrutiny was 'probably moderately successful', it was sporadic and unsystematic, "scrutiny is too unpredictable with long intervals between visits. Also accountability to other bodies, especially stakeholders, is increasingly seen as important and this acts to ensure efficient and effective regulatory action."[23]

1.32 Parliament must make better use of the work of others so that its scrutiny is more coherent and systematic or risk being superseded by other non-parliamentary forms of accountability.

1.33 There are areas where Parliament has used other methods of investigation to buttress its activity. Despite limited expectations at its inception in 1967, the Parliamentary Commissioner for Administration (PCA or Ombudsman), has been successful. The office has responsibility for investigating cases of maladministration by public bodies, and has built up a reputation for high calibre investigative research and persuasive argumentation in its reports. The strength to Parliament is that although the PCA is mostly concerned with the investigation and resolution of individual cases of maladministration, MPs are able to use the broader lessons of such cases for the improvement of policy and administration. And despite having few formal powers of redress, its findings carry authority and almost all the PCA's recommendations have been accepted by Government.[24]

1.34 The number of cases referred to the Parliamentary Ombudsman has continued to rise since 1967. Between 1990 and 1999, the number of cases per year increased from 1002 to 2108.[25] The success of the PCA is illustrated by the fact that it has spawned a host of other public and private sector ombudsmen (see figure 1B), so that most of public service is covered by one ombudsman or another. Although there are plans to co-ordinate the system, the vast bulk of information generated by these bodies is not used by Parliament.

Figure 1B – Ombudsmen

Banking Ombudsman*
Building Societies Ombudsman*
Estate Agents Ombudsman
Financial Ombudsman Service (set up by the Financial Services & Markets Act 2000)
Funeral Ombudsman
Health Service Ombudsman
Housing Association Ombudsman Scotland
Independent Housing Ombudsman
Insurance Ombudsman*
Investment Ombudsman*
Legal Services Ombudsman
Local Government Ombudsman
Northern Ireland Ombudsman
Pensions Ombudsman
Personal Insurance Arbitration Service*
Personal Investment Authority Ombudsman*
Police Complaints Authority
Scottish Legal Services Ombudsman (appointed by Sec of State for Scotland)

*to become part of Financial Ombudsman Service when FSM Act 2000 comes into force

---

[23] Appendix 2, Evidence 24
[24] Giddings, P., (1998), 'The Parliamentary Ombudsman: a successful alternative?', in Oliver, D., & Drewry, G., (Eds for the Study of Parliament Group), *The Law and Parliament*, Butterworths: London, p. 128
[25] The Parliamentary Ombudsman, *Annual Report*, 1999–2000, HC 593, p.14

1.35 The success of the Ombudsman system can be viewed as part of a wider trend where accountability is conceived in terms of the individual. Since the introduction of the Citizen's Charter in 1991 there have been an increasing number of public service charters covering health and education which seek to guarantee the rights of the individual and right to redress when things go wrong. At the same time there has been a rapid increase in applications for leave to apply to judicial review, rising from 558 a year in 1981 to 3,208 in 1994.[26] It is difficult to ascertain exact figures on how many cases reach the courts and how many are upheld[27] but the figures show a greater propensity for individuals and organisations to use the courts to challenge government decisions. The fact that the vast majority of cases fall into one of three areas – either crime, immigration or housing – illustrates the extent to which individuals are using this course in order to seek redress from government.

1.36 Such developments have undoubtedly strengthened the public accountability of Government, but as Philip Giddings observes they "suggest that the British cultural preference for the political method of complaint-redress has now changed, reflecting a decline in confidence in our political system and, perhaps especially, our politicians."[28] However, these new forms of accountability should not be viewed as alternatives to Parliament, but as complementary. The work of other regulatory and scrutiny bodies generates a huge amount of information and expert opinion on the performance of Government. They provide new opportunities for Parliament to scrutinise and challenge departments. However, MPs have failed to use these new mechanisms in any systematic way.

The public and Parliament

1.37 It therefore should not be too surprising that levels of confidence in politics are low and declining. The British Social Attitudes Survey shows a declining level of trust in Government over the last 25 years from 39% in 1974 to 16% in 2000, and a similar drop in the number of people who believed the system of Government worked well from 48% in 1973 to 35% in 2000.[29] The ESRC-funded 'Citizen Audit', also showed low levels of support. They asked 3,140 people to rate from 0 to 10 how far they trusted various institutions (0 – do not trust at all, 10 – trust completely). The survey found that 11% did not trust the House of Commons at all, 14% did not trust Government at all, and 16% felt the same way about politicians as a breed.[30]

1.38 Ofwat's evidence to the Commission reflects the tone of many contributions regarding the position and role of Parliament in relation to Government,

---

[26] Weir, S. & Beetham, D., (1999), *op cit.*, p. 446

[27] In response to enquiries from Margaret Hodge MP in 1997 five departments replied that they did not keep such records on grounds of disproportionate cost. One of these was the Home Office which stated that it had been involved in 'several thousand' cases, and estimated that its decisions had been upheld in around 90% of cases. Cited in Weir and Beetham, *ibid.*

[28] Giddings, P., (1998), 'The Parliamentary Ombudsman: a successful alternative?', in Oliver, D., & Drewry, G., (Eds for the Study of Parliament Group), *The Law and Parliament*, Butterworths: London, p. 126

[29] *'Is there a crisis of Democracy?'*, CREST conference, 28 March 2001. Presentation by John Curtice and Roger Jowell

[30] The Commission is extremely grateful to Patrick Seyd of Sheffield University for providing these figures.

> "In examining the role Parliament has to play in this process, it is necessary to recognise the powerful influence of the media and well-organised powerful pressure groups. Increasingly it is these who are leading the process of scrutiny and challenging the accountability of government."[31]

1.39 In many ways Parliament, pressure groups and the media work to reinforce this impression. The media require NGOs and pressure groups to provide non-parliamentary opinions and analysis of government policy. Such analysis will often be the basis for interviewing ministers. Pressure groups themselves use the media effectively to promote their point of view and generate public interest in the issues. Between them they provide a regular challenge to Government decisions. Parliament appears not to have fully adapted to their existence. A submission to the Commission from the Green Party expressed surprise that "Parliament has not yet found a structured and regular manner in which to use the wealth of information and research generated by the various pressure groups and NGOs that now exist."[32]

1.40 Perhaps more significantly, the media has superseded Parliament so that the main arena of British political debate is now the broadcasting studio rather than the chamber of the House of Commons. Parliament rarely sets the agenda for the day's news stories. The style of parliamentary proceedings, the lack of topical debates in the chamber, and the odd hours of the Commons, means that it is not frequently a feature of the daily news bulletins. The quality of debates in the chamber, the length of contributions and the rules which govern them, put them beyond the understanding and interest of most voters. Television allows politicians to communicate directly with voters much more effectively than anything they say in the chamber.

The parliamentary perspective on accountability

1.41 MPs appear to share this view of Parliament's ineffectiveness. As part of the Commission's research a questionnaire was sent to every Member of Parliament, asking for their views on how well they thought Parliament performed in a number of areas, what they thought were the key functions of Parliament, and how they saw their own roles inside and outside Parliament. The results of the survey appear throughout the report and the full results are available in appendix 4.[33]

1.42 MPs were asked to rate Parliament's performance between 1 (very effective) and 5 (not effective at all), and asked "Overall, how effective is Parliament at holding government to account for its actions?", 26.8% thought it was quite or very effective, 40.2% thought it was neither effective nor ineffective, and 31.3% thought it quite or very ineffective. However, in response to the question "How effective is Parliament in scrutinising government activity in the following areas?", as figure 1C shows, MPs share many of the concerns expressed about Parliament's ability in certain core areas.

---

[31] Appendix 2, Evidence 25
[32] Appendix 2, Evidence 9
[33] The survey elicited 179 responses from MPs. 55 Conservative, 101 Labour, 14 Lib Dem, and 9 others.

1.43 MPs appear to be ambivalent about Parliament's efficacy in relation to policy making, public services and expenditure, with opinion evenly divided. However, in most other categories a majority of MPs believed that Parliament is quite or very ineffective. Almost two thirds shared this view about scrutiny of cross-cutting issues and over 78% about the council of ministers. In relation to scrutiny of outside bodies 72.6% thought Parliament was quite or very ineffective at scrutinising the utility regulators, 63.7% thought the same about scrutiny of executive agencies and 81.6% with regard to scrutiny of quangos.

Figure 1C – The effectiveness of Parliament

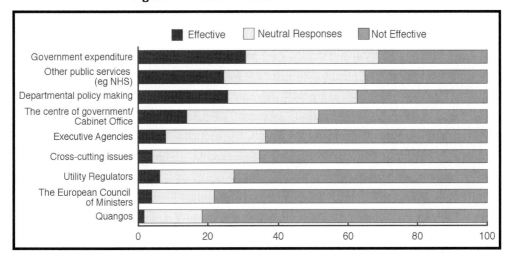

1.44 This verdict from MPs themselves reinforces the impression that Parliament needs to engage more directly with the concerns of the public, draw more systematically on the work of non-parliamentary regulators and inspectorates, and adapt to the changes in the structure of Government.

Clarifying the role of Parliament: Parliament at the apex

1.45 The Commission believes that the effectiveness of Parliament requires a clarification of its role and its relationship to other mechanisms of accountability. Parliament alone cannot guarantee accountability across the entire range of Government activity. Although new forms of scrutiny and accountability have emerged Parliament has a unique role in making their work relevant. Parliament's role is in disentangling the key political issues from technical scrutiny, interpreting their significance and using this as the basis on which to challenge Government. Parliament should be the apex of the system of scrutiny.

1.46 Parliament performs certain functions which cannot be performed by any other institution. On the basis of available evidence Parliament calls ministers to account for their actions. Its role is to seek information and explanation from Government and, where necessary, seek amendatory action. Parliament performs an oversight role ensuring that lessons are learnt and that mistakes are not repeated. It provides political accountability from ministers and civil servants so as to improve the quality of government on behalf of the public.

1.47   Different forms of accountability are now provided by a range of non-parliamentary institutions, but these can only supplement and not replace accountability to Parliament. As the Public Service Committee has noted, accountability might be provided "by Charters, through the Ombudsman, through the courts, even; and we welcome that. Accountability to Parliament should not preclude accountability to the public; and vice versa. Parliament needs to retain and protect its role; and to do so, it has to be more effective in fulfilling it."[34]

1.48   The Commission believes that the effectiveness of Parliament, and the effectiveness of other scrutiny and accountability mechanisms, relies on the interaction between them. Parliament should make all the accountability structures relevant. The reports of the privatised utility regulators, the ombudsman or the Data Protection Commission provide an expertise beyond the scope of Parliament or its committees. However, the impact of these reports on the quality of government, relies to a large extent on Parliament developing their findings and using them in holding the Government to account. Parliament should illuminate the key political issues for the public, by bringing expertise to politics and politics to expertise. In this sense Parliament's job is to add value to the work of others, in so doing it will be more effective in its pursuit of ministerial accountability.

1.49   Parliament should provide the framework for accountability. Parliament's relationship with other bodies needs to be systematised so that they complement one another. This requires parliamentary reform which provides greater direction for MPs and Peers in their work in the chamber and in committee.

Conclusion: The reform of Parliament

1.50   Parliament must adapt to the changed context in which it now operates. Despite the fact that its standing and role have been eroded by events, the pace of parliamentary reform has been slow. It has failed to adapt adequately to the challenges it faces.

1.51   In 1997 the Labour Government established a new 'Modernisation Committee' chaired by the Leader of the House of Commons. Its first report set out its objectives and its desire to examine four specific areas: the legislative process; the accountability of government to Parliament; the parliamentary calendar and procedural changes. Between 1997 and 2000 the Committee published fifteen reports and has achieved some significant changes.[35] Some of its recommendations have been relatively minor and some have simply encouraged (or acknowledged) greater experimentation, rather than formalising procedures into standing orders (see for example HC190 *The Legislative Process*).

---

[34] Public Service Committee, (1995–6), *Ministerial Accountability and Responsibility*, HC 313-I, para 173
[35] Changes include provision of the introduction of a parallel chamber in Westminster Hall, carry-over of bills from one session to the next, changing the hours of Thursday Sittings, greater use of committees to scrutinise draft legislation and programming of bills.

1.52   The history of recent parliamentary reform has been one of improving the efficiency of Parliament, but not its effectiveness. Changes have tended to focus on long overdue and much-needed reforms that improve the working conditions of MPs. However, since the introduction of the departmental select committees in 1979 there has been little attempt to address issues of accountability or the balance of power between Parliament and the Executive. The Modernisation Committee stated in its first report that ministerial accountability was one of the four principle issues it would address. However, despite tackling a number of other subjects,[36] the Committee did not broach the issue. This is despite the continued interest of the Public Administration Committee and, most significantly the reports of the Liaison Committee during 2000.[37]

1.53   The Commission believes that **if Parliament is to improve its effectiveness, reform must be based on underlying principles which improve Parliament's relationship with the public and outside bodies. Parliament needs to be at the apex of the network of regulatory bodies and alternative scrutiny mechanisms.** It should seek to commission work and draw effectively on the findings. However, the changes envisaged in this report are not just a matter of reforming parliamentary procedure but require a more qualitative shift in perceptions of the proper role of Parliament, the ethos of the House of Commons and the role of MPs, and the way in which Parliament interacts with the public and outside organisations.

Principle I – Parliament at the apex

If Parliament is to improve its effectiveness, reform must be based on underlying principles which improve Parliament's relationship with the public and outside bodies. Parliament needs to be at the apex of the network of regulatory bodies and alternative scrutiny mechanisms. (para. 1.53)

---

[36] The Modernisation Committee has published 15 reports since 1997. (2000–2001) *Sittings in Westminster Hall: Report, Proceedings and Appendices of the Committee*, HC 906; (2000–2001) *Thursday Sittings: Report and Proceedings of the Committee* HC 954; (2000–2001), *Programming of Legislation and Timing of Votes: Report and Proceedings of the Committee*, HC 589; (2000–2001) *Facilities for the Media: Report and Proceedings of the Committee*, HC 408; (1998–9) *Work of the Committee: Second Progress Report*, HC 865; (1998–9) *Thursday Sittings*, HC 719; (1998–9) *Sittings of the House in Westminster Hall*, HC 194; (1998–9) *The Parliamentary Calendar: Initial Proposals*, HC 60; (1997– 8) *The Scrutiny of European Business*, HC 791; (1997–8) *Voting Methods*, HC 779; (1997–8) *Consultation Paper on Voting Methods*, HC 699; (1997–8) *Conduct in the Chamber*, HC 600; (1997–8) *Carry-over of Public Bills*, HC 543; (1997–8) *Explanatory Material for Bills*, HC 389; (1997–8) *The Legislative Process*, HC 190

[37] The Liaison Committee published three reports during 2000– 2001 (see bibliography) and took the unprecedented step of taking oral evidence from the Leader of the House of Commons, Margaret Beckett on 11 July 2000

Chapter Two

Building a culture of scrutiny in the Commons

2.1　Procedural reform alone will not improve the quality of parliamentary scrutiny. Parliament is only as effective as its Members. Proposals for reform may include giving Parliament a range of statutory powers to demand information or call ministers and their officials to account, but the effectiveness of the institution relies on its members' willingness to use the powers at their disposal. This in turn requires that every MP regards the pursuit of accountability as an integral part of their work in the Commons.

2.2　Every MP must balance a number of competing roles. They must represent the interests of their political party and their constituency, as well as discharging their parliamentary duties. The Commission acknowledges that for most MPs, the scrutiny of government is only one role amongst many. Regardless of any reform, the party will remain the dominant factor in the life and loyalties of most MPs. However, the Commission is concerned that the dominance of the party in the structure and ethos of the Commons means that for many MPs, their party role too often overshadows their parliamentary role. As a result, parliamentary scrutiny and oversight are not as effective as they might be.

2.3　Evidence to the Commission emphasised that the effectiveness of Parliament required a change in attitude as well as procedure, and solutions which sought to create a new ethos. Michael Ryle, a former clerk of the Commons told us that reform should focus on making Parliament more effective rather than simply increasing its constitutional powers.[38] Dr Nicholas Baldwin argued that

> "reform of the House of Commons, and the effectiveness of any reform, depends ultimately upon the attitude of the Members of Parliament themselves and upon their ability to exert a 'parliamentary' attitude over and above the attitude of the frontbenches . . . In short, changes in the procedures and machinery of the House of Commons designed to enhance its ability to scrutinise the Executive will be to no avail whatsoever unless there are also changes in its own collective character."[39]

2.4　Professor Michael Rush made a similar point to the Commission stating that although certain procedural changes have enhanced the ability of Parliament to hold Government to account, "ultimately it is attitudes that are crucial. This is not to argue that no useful procedural changes can be made, rather that their efficacy depends on Members being willing to use them to good effect."[40]

2.5　The Commission recognises that the institutional structure of Parliament and the dominance of parties means that MPs have very different and often contradictory views about their own role, and that of Parliament. Many of these problems relate to the absence of separation of powers and the Commission recognises that for as long as the political parties are the principal means for organising parliamentary

---

[38] Appendix 2, Evidence 30
[39] Appendix 2, Evidence 2
[40] Appendix 2, Evidence 29

business, the executive will dominate Parliament. The Commission's recommendations seek to redress some of the balance between the executive and Parliament in the Commons. The Commission also sought recommendations which would promote cultural change by offering MPs greater opportunities and incentives to reconcile their roles in a manner that does not lose sight of the public interest.

The institutional structure of the Commons and parliamentary roles

2.6   What MPs do at Westminster is, of course, decided by the individual MP. There are few obligations on the Member of Parliament, there is no job description and MPs enjoy a great deal of leeway in defining who they represent, and how they represent them. In a landmark survey of Members of Parliament Donald Searing[41] found eight distinct roles which individual MPs could play whilst in the Commons, four of these were backbench roles – policy advocate, ministerial aspirant, constituency member, Parliament man – and four were leadership roles – parliamentary private secretaries, whips, junior ministers, senior ministers.

2.7   He found that in so far as MPs consciously chose a particular role, their decisions were based on both institutional and political factors. The opportunities provided by the institution were obviously a significant factor but these were tempered by MPs' own political ambitions, which rely on the support and patronage of the political party. In short, the structure of the institution, and its formal and informal rules, will "define the essential tasks that need to be performed."[42] At Westminster the two most important factors which determine activity are the dominance of the governing party over the activity of the Commons, and the influence of the parties over their MPs.

2.8   Westminster is characterised by the dominance of the executive. Although this is common in many democracies, especially where the executive is drawn from the legislature, evidence to the Commission from Professor Thomas Saalfeld shows the extent of executive dominance at Westminster is far greater than for many other parliaments.[43] The extent of this control is conveyed in Standing Order 14 of the House of Commons which states that "save as provided in this order, government business shall have precedence at every sitting".[44]

2.9   The organisation of business in the chamber of the Commons is determined by the governing party. It allocates the timing for all debates and legislation, and although in practice this relies on negotiation with the Opposition parties through the 'usual channels', the Government will time debates to its own advantage. The notion that the Government shall get its business dominates procedures in the chamber and standing committees. This has a number of implications for Parliament as an institution. It means that Parliament is informed of its business by a Cabinet minister,

[41] Searing, D., (1994), *Westminster's World: Understanding Political Roles*, Harvard University Press: Cambridge, Mass.
[42] *ibid*, p.34
[43] Appendix 2, Evidence 31
[44] *Standing Orders of the House of Commons – Public Business*, (2000), HC 518

the Leader of the House, on a weekly basis who announces the content for each day the following week and provisional business for the week after. Although the Labour Government has introduced reforms which seek to bring a greater predictability to parliamentary business the current system means that it is impossible for MPs to plan their work too far ahead.

2.10   The effect on the ethos of the Commons is to emphasise the distinction between executive and legislature. MPs conceive their role according to their position, and the position of their party, in relation to the Government. There is little sense that Parliament owns its business or determines its own workload, nor much sense of Parliament acting collectively as an institution. In some respects this atomises and individualises the work of MPs, with each MP acting as "his own public relations officer."[45] Although Parliament has certain collective functions, its ability to deliver them is limited by the fact that it has no collective ethos, "The idea of 'Parliament' as a political force, or as a whole, is simply a myth. Parliament in this sense simply does not exist."[46]

2.11   The only collective activity inside the Commons is orchestrated by the political parties and the only realistic career path for the ambitious MP is through the structures of the political party. The vast majority of activity in the Commons chamber is organised along party lines and the whips on both sides play a significant role in marshalling the contributions of their MPs. The knowledge that whips and party leaders will determine their political career has a significant bearing on MPs' behaviour, and it is those traits which emphasise the party political divide that are most likely to get a backbencher noticed. Promotion is more likely to be the result of partisan activity – toeing the party line, asking the right questions, scoring points off the Opposition – than pursuing the accountability functions of Parliament.

2.12   Given these factors it is not surprising that MPs' conception of their role inside Parliament is dominated by the party. But Parliament is built around two separate confrontations.[47] The first is the party political battle between Government and Opposition parties, which is reflected in the very shape of the chamber. The second is that between those MPs that are members of the Government and all other Members of Parliament. In theory, all MPs who are not part of the executive have a responsibility to scrutinise and hold government to account. However, there appears to be a disjunction between the way in which MPs think of their own role and how they see the role of Parliament as an institution.

2.13   The Commission's survey of MPs[48] asked politicians to comment on their role and goals, the role of Parliament as an institution and to rate how effectively Parliament carried out its core task. Regardless of party, MPs felt that the two most important functions of Parliament were the scrutiny of legislation and the scrutiny of Government departments. Over 90% of Members stated that such roles were very or quite important. As Fig 2A shows, when asked which was the most important function of Parliament, scrutiny of legislation came first with 37%, whilst 15.6% named scrutiny of government departments.

---

[45] Griffith, J.A.G. & Ryle, M., (1989), *Parliament: Functions, Procedure and Practice*, Sweet & Maxwell: London, p. 6
[46] Weir & Beetham, *op cit*, p. 376
[47] Griffith, J.A.G. & Ryle, M., *op cit*, pp. 13–15
[48] Appendix 4

Figure 2A – Which do you think is the most important role for Parliament?

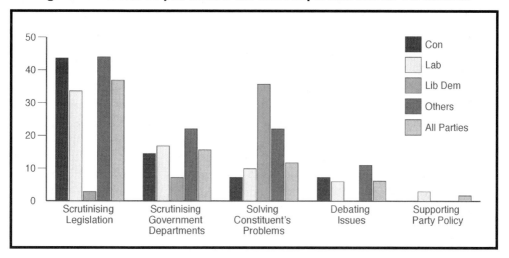

2.14 MPs also attach a great deal of importance to parliamentary duties when thinking about their own role as an individual MP within Parliament. Just over 80% regarded holding the government to account as very or quite important and over 70% thought in similar terms about the scrutiny of legislation. The survey revealed the importance of the political party in shaping the thinking of MPs with more than two-thirds regarding voting with their political party as very or quite important, and when asked how important were the interests of the political party in determining their behaviour 71.5% stated they were quite or very important. However, it is worth noting the very high level of support for the constituency role, almost 90% regarded the solution of constituent's grievances as very or quite important and over 80% thought similarly about protecting the interests of the constituency.

2.15 Asked to rank these possible roles in order, scrutiny of government came first with 33%, followed by protecting the interests of the constituency, dealing with constituents grievances, and then, perhaps surprisingly, scrutiny of legislation. Voting with the political party was regarded as most important by only 2% of the poll.

2.16 The fact that MPs place such a high value on their parliamentary roles might be regarded as heartening for the effective functioning of Parliament. However, when the figures are broken down by party a different pattern emerges. The figures show the extent to which party membership influences the MPs perception of their role. Opposition MPs give a greater precedence to the 'parliamentary' roles – scrutiny of departments and legislation – than the Government MPs. As figure 2B shows, whereas more than half of Conservative MPs regard holding government to account as their most important task, only a quarter of Labour MPs regard this as their priority. It is the constituency roles (dealing with grievances and protecting constituency interests) which is the overriding concern of more than 40% of Labour MPs.

Figure 2B – Which is the most important role of the MP?

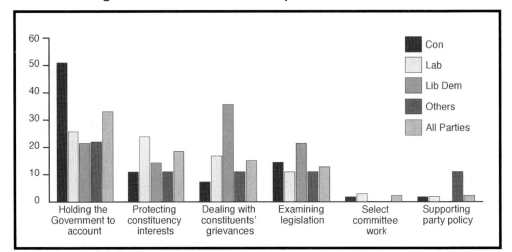

2.17 The extent to which MPs tend to define their own role according to their party's position in government or opposition was further emphasised in evidence submitted by Professor Michael Rush. In a survey conducted by the Study of Parliament Group MPs were asked to rank the constituency role, influencing policy, supporting the party or scrutinising government, in order of importance. In 1994, the most important role for Conservative MPs was representing the constituency, and scrutiny of government the least important. By 1999 the constituency was the second most important role, after the scrutiny of government.[49]

2.18 The findings show that MPs take their parliamentary duties seriously and give them a high priority. There is a discrepancy between the politician's view of the proper role of Parliament and how they rank their own priorities as an MP. It appears that in practice their activity will be largely determined by party political considerations. Scrutiny, it seems, is a task for the Opposition, not for the Government's own MPs. Whilst Parliament has certain collective duties in relation to Government, it does not appear to have the collective ethos which ensures the effective performance of these duties. This may reflect the ambitions of MPs; as figure 2C shows whilst around 60% expressed a desire to serve on a select committee it appears that relatively few saw this as the basis for a parliamentary career. Less than half this number saw chairing a select committee as an important goal (a third of MPs regarded it as unimportant), whilst a slightly higher number wished to become a junior minister and almost 40% expressed a desire to serve in cabinet.

[49] Appendix 2, Evidence 29

Figure 2C – Importance of parliamentary roles to MPs

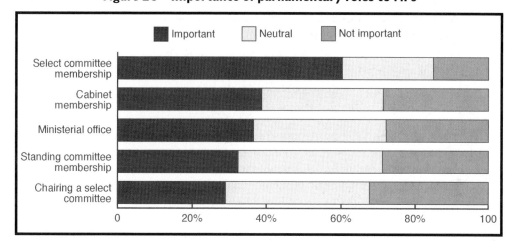

2.19 The Commission believes that reform of the Commons must seek to find ways of allowing MPs to balance their party role with their parliamentary role. Reform should give MPs the opportunity, ability and incentives to pursue their parliamentary roles. The Commission believes that the principal means for this is through the system of select committees. However, the effectiveness of the committee system in changing the ethos also requires that greater attention is paid to the training and support of MPs in their work. Although the Commission believes that reforms to the select committees would improve the effectiveness of Parliament, a change in culture will require that this 'parliamentary' activity is fostered and co-ordinated, so that MPs have a better understanding of their roles and how they impact on the role of Parliament. The Commission believes that a Parliamentary steering committee should be established to provide greater co-ordination of activity.

Enhancing the select committees

2.20 The Commission believes that the system of select committees provides opportunities for MPs to play a more productive parliamentary role. The select committees avoid many of the most sterile and partisan aspects of parliamentary activity in the chamber and standing committees. One of the principal recommendations of this report is that Parliament should become a more committee-based institution, and many of our other proposals stem from this central theme. The Commission believes that to be more effective in holding the Government to account, Westminster must look to the committees.

2.21 In subsequent chapters we examine the performance of the departmental select committees since their establishment in 1979 in holding government to account, their relationship with the chamber of the House of Commons, and make recommendations to improve their effectiveness. This chapter focuses on their value in changing the culture of the Commons and providing an alternative source of activity to the party political roles. The recommendations aim to highlight the committees' role in fostering cultural change in Parliament.

2.22   The committees have two main potential strengths. First, the activity of the committees is not determined by party political considerations, and they allow MPs to develop their parliamentary role. Relatedly, they provide an important arena for scrutiny where activity is not prescribed by the Government. Second, development of the committees could provide MPs with an alternative career path which does not rely solely on the patronage of the political parties.

Committees as forums for parliamentary activity

2.23   The introduction of the departmental select committees in 1979 has shown that the conflict between MPs' differing roles can be resolved, to quite a large extent, by the correct institutional framework. Part of the argument for their introduction was that it would change their perceptions of their own roles. Professor Anthony King, writing in 1976, argued that MPs on select committees see themselves primarily as parliamentarians rather than party MPs,

> "concerned with investigating the quality of the performance of the executive (of whichever party), with protecting the rights of the citizen against the executive (of whichever party), and with asserting the prerogatives of backbench MPs (irrespective of party)."[50]

2.24   According to Rt. Hon Robert Sheldon MP, the chair[51] of the Liaison Committee and a former chair of the Public Accounts Committee, these hopes have to a large extent been borne out. Speaking in a debate in November 2000 about the Liaison Committee reports designed to reform the select committees,[52] he pointed out their value and strengths,

> "In each select committee, there has been a search for bipartisan agreement. Point scoring has a part to play on the Floor of the House, but it has no role in Select Committees . . . We understand that the first priority of hon. Members is to support or oppose the Government, but it is possible, in a Select Committee, to move away from that confrontation and look at the facts of a matter. It is interesting that the trust and confidence that grows between Select Committee members means that it is more difficult for them to play the party game at the expense of the investigative role that is their proper task."[53]

2.25   The strength of the select committees is that they are largely free from the interference of the political parties. Although the Institute of Directors raised concerns in their submission to the Commission about the process of appointment to committees[54] (which we deal with in more detail in the next chapter), once they have been established the committees tend to derive their influence from effective cross-party collaboration. As a result the committees provide a forum which allows MPs from all parties to reconcile their conflicting roles in the pursuit of the public interest. The lack of overt party politics in the committees means that, in distinction to other parts of Parliament they "can be the focus of public input and the pipeline between the constituents and the government."[55]

---

[50]   King, A., (1976), "Modes of Executive-Legislative Relations: Great Britain, France and West Germany", *Legislative Studies Quarterly*, Vol. 1, No. 1, p. 19

[51]   The words 'chair' and 'chairs' are used in place of 'chairman' and 'chairmen' throughout the report. The Commission acknowledges that the latter are the formal titles used inside the Houses of Parliament but find it preferable to use the terms which do not specify gender.

[52]   Liaison Committee, (1999–2000), *Shifting the Balance: Select committees and the Executive*, HC 300

[53]   HC Debs, 9 November 2000, vol 356, col, 474

[54]   Appendix 2, Evidence 13

[55]   Commonwealth Parliamentary Association Study Group, (1999), *Parliamentary Committees: Enhancing Democratic Governance*, Cavendish Publishing: London, p.7

Committees as an alternative career path

2.26   Although the committees provide an alternative focus for parliamentary activity, the impact on Parliament as a whole is limited by their size and status. They provide one possible role in Parliament. But only a limited number of MPs can take advantage of these opportunities and the incentives for backbenchers to engage in this activity are often only as a possible stepping stone towards promotion, and other roles as a minister or shadow spokesperson. Lord Naseby told the Commission that the select committees seem "to be treated as a training ground for potential ministers and to sideline certain MPs seen as incapable."[56]

2.27   The Commission believes that the impact of the committees on the culture of the Commons requires them to play a more important and extensive role. The committees should provide an additional and alternative career path to the ministerial ladder.

2.28   The first problem is that select committees do not provide a job for every MP in Parliament. At the end of February 2001 there were 325 MPs serving on select committees. However, excluding the domestic committees and those that do not perform a scrutiny function (such as Accommodation and Works, Broadcasting, and Information) this number drops to below 300. Fewer than half the MPs in Parliament serve on a committee designed to scrutinise and hold the Government to account.

2.29   The Commission believes that committee activity should be integral to the work of every MP and **recommends that every backbench MP should be expected to serve on a select committee**. The Commission does not believe that MPs should be coerced into this activity, and accepts that there are some MPs, perhaps former Prime Ministers or senior ex-ministers, who would be unlikely to want to engage in committee work. However, the expectation of committee service should act as a powerful pressure on individual MPs and provide the impetus for a new ethos to develop in Parliament. The increased membership would mean expanding the size of the committees and require alterations to their structure and support which we examine in the next chapter.

2.30   With almost every backbencher serving on a committee the Commission believes that the status of the committees would be enhanced. However, the Commission believes that MPs should be given further incentives to take this work seriously and provide the basis for an alternative career path.

2.31   Reform should, in the first place, tackle the number of MPs on the payroll vote. There are around 110 ministers in the Government, the vast majority of which are in the Commons. Although the Commission makes no specific recommendations on reducing the number of ministers it is concerned that in addition to these ministers there are 53 positions for parliamentary private secretaries (PPSs).[57]

---

[56] Appendix 2, Evidence 20
[57] Figures correct at April 2001.

2.32 One of the most significant features of the early part of the 1997 Parliament was the large number of MPs who left committees to take up positions in Government. The turnover of membership on some select committees since 1997 has been staggering: for example, between 1997 and November 1999 the Social Security Committee had a turnover of 64% and the Treasury Committee had a turnover of 42%. The Public Administration Committee had a turnover of 64% in the session 1999–2000 and the Education and Employment Committee 47% during the same session.[58] The Commission agrees with the analysis of the Liaison Committee about the implications of this situation,

> "Ministerial office has a powerful attraction for many back-benchers on the government side of the House. But it is a matter of concern when able and effective select committee members – and sometimes even chairs – are so easily tempted by the lowliest of government and opposition appointments. We must be realistic about this; many Members understandably aspire to be Ministers, and of course former Ministers bring valuable knowledge and experience to their service on select committees. . . . What we would like to see is a better *balance* between the attractions of government office and of service on select committees."[59]

2.33 The Commission acknowledges that it is inevitable that some members will, quite rightly, wish to take up posts in the government or on the frontbench. But the Commission wishes to promote a more effective Parliament and believes that the current number of MPs on the payroll vote seriously weakens Parliament's ability to carry out its collective functions. **The Commission recommends that all but the largest government departments should have only one PPS.** The Commission recognises that there may be exceptions, with the larger departments such as Environment, Transport and the Regions requiring more than one PPS, but believes that the number of PPSs must be drastically reduced.

2.34 In addition the prospect of committee service must be made more attractive and should provide specific incentives for MPs. Evidence from Age Concern to the Commission reflected the views of many in stating that committees would be more effective if "Committee membership, especially the chairmanship, was better resourced and considered on a par with ministerial office."[60] The Commission also noted that Lord Wakeham's Commission recommended that salaries should be paid to those members who chair significant committees in the second chamber.[61] The Commission agrees with these views and believes that **key posts on select committees should be paid and MPs chairing committees should receive a salary equivalent to that of a minister.**[62]

---

[58] Liaison Committee, (2000–2001), First Report, *Shifting the Balance: Unfinished Business*, HC 321-I, para 129
[59] Liaison Committee, (1999–2000), HC 300
[60] Appendix 2, Evidence 1
[61] Royal Commission on the reform of the House of Lords, (2000), *A House for the Future*, Cm 4534. TSO: London, para 17.12
[62] The current entitlements for MPs and ministers is as follows. Backbench MP £48,371, Under secretary of state £74,424, Minister of State £82, 697, Cabinet Minister £114, 543. Source: Review Body on Senior Salaries (2001), *Report No. 48: Review of Parliamentary Pay and Allowances*, Cm 4997-II, p. 5

2.35   The position of committee chair can be onerous, with few rewards. We recognise that there are differing views about the desirability of paying chairmen. During our meeting with the Liaison Committee a number of committee chairs expressed concern that payment and the increased in stature of the post would consolidate the control of the whips.[63] Others believed that it might damage the collegiate nature of some committees, encouraging other members to think that the chair should do all the work. However, others remarked that remuneration would provide the necessary status and recognition and might discourage chairs from taking unpaid PPS jobs and, if the pay were sufficiently high, discourage them even from taking ministerial positions.

2.36   The Commission recognises that there are genuine concerns but we are not convinced that the disadvantages outweigh the benefits. The influence of the whips over the committees exists regardless of payment and we believe that our other recommendations regarding committee membership and selection overcome many of these concerns. As for the collegiate nature of the committees, some chairs undoubtedly consider that they already have to shoulder almost the entire burden of work. But in the following chapter we recommend the creation of new posts on the select committees to share the work and extend the scope of committee inquiries.

2.37   The next chapter examines the staffing of the committees in more detail, as our recommendations are linked specifically to improving the outcomes and increasing the responsibilities of select committees. However, enhancing the status and performance of committee will also require more resources and support. In addition to payment of the chairs, committees should be provided with more staff, greater allowances, research or travel budgets.

Enhancing understanding of parliamentary roles

2.38   The effectiveness of Parliament in this area also requires that MPs and committees are properly trained and supported in that role. At one level the provision of training is essential to the creation of a new ethos in Parliament. MPs and prospective MPs are presently trained by their political parties to be effective political campaigners, constituency workers and press officers. The parties do not teach them how Parliament works. In the Commission's private meetings with MPs almost all stated that they came to Parliament with little or no understanding of what was expected of them or how to do the job. This was borne out by the Commission's survey of MPs which showed that almost two-thirds of MPs said they had received no training at all. As a result only 40% of our survey felt that they were prepared for the job by the time they reached Parliament.[64]

---

[63] Appendix 3
[64] Appendix 4

2.39   Although the House authorities provide an introductory course less than 4% of our poll attended. For most MPs the job is learnt from older MPs or simply by trial and error.[65] Developing the culture of the Commons so that it becomes a place where MPs can reconcile their various roles in the pursuit of the public interest requires a more rigorous approach to induction and training. **The Commons should build on current practice and provide continuing training for MPs related to their work on committees, parliamentary procedure and specialist subject policy areas.**

2.40   Given the importance the Commission attaches to the committees we believe that MPs should be properly trained for such work. At present MPs are given no training for their work on select committees yet the committees' effective scrutiny of ministers and civil servants requires certain specific skills. New MPs are expected to develop expertise in the particular specialist subject, often from scratch. They are also expected to develop a mixture of forensic, interrogation and accounting skills. Former minister Rt Hon Michael Jack highlighted the issue succinctly for the Commission, "Unless you have been in government yourself, it is sometimes quite difficult to understand just how closed Ministers are being in the way they conduct themselves. I think there would be merit in Members being given training in the art of thorough probing, to ensure that whenever the government were questioned, it was done as thoroughly as possible."[66]

2.41   The Commission also believes that such training will be of benefit to Government. Better trained, more capable MPs are likely to become more competent ministers. The transition to a ministerial post, as described to the Commission by one senior civil servant, marks a shift 'from oratory to activity'. The Commission believes that the sorts of expertise and skills developed on select committees are likely to be of greater use to prospective ministers than activity in the chamber.

2.42   The Commission's discussions with individuals and organisations revealed some concern that MPs would baulk at the prospect of training. However our research suggests that the increasingly professional breed of new MPs brought in at each election is likely to have had experience at relatively senior levels in both the public and private sectors where continuing training and induction were mandatory. The experience of Parliament therefore is often a shock for new Members. Put simply, it does not match the professional standards that most new MPs were used to in their previous career. The survey showed that of those who expressed an opinion there were a significant proportion who wanted further training. The most popular area was information technology where 64% wanted further training, 44% wanted training in subject specific policy areas and, perhaps most significantly, 45.5% wanted further training in parliamentary procedure.[67]

2.43   The Commission believes that Parliament has collective functions and MPs need to be trained to perform them effectively.

---

[65] See Rush, M., & Giddings, P., (2000) 'Learning to be a Member of Parliament', in Power, G., Ed., *Under Pressure: Are we getting the most from our MPs?*, Hansard Society: London
[66] Appendix 2, Evidence 14
[67] Appendix 4

Leadership and co-ordination in Parliament

2.44 Changes to committee membership and training will not themselves alter the ethos of Parliament. Cultural change needs to be reinforced. This is unlikely to come from the Government. The Commission believes that in order to perform its collective functions more effectively Parliament requires a leadership and co-ordinating body.

2.45 **The Commission believes that Parliament should have a steering committee responsible for the management of the parliamentary timetable.** This would bring a greater certainty to the parliamentary timetable and involve the main political parties in the management of business. In addition, **the Liaison Committee should be restructured to provide a greater degree of leadership and co-ordination for parliamentary activity.** The Commission believes this would bring greater co-ordination and effectiveness to the efforts of the select committees.

Parliamentary steering committee

2.46 The idea of a steering committee to organise business is not new and has been recommended by other reviews of Parliament, not least by the Hansard Society Commission on the legislative process[68] and more recently by the Norton Commission report on strengthening Parliament.[69] It is not unusual for modern Parliaments to have a steering committee which decides and manages parliamentary business, and the model has been incorporated into the Scottish Parliament under the title 'Bureau'.

2.47 The Scottish Parliament Bureau was intended to replace the Westminster system of Government-dominated and secretive 'usual channels'. Chaired by the Parliament's Presiding Officer, the Bureau consists of representatives of parties with five or more MSPs. Votes on the Bureau are weighted according to party size. This means that, in practice, the executive can be assured of its business, but it gives a formal role to the other parties in the decisions on the timing of business.

2.48 Although, in practice the use of the Bureau has not entirely done away with some elements of the 'usual channels' it has meant that business is formally timetabled. The Bureau has become a key forum for discussion and negotiation on many complex or controversial aspects of parliamentary administration and operation, not just the arrangement of its formal business. The fact that there are apparently extremely few occasions where the Bureau proceeds to a formal vote can suggest an impressive degree of cross-party consensus, or, alternatively, either the presence of informal, but decisive, pre-meetings or the ceding of the initiative to the Executive as occurs at Westminster.

---

[68] Hansard Society, (1992), *Making the Law: Report of the Hansard Society Commission on the Legislative Process*, Hansard Society: London

[69] Commission on Strengthening Parliament, Chaired by Lord Norton of Louth, (2000), *Strengthening Parliament: The report of the Commission to Strengthen Parliament*, Conservative Party

2.49 The Commission believes that a steering committee at Westminster should be made up of representatives of all parties with more than ten MPs. Votes on the steering committee would be weighted to reflect the strength of the parties in Parliament. The Government would therefore be assured of getting its business. However, the system would put the management of business on a formal footing and overcome many of the problems inherent in the informal agreements of the 'usual channels'.

A parliamentary executive

2.50 The Liaison Committee, consisting of the chairmen of the select committees, brings together some of the most senior backbench MPs, with representatives of all parties and many different parliamentary and former government backgrounds. In theory, the experience and status of many of the Committee's members would make them ideally placed to provide leadership. However the Liaison Committee has in the past tended to concentrate on the internal administration of select committees and has failed to make much wider impact. Its greater activity in 2000 suggested that it might be developing a higher profile on behalf of Parliament. It published two reports in the 1999–2000 session on reform of the select committee system: *Shifting the Balance: Select Committees and the Executive*[70] and *Independence or Control?*,[71] which was the committee's response to the Government reply to the first report. A third was published in March 2001, *Shifting the Balance: Unfinished Business*,[72] which further developed some of the committee's proposals.

2.51 One particular proposal, to change the way that members are appointed to select committees, indicated that it was serious about developing a genuine parliamentary leadership. The Liaison Committee believed that the Whips had assumed too much influence in nominating members to serve on select committees. This influence it believed had three unwelcome consequences: long delays in setting up committees at the beginning of a Parliament, long delays in appointing a replacement when a Member leaves a committee and, in our view most important, members had been kept off committees, or removed from them, on account of their views.

2.52 It proposed that the Liaison Committee should be renamed and reconstituted as the Select Committee Panel and would propose to the House the names of Members to serve on select committees. In the early weeks of a Parliament, before a Liaison Committee was established, it proposed that the House should appoint a chair of Committees and two Deputy chairs of Committees, senior and respected Members of the House, who would invite names for membership of committees, with a deadline for submissions. They would propose to the House the membership of each committee not more than a fortnight after that deadline. Under this proposal Members would be free to propose themselves, or others, with information about qualifications and suitability; and the Whips could make their own suggestions; but the final decisions on nomination would be made by the chairs and Deputies. The Liaison Committee believed that "this system would be transparent and fair, and that it would protect the independence of select committees."[73]

---

[70] Liaison Committee, (1999–2000), HC 300
[71] Liaison Committee, (1999–2000), HC 748
[72] Liaison Committee, (2000–2001), HC 321
[73] HC 300, para 20

2.53   The Government entirely rejected these proposals. It rejected both the analysis (that the Whips had unwarranted influence and consequences that flowed from that) and the proposed solutions. The Liaison Committee responded in forthright terms.

> "There is widespread disquiet, both amongst Members and outside the House, about a system which is not open, and which is not clearly independent of the Government and the party managers. Those being scrutinised should not have a say in the selection of the scrutineers. We believe that the present system does not, and should not, have the confidence of the House and the public."[74]

2.54   The Liaison Committee appears to have been comprehensively defeated. Indeed it might have been practically difficult to have adopted the proposals in that particular form, even if the Government were minded to do so. But it was clear that the Government was not prepared to accept even the spirit of the proposals.

2.55   **The Commission believes that part of the answer lies in reforming the Liaison Committee itself.** It is a large and unwieldy body, its membership straddles departmental, cross-cutting, procedural and domestic committees, and it has 33 members in total. The first small change would involve removing the domestic committees, which were only ever envisaged as advisory, and their presence on the Liaison Committee is anomalous.

2.56   **The Liaison Committee should be reduced in size and should elect its own executive body of six MPs.** It should also adopt a new name which illustrates more clearly its role within Parliament, such as the Select Committee Panel or Parliamentary Executive Committee. The new body, and specifically its own executive, would be responsible for the membership of the committees and the co-ordination of their activities. We envisage that the individual committees would retain some autonomy but the new Panel would perform an important function in agreeing targets and activity with committee chairs (see paras 3.23–3.26). **We believe that the Liaison Committee has the potential to provide a focus for Parliament's role in the scrutiny of Government and wider parliamentary reform.**

Conclusion: Changing the culture

2.57   It is impossible to provide a set of detailed recommendations that guarantee a change in the ethos of the House of Commons. As we stated at the outset of this chapter the most significant determinant of Parliament's effectiveness will be the activity of its Members. The way in which those Members perform will depend on a number of factors, the strength of the political parties in Parliament, the conditions in the MP's constituency, the level of party discipline and the political issues of the day. However, the Commission believes that Parliament should provide a forum where MPs can reconcile these differing interests in the pursuit of the public interest. The Commission acknowledges the very important role played by party politics in illuminating issues of public concern, but such a role works only in certain situations at certain times. If party political interests override all other factors, the public interest is often lost. The Commission's principal objective is that Parliament engages with and articulates issues of public concern.

---

[74] HC 748, para 28

Principle 2 – Parliament must develop a culture of scrutiny

The task of holding Government to account should be central to the parliamentary work of every MP but, in practice it is often defined solely in party political terms. Reforms should seek to enable MPs to balance their party role with their parliamentary role in the pursuit of the public interest. The Commission believes this should be achieved mainly through the system of select committees.

Recommendations

1. To develop a culture of scrutiny and allow all MPs to pursue their scrutiny function every backbench MP should be expected to serve on a select committee. (para. 2.29)

2. The high turnover of MPs on committees is partly a result of the large number of MPs on the payroll vote. This should be reduced, so that all but the very largest government departments are limited to one PPS. (para. 2.33)

3. Reforms should seek to improve the attractiveness of committee service and create a parliamentary career path for ambitious MPs. Key posts on select committees should be paid and MPs chairing committees should receive a salary equivalent to that of a minister. (para. 2.34)

4. The Commons should build on current practice and provide continuing training for MPs related to their work on committees, parliamentary procedure and subject specialist policy areas. (para. 2.39)

5. Fostering a culture of scrutiny requires greater leadership and co-ordination of parliamentary activity. Parliament needs a steering committee or bureau which formally organises parliamentary business. (paras 2.47–2.49)

6. In addition, the Liaison Committee should be restructured and re-named to provide a greater degree of leadership and co-ordination for parliamentary activity. The committee should be reduced in size and elect its own executive body of six MPs. It should play a greater role in determining the membership of the committees and oversee their work. (paras 2.50–2.56)

Chapter Three

Reforming the select committees

3.1   The system of departmental select committees, responsible for the scrutiny of policy, administration and expenditure of Government ministries was established in 1979. They provided Parliament, for the first time, with a structure for systematic inquiry into the full range of Government activity. The committees are the main parliamentary vehicle for monitoring the work of Government and should provide a permanent watch over departments of state.

3.2   Since their inception they have generally been regarded as a successful innovation. Academics and parliamentarians alike have acknowledged their contribution to the effectiveness of Parliament. Successive reports from the Liaison and Procedure Committees have cited their importance in holding ministers to account, so that they have "provided a far more rigorous, systematic and comprehensive scrutiny of ministers' actions and policies than anything which went before."[75] This view was supported by evidence to the Commission. Sir Ian Byatt, director general of the water industry regulator Ofwat, commented that "The work of select committees represents an effective means of scrutiny . . . they bring out important issues of public interest."[76] The Consumers' Association expressed a similar view, "select committees can and often do play a useful role in challenging Government and other bodies, improving the transparency of decision making, and in some cases leading the Government to rethink its position."[77]

3.3   However, the success of the committee system is limited. Despite the generally favourable view of their work the quality of scrutiny is variable and unsystematic. The Liaison Committee report, *Shifting the Balance*, published in 2000, which provided an overview of the system of select committees, commented that although their introduction should be regarded as an undoubted success, their performance "has not been consistent and success not unalloyed. In each of the five Parliaments since 1979, different committees have shone; some have found it difficult to surmount the difficulties they have encountered."[78]

3.4   The Commission believes that the system of departmental select committees provides the basis for a more effective system of scrutiny. Select committees should bring coherence to the various methods for scrutinising Government. Their increased effectiveness thus relies on them raising their objectives and engaging more systematically with external scrutiny mechanisms.

---

[75] Procedure Committee, (1989–90), *The Working of the select committee system*, HC 19-I, para. 67
[76] Appendix 2, Evidence 25
[77] Appendix 2, Evidence 4
[78] HC 300, para 41

3.5   The Commission sees the committees' unique role as mediating between the technical investigations of the regulators, inspectorates and even judicial inquiries and the work of Parliament. The scrutiny of Government is likely to be more effective where the select committees are able to disentangle the issues of political significance from external investigations and use these as the basis for questioning ministers. They thus become a sifting mechanism for issues of importance and offer an interpretation of their significance. The effectiveness of the committees therefore relies on them bringing added value to other forms of scrutiny, making all other structures of accountability relevant, by identifying the public interest and linking it into the parliamentary process.

The work of the select committees

3.6   One of the principal reasons for the apparent success of the select committee system is because of the qualitative shift in Parliament's performance compared with the situation before 1979. Select committees had been a feature of Parliament for some time, but they tended to be either *ad hoc*, temporary and/or not related to a department. During the Labour government of 1966–70 a series of subject specific committees were established to monitor areas such as agriculture, education and science, and race relations. However, the departmentally related committees were not reappointed in 1970 (with the exception of overseas aid) and the general opinion of the select committees was poor.[79]

3.7   The 1979 reforms offered interrogation of all departments by a greater number of MPs in a more systematic fashion than Parliament had previously experienced. The fact that the committees were tied to ministries meant the MPs could legitimately roam over the activities of the department and call ministers and civil servants to account for their decisions. Moreover, the prolonged and intensive questioning in committee hearings offered a much more effective means of getting answers from ministers, and the ability to use that information to highlight key issues.

3.8   The benefits of the system were summed up neatly by former clerk Michael Ryle in his evidence to the Procedure Committee in 1990 – the committees had enabled more frequent and systematic examination of government policies, the provision of more information about the workings of government, improving the contact between Parliament and the people, opening up the arguments of pressure groups, and increasing the influence of Parliament on Government.[80]

3.9   However, as we have noted, the system is far from perfect. The committees operate on a limited budget and tend to have only between three and six staff each, which inevitably affects the range and scope of their investigations. Their inquiries cannot match the level of detail provided by many external scrutiny bodies. The committees must pick their subjects carefully, and as a result the quality of scrutiny is less than systematic and varies from committee to committee. An examination of the committee

---

[79] See for instance Walkland, S.A., & Ryle, M., (1977), *The Commons in the Seventies*, Fontana: London
[80] HC 19-II

system between 1997 and 1999 reveals tremendous variation in the subjects and workrate of the various committees.[81] In that period the Committee on Environment, Transport and the Regions produced 33 reports, whilst the Scottish Affairs committee published only four. Although this is perhaps not the most reliable gauge of a committee's effectiveness (and these two committees are, for different reasons, atypical), it does signal a disparity which underlies many of the problems in the committees, and concerns relating to the quality of oversight, the failure to deal with key issues, and concerns about impact and effectiveness of committee reports.

Autonomy of committees

3.10   The fact that there is very little standardisation of committees' work is partly a result of the fact that each committee has complete autonomy over its inquiries. Standing orders relating to the select committees give them a free hand in determining which issues they investigate and how they investigate them,

> "Every select committee shall have leave to report to the House its opinion and observations upon any matters referred to it for its consideration . . . and also to make a special report of any matters which it may think fit to bring to the notice of the House."[82]

3.11   In some respects this can be regarded as a source of influence in that it gives committees the freedom to range widely over the array of Government activity. But in other ways it is a weakness of the system as a whole. Whilst the selection of subjects will be influenced by the resources available, the determining factor will be the attitude of the committee chair. The chair will ultimately decide the subject of their inquiries and the amount of time that the committee spends on those subjects. Several members of the Liaison Committee told us that their decisions were, more often than not, influenced by a consideration of how interested they thought the committee's Members would be in a particular subject. When one committee chair was asked why the select committees spent so little time on scrutinising the finance of their departments, he mournfully replied that it was impossible to get MPs to turn up at meetings which were discussing finance, because "They're simply not interested."

Figure 3A – Subject matter of committee reports 1997–9

Subject matter	No. of reports	Percentage
Administration	153	59.3
Expenditure	88	34.1
Policy	199	77.1

The total number of committee reports published during the period between 1997–1999 was 258. The figures reflect the fact that most committee reports cover more than one subject matter.

---

[81] For full findings see appendix 5

[82] *Standing Orders of the House of Commons – Public Business*, (2000), HC 518, No. 133

3.12 As our research shows, the latitude given to committees means that they spend a greater proportion of their time investigating policy matters than they do the ministry's finance or administration. The fact that more than three quarters of the reports covered policy matters, compared with around a third for finance bears out the above committee chair's view that MPs find policy more interesting. It is a view reinforced by the former minister Rt Hon Michael Jack MP, "there is a strong temptation by select committees to produce reports on subjects which they themselves find interesting. I believe this inevitably means that they do not spend as much time as they might shadowing the activities of government departments on a day to day basis."[83]

3.13 The desire of the chair to maintain the interest of committee members and ensure cross-party support will also have an influence on the choice of subjects and the rigour with which they are investigated. Commentators have remarked that committees are not very effective with post mortem enquiries, such as Arms-to-Iraq or BSE because they tend to be extremely contentious and occur within the lifetime of one administration. As such the Government majority on the committee is put under extreme pressure to dilute their findings. At the other end of the legislative process committees have in the past occasionally avoided issues likely to be the subject of forthcoming legislation. This approach, described by Butler, Adonis and Travers in their book about the genesis of the poll tax, was termed the 'Rossi doctrine' after Sir Hugh Rossi, the chair of the environment committee which failed to examine the proposed tax. Although committees have shown a greater willingness to address forthcoming legislation since then, as Butler *et al* note, such an attitude consigns select committees to the political car park.[84]

Engagement with external scrutiny bodies

3.14 The autonomy of the committees and their limited resources has a further impact on the rigorousness with which they pursue issues raised by external scrutiny bodies. It is estimated that over 500 bodies present reports to Parliament, some on an annual basis, others less frequently. During the 1999–2000 session of Parliament 247 reports were officially laid before MPs.[85] However, whereas the National Audit Office keeps a record of those organisations obliged to submit a financial report, the Commons has no such central list of bodies which lay reports before the House. It appears that it is the duty of those bodies to fulfil their statutory obligations rather than Parliament's duty to ensure that they do so. In the two sessions 1997–9, only 13.7% of committee reports (21) dealt with the work of the regulators, who are obliged to report to Parliament.[86] This figure is put into starker contrast when one excludes the reports of the Committee on Public Administration on the Ombudsman (1), the Health Service Ombudsman (2) and the Northern Ireland Ombudsman (1).

---

[83] Appendix 2, Evidence 14
[84] Butler, D., *et al*, (1994), *Failure in British Government: The politics of the poll tax*, Oxford University Press, p.231
[85] The Commission is indebted to the House of Commons library for compiling these figures.
[86] Appendix 5

3.15 The lack of systematic engagement with the work of the regulators and inspectorates was a cause of concern in evidence submitted to the Commission. The evidence from Elizabeth France, the Data Protection Commissioner, is particularly relevant. The Office of the Data Protection Commissioner (ODPC) is directly answerable to Parliament, via an annual report laid before each House of Parliament, for issues relating to data protection. Specifically, the Home Affairs committee is responsible for scrutinising the work of the Commissioner and the Commission's annual report is sent individually to each member of the committee. However, the Commissioner was concerned about the extent to which the committee were aware of such work and the implications of this for accountability,

> "The Commissioner does understand that data protection is only one of a range of subjects of interest to the committee and the pressure there must be on their time. However, the Commissioner has yet to appear before the committee to discuss her Annual Report and the general work of her office. The previous Data Protection Registrar appeared before the Home Affairs committee on just one occasion to discuss his Annual Report."

> ". . . as a public servant responsible for spending a large sum of money her actions should be subject to effective review by Parliament. However, she also believes that the work of the ODPC would be enhanced if it were to be routinely scrutinised and endorsed by a select committee. Further it would give the Commissioner an opportunity to raise issues of concern."[87]

3.16 As Elizabeth France notes the committees have limited resources and a wide subject area to cover. However, the concerns of the ODPC raise questions about the extent to which committees are systematic in their coverage of the Government's work. This is a problem for Parliament as the committees' work should not simply be post hoc investigation, their oversight of government should also provide a trip-wire for administrative or policy failure.

3.17 In addition, as the evidence suggests, parliamentary engagement with the work of bodies such as the ODPC would not only strengthen Parliament, but would also strengthen the external scrutiny mechanisms through MPs' interest and involvement. The vast amount of information generated by expert scrutiny bodies brings with it the potential for an enormous strengthening of scrutiny and accountability. However, committees need to be more systematic in their use of such information.

3.18 Concern about the ability of committees to cover a wide range of issues has resulted in the creation of non-departmental scrutiny committees such as the Environmental Audit Committee. The Data Protection Commissioner suggested to us that this was a possible model to be developed, and that "there may be value in creating a cross-departmental select committee exclusively dealing with information issues, including freedom of information and data protection."[88] A similar suggestion was made by Dr Nicholas Baldwin who argued for a 'democratic audit' committee which would examine legislative proposals regarding possible clashes with the Human Rights Act, the Freedom of Information Act and devolved Parliaments.[89]

---

[87] Appendix 2, Evidence 23
[88] Appendix 2, Evidence 23
[89] Appendix 2, Evidence 2

Impact of committee work – does it have any effect?

3.19 If the committees are not rigorous in their relationship with external scrutiny mechanisms, they are also isolated from many other areas of activity inside Parliament. The committees have no formal relationship with the chamber and do not examine legislation. As a result, of the 396 departmental select committee reports published between May 1997 and November 2000, 29 were debated in the main chamber,[90] and since its inception in November 1999 to the end of the 1999–2000 session, 13 were debated in Westminster Hall.[91] However, none of these were put to a vote.

3.20 This detachment from the main business of the chamber detracts from the committees' work. Some committees have scrutinised draft legislation since 1997 and have had an impact on the subsequent passage of the bill through Parliament, but such activity is sporadic and there are concerns that the terms of scrutiny can be dictated by the Government department.[92]

3.21 As to the effect of committee reports, their impact is notoriously difficult to measure and there are few concrete examples of where committees have significantly altered Government policy. However, the committees do little to check how far their recommendations have been taken up. The work of shadowing Government and ensuring that mistakes are rectified would require the committees themselves to return to their reports and assess whether the department has taken the necessary action. The committees would provide the criteria by which their own effectiveness could be judged.

3.22 Although the introduction of the departmental select committees in 1979 improved the quality of scrutiny and accountability at Westminster, the system provides a partial form of scrutiny. Its flaws mean that it does not guarantee accountability. **The Commission believes that in order to improve accountability through the committees their duties should be more closely specified, their relationship with external scrutiny mechanisms formalised and their input into the other areas of parliamentary activity increased.**

Improving scrutiny

3.23 The effectiveness of the select committees requires that their role is clarified. The committees have a political function. Committees should leave it to others to establish the facts of a case. Even with increased members, staff and resources the select committees would struggle to match the expertise available outside the walls of Westminster. Detailed forensic investigation is not the strength of these committees, and to engage in such activities is a waste of time and resources. As one academic has put it, "it is pointless for a Parliamentary committee, comprised as it is of politicians, to investigate that which is not of political significance."[93]

---

[90] The Commission is grateful to the Journal Office of the House of Commons for these figures.

[91] Modernisation Committee, (1999–2000), *Sittings in Westminster Hall*, HC 906, paras 10–11

[92] See Power, G., (2000), *Parliamentary scrutiny of draft legislation 1997–1999*, Hansard Society/Constitution Unit: London

[93] O'Keefe, P., 'The Scope and Function of Parliamentary Committees', cited in the Report of the Commonwealth Parliamentary Association Group, *op cit*, p.142

3.24 The principal task of the select committees should be to extract the issues of political significance from the technical scrutiny provided by the regulators and inspectorates. This would add value to their work and strengthen parliamentary scrutiny if it is used as the basis on which to challenge ministers, civil servants and others. However, the effectiveness of Parliament relies on it engaging with the work of such bodies in a more systematic fashion. **In the first place, both Houses should maintain a central list of all those organisations obliged to report to Parliament. This list should be distributed to every committee, so that every departmental select committee is aware of the organisations which come under their jurisdiction.**

3.25 The Commission believes that in order to make scrutiny more systematic **the select committees should be given a set of core duties. The committees should retain the freedom to initiate inquiries according to the interests of the committee or to respond to emerging issues.** One of the system's strengths is its flexibility and its ability to adapt to changing circumstances. This adaptability should not be lost. But **to improve the coverage of issues, to utilise the work of the regulators and to give the committees a continuity to their work they should meet pre-agreed objectives over the course of a Parliament. These objectives would provide a set of criteria against which their performance can be judged.**

3.26 We do not believe that an external Commission such as ours should detail the activities of a select committee. The objectives would vary from committee to committee and the Commission believes that **the specific objectives should be agreed with the reformed Liaison Committee, which would also be responsible for monitoring progress over the Parliament**. This would take the form of a concordat between the Liaison Committee and the relevant select committee (see figure 3B) agreed at the beginning of each parliamentary session. The purpose of the core tasks would be to make scrutiny more systematic, as such **these objectives might include; balancing inquiries between administration, finance and policy of their department; monitoring all departmental reports, business plans and performance indicators; conducting a regular cycle of work on activities of the regulators, executive agencies, quangos and other associated bodies within their department's purview; and review the progress of the department following the committee's previous reports.**

Figure 3B – Model concordat of select committee duties

The Liaison Committee has agreed the following concordat with the [example] Committee

That it will publish, within six weeks of the end of each Session (except where a dissolution occurs), a report setting out its achievements against the following targets.

Expenditure
- To examine and report on the main Estimates and annual expenditure plans of its department by 30 June each year.
- To examine and report on the resource accounts of its department by 31 March each year.
- To consider each supplementary estimate presented by its department, and report to the House whether it requires further consideration, within 28 days of the presentation of the supplementary Estimate.
- To report annually on its department's performance against its service level agreements.
- To report, at least once in each Parliament, on the impact of efficiency savings on the running costs of the department and their impact on the effectiveness with which it delivers services to the public.

Administration
- To consider the reports and accounts of each executive agency within the department, and report annually at least on whether any raise matters of particular concern.
- To take evidence and report on, over the cycle of a Parliament, each agency within the department of which the budget exceeds 4% of the overall departmental budget.
- To take evidence and report on, over the cycle of a Parliament, not fewer than one in four of the remaining agencies within the department.
- To take evidence and report on, over the cycle of a Parliament, each NDPB sponsored by the department which has an annual budget in excess of £10 million.
- To consider, and if appropriate take evidence and report on, each major appointment made by the relevant Secretary of State.

Policy
- To examine and report on any major policy initiative announced by the Department.
- To examine each Minister in the department, at least annually, on their discharge of their particular policy responsibilities.
- To keep under consideration the department's compliance with Freedom of Information legislation, and the quality of its provision of information to Parliament by whatever means.
- To consider each item of delegated legislation made by the department, and draw the attention of the House to those which raise particular questions of policy which require debate or other consideration.
- To consider each treaty signed by HMG falling within the area of responsibility of the department, and draw the attention of the House to those which raise particular questions of policy which require debate or other consideration.
- To consider and report on any draft legislation proposed by the government and referred to it by the House.

The annual report of the Committee will also itemise its expenditure in the relevant period on research, specialist advice, travel and entertainment.

At the beginning of each Parliament, within three months of its appointment (allowing for periods when the House is adjourned), the Committee will publish a report setting out its strategic plan for achieving the above targets, and any other matters relating to the discharge of its responsibilities that it thinks fit.

3.27 Such tasks may appear onerous; however, the Commission does not believe that each of these should be undertaken as a major, or even medium-scale inquiry. In most cases it is envisaged that the committees will not need to take evidence. The purpose of the core tasks is to ensure that the committee is at least taking note of the activity within their department and its associated bodies in a more regular fashion. This should enable them to identify significant issues at an earlier stage and if the committee feels it necessary this can be the starting point for a more detailed investigation.

3.28 Evidence from Andrea Ross-Robertson from Dundee University stated that identifying core objectives would improve the effectiveness of the committees. These "criteria could be set out in its order of reference. If the committee's remit has a clear purpose and if it has been appropriately interpreted by the committee, then assessing the committee's output against it objectives is a useful means of judging its effectiveness."[94] Such a procedure is already adopted by the Defence committee and **the Commission believes that select committees should have a set of objectives and performance indicators by which their performance could be judged. This would provide a public measurement of their effectiveness**.

Systematising scrutiny – improving the coverage of select committees

3.29 The introduction of core duties will increase the workload of every committee. It will require that committees are better-resourced and staffed and this is examined in more detail later. However, in the previous chapter we recommended that every backbench MP should serve on a select committee. We believe that the increased number of MPs serving on select committees will improve their capacity to cope with these extra demands and allow the committees a variety of options in their approach to their duties.

3.30 The Commission was struck by the work of the select committee on Environment, Transport and the Regions. This committee has 17 members, compared with the usual 11 members for other committees. The size of the committee means that its work is conducted through sub-committees operating in each of the subject specific areas. The fact that this committee was able to produce 33 reports over the course of the two parliamentary sessions 1997–1999 suggests that a similar approach by other committees may improve their productivity and scope of their scrutiny.[95]

3.31 The Commission believes that **the principal method of work for these enlarged committees should be through a series of sub-committees with specific remits for examining different aspects of departmental activity. The Commission believes that this would markedly improve the breadth and depth of scrutiny.**

3.32 The benefit of such a system is highlighted in the concerns of Sir Ian Byatt, the Director-General of Ofwat. As he points out, departments produce a plethora of information, but the committees largely fail to make use of it,

---

[94] Appendix 2, Evidence 27
[95] Appendix 5

> "The Government has been concerned to focus on target setting, public service agreements (PSAs) and many other initiatives. It would appear there is little structured evaluation or scrutiny by Parliament on the beneficial outcomes or otherwise to be achieved by Government objectives . . . Trying to engage select committees in the production of PSAs and Resource Accounting, each designed to improve openness and accountability seems to have attracted little attention or interest in Parliament."[96]

3.33 Each of the subject based sub-committees could be established with responsibility for monitoring the statistics produced by the department, but also by the bodies related to the department. The sub-committees would be given responsibility for reporting to the main committee issues of significance. It would be for the committee to decide whether such information merited a larger inquiry.

3.34 The Commission believes that the flexibility of the committees and the range of issues covered would be enhanced by adoption of the rapporteur system. Rapporteurs are common in European Parliaments but are little used in Westminster-style legislatures. The rapporteur would be a committee member, chosen by members of the committee to prepare background papers and research on a specific subject of interest to the committee. The rapporteur might have responsibility for monitoring a subject for the course of a Parliament. The benefit of the system is that it allows individual Members to play a greater role pursuing issues of particular interest, and as such broadens the scope of the committee without limiting their inquiries. **The House of Commons should allow committees to experiment with the use of rapporteurs who would gather evidence and produce background papers for the whole committee.** The Liaison Committee or Procedure Committee should evaluate the performance of the system.

3.35 Sir Ian Byatt's concerns about Parliament's treatment of finance were echoed in other evidence to the Commission. The Commission believes that, given the importance of monitoring expenditure in the process of holding government to account, Parliament must pay far greater attention to these sorts of indicators than it does at present. Chapter five deals with Parliament's scrutiny of government expenditure in more detail and includes a series of recommendations to improve accountability in this area. It is sufficient to state here that the Commission believes every departmental select committee should have an audit sub-committee, specifically responsible for examining the finances of the department (see para 5.20).

3.36 The Commission acknowledges that the increased workload will put extra pressure on MPs, even with enlarged membership and extra resources. The Commission believes that this extra work must also be reflected elsewhere in Parliament so that MPs are given more time to pursue their committee work. The most valuable resource available to select committees is time; the time of MPs to attend meetings and read briefings; the time of the staff to undertake the many tasks select committees should carry out; and the time in the parliamentary week, with the competing demands of the chamber, standing and select committee committees. The Commission believes that select committee work is at present squeezed by other functions and duties. Select committee activity should be a priority of MPs and the House as a whole; our recommendations are designed to ensure that they have the time and resources to function effectively. As such in the next chapter we recommend that one day a week should be devoted to committee work when the chamber does not meet (see para 4.28).

---

[96] Appendix 2, Evidence 25

Ensuring accountability – improving impact

3.37 Although improved resources and membership are likely to enhance the productivity of the committees it does not necessarily follow that this will improve their effectiveness. The powers of the committees are limited in their access to information and Ministers, and in their ability to enforce their findings. Although standing orders give committees the power to compel witnesses to attend this does not apply to Ministers or specific Government papers. And as one select committee chair told the Commission at a private meeting, the only power he possesses is to embarrass the Government occasionally. Committees have few formal powers for ensuring their reports are taken notice of or their recommendations implemented and they usually rely on a wily chair able to generate media coverage.

3.38 However, it is not clear that increasing committees' formal powers would dramatically improve their performance. Rather, as the comment from the above committee chair suggests, the impact of the committee's report will depend on the way in which the committee handles it. The Commission believes that select committees have significant scope to improve their effectiveness within their existing powers.

3.39 In evidence to the Commission, Age Concern suggested that select committees should follow up their reports with a review of progress, perhaps at the end of each parliamentary session.[97] David Millar a former clerk in the House of Commons made a similar proposal,

> "Each select committee should be obliged, by sessional order or by decision of the Liaison Committee, to follow up the degree of implementation of its recommendations, e.g. three or five years after their publication, and to report upon them. This would highlight government failure to implement; enable interested parties to point out the desirability (in many cases) of their implementation; and attract media attention"[98]

3.40 The Commission agrees with this analysis. **The impact of committee reports will be determined by the assiduity with which their recommendations are monitored and followed up. Committees should publish a periodic review (two to three years after the original report) assessing how far their recommendations have been implemented.**

3.41 There is some concern about the quality of government replies to committee reports, although our research shows that committee clerks are generally quite satisfied with the quality of Government replies with only 17% regarding the responses as unsatisfactory or highly unsatisfactory.[99] We have no way of knowing whether committee chairs would share these views, and the Liaison Committee in 2000 stated that,

> "Too many are superficial – and give the impression that they have been drafted with only a cursory look at the summary of recommendations, ignoring the analysis and argument in the body of the report . . . The format of replies sometimes borders on the casual. A Government reply should not be given by letter or written answer."[100]

---

[97] Appendix 2, Evidence 1
[98] Appendix 2, Evidence 19
[99] Appendix 5
[100] Liaison Committee, (1999–2000), HC 300, para 47

3.42 Age Concern suggested that Ministers ought to be obliged to respond to committee reports through oral hearings as a way of improving both the status of the report and the quality of reply.[101] **Government replies should conform to a set of minimum standards. These should include an undertaking that a reply should address each of the committees' specific recommendations and oblige Government to formally publish their response.** However, once again the extent to which such standards of reply are maintained is likely to rely on the persistence of the committee in following up substandard replies.

Making committees relevant to Parliament

3.43 The Commission's proposed reforms are intended to make select committees the engine of parliamentary activity. By expecting every backbench MP to serve on a committee and increasing their responsibilities we hope that their status will be enhanced. However, the committees' vital role in filtering evidence and highlighting issues of political significance needs a parliamentary outlet, and **the Commission believes that reform should integrate the committees into the activity of other parts of Parliament**. The Commission believes that committees should have a greater impact on the debates in the chamber and the scrutiny of legislation.

3.44 As we have noted committee reports are irregularly debated and very few are put to a vote in the chamber. The introduction of Westminster Hall has increased the opportunities for debating committee reports, but the attendance at such debates is often poor and can sometimes include only the members of the relevant select committee. In many ways, the use of Westminster Hall reflects the low priority given to committee work. Part of the problem is that reports are rarely considered on a substantive motion, but rather on a motion to adjourn the House. This means that even when a vote is taken it is not related to the recommendations of the report.

3.45 The Liaison Committee studied this matter in some detail and recommended that there should be a half hour debate once a week after question time on a committee report published within the previous fortnight.[102] The Government rejected this proposal on the grounds that two weeks was not enough for ministers to develop a considered response.[103]

3.46 However, the point of this recommendation is not simply to create more time for select committee debates, as many of these are of low quality and often attract only the members of the committee to the chamber. The Liaison Committee itself noted that their proposal was to provide a half hour at prime time to highlight topical issues and encourage an exchange of views between MPs and Government. In a subsequent report the committee refined its recommendations suggesting a "more question-based event" perhaps along the lines of starred Questions in the Lords.[104] The Commission

---

[101] Appendix 2, Evidence 1
[102] HC 321 (2000–2001), paras 28–35
[103] The Government's Response to the First Report from the Liaison Committee on Shifting the Balance: Select Committees and the Executive, (May 2000), Cm 4737
[104] Liaison Committee, (2000–2001), HC 321, paras 31–35

supports the proposal of the Liaison Committee. **There should be regular opportunities for short debates/questions on recently published reports during a peak period in the chamber, to which ministers should give the Government's preliminary response.**

3.47 **The Commission also believes that the work of the select committees should have a greater bearing on parliamentary scrutiny of legislation.** Several members of the Commission believed that select committees should be responsible for examining legislation, and we received evidence from a variety of sources reinforcing this point of view. It is argued that the expertise built up on select committees means that bills would receive a much closer level of scrutiny than under the current system of standing committees.

3.48 The counter argument, equally fervently expressed, is that if select committees were given a legislative role this would dominate their activity and weaken their ability to scrutinise and hold ministers to account. In the Scottish Parliament where committees undertake both accountability and legislative functions this appears to be the case in some areas. The Justice and Home Affairs Committee, for example, in its first year examined four pieces of legislation and was unable to initiate any of its own inquiries. By comparison other committees had very few pieces of legislation to deal with and were able to scrutinise in greater detail their department's work.

3.49 Although our remit does not extend to parliamentary scrutiny of legislation **the Commission believes that the expertise of select committees should be deployed much more effectively in examination of legislation.** However, a range of options exist between the current system and the creation of new dual-purpose committees. Since 1997 the Government has made a greater effort to publish bills in draft and use the select committees in their scrutiny. Dr Lynne Jones MP suggested that pre-legislative scrutiny committees should be made up of interested MPs and that the same MPs should make up the standing committee.[105] Age Concern informed the Commission that they were

> "attracted to the notion of combining select and standing committees so that they can together better scrutinise legislative proposals but first await consideration of the pre-legislative committee experiment. Most legislation emanates from Whitehall and has been consulted upon with interested parties well before it reaches Parliament. This process should involve Parliament earlier, perhaps by using select committees."[106]

3.50 The Commission recommends that Parliament experiment with various methods for involving select committees in the legislative process. The larger select committees working through a variety of sub-committees mean that scrutiny of legislation need not dominate the activity of the entire committee. **Committees should play a greater role in the scrutiny of draft legislation, but this relies on earlier publication by departments so that committees have sufficient time to examine the draft bills. In addition, one or two dual-purpose committees, conducting departmental inquiries and scrutinising legislation, should be established on a pilot basis and their performance evaluated by the re-organised Liaison Committee.**

---

[105] Appendix 2, Evidence 16
[106] Appendix 2, Evidence 1

Resources

3.51 Our recommendations for enhancing the functions of select committees would require a consequent increase in staffing and resources. At present the annual cost of the select committee system is £7.7 million, this compares with the £394.9 billion of central government expenditure each year.[107] A recent report on the governance of the House of Commons highlighted the core issues,

> "Resourcing a Parliament effectively is an extremely difficult business. The House of Commons is no exception. The House has no mission statement; Members of Parliament have no job description. The Parliamentary process is to a great extent reactive, and the type and scale of activity is often dictated by external events . . . Yet the effective operation of the House is of enormous constitutional and public importance. The elector (and taxpayer) expects Governments to be held to account; constituents to be represented and their grievances pursued; and historic Parliamentary functions to be extended and adapted to changes in the wider world. . . These things do not come cheap, and no-one should expect them to. Seeking to hold to account a complex, sophisticated and powerful Executive; dealing with an unremitting burden of legislation; and meeting ever-increasing expectations on the part of constituents; all this requires substantial, high quality support."[108]

3.52 The resources available to Parliament in its scrutiny function need to be examined strategically, and to be planned and managed as a whole. This is currently impossible in the way the Houses are organised and managed. There are various sources of expertise available to Parliament and politicians – the generalist administrators and policy analysts of the clerk's departments, the specialist staff directly employed by individual committees, the specialists in the House of Commons Library, the Parliamentary Office of Science and Technology, the National Audit Office, the legal services of the two Houses, and the "freelance" special advisers employed on an *ad hoc* basis by select committees. To these could be added the individual research assistants employed by Members and Peers. However, these resources are disconnected, largely unaware of the opportunities for co-operation and co-ordination, and occasionally engaged in direct and damaging competition with each other.

3.53 Those who are charged with managing Parliament's scrutiny function – for the most part the clerk's departments of the two Houses – have no strategic direction from their employers and little freedom of action to innovate and develop the scrutiny function within broad guidelines. It might be supposed that the relationship between a committee and its staff would be similar to that between a Minister and his department – the one making key decisions and giving strategic direction, the other implementing those decisions, examining and evaluating alternatives, developing services to deliver that strategy more economically and efficiently, and carrying forward day by day work within the broad framework of political direction.

3.54 In fact, it seems that these relationships are ill-defined and often dysfunctional. On occasion the roles seem to be reversed, with staff trying to give strategic direction and chairs and members concerning themselves only with the grammar of their draft reports.

---

[107] Liaison Committee, (2000–1), *Shifting the Balance: Unfinished Business*, HC 321, para 142
[108] *Review of Management and Services: Report to the House of Commons Commission*, (1998–99), HC 745, paras. 2.1–2.3

3.55 Rational strategic planning of scrutiny activity cannot happen in such a context, and rational manpower resource planning cannot take place without any definition of the task to be done or any output measures against which to judge whether the organisation is hitting its targets. We have proposed elsewhere a model 'concordat' between the Liaison Committee and a departmental committee (see Figure 3B). We believe that making explicit and transparent the expectations of a committee from its staff in a similar way could begin to clarify the resource to task allocation for committee staff, and provide a framework within which the managers of those staff could become more creative and innovative in delivering an effective scrutiny function to each House. **The provision of extra staff resources to select committees should be tied to a clarification of the committees' roles and their core tasks. Extra staff or secondments should be related to their agreed functions and duties**.

3.56 More generally, the Commission sees a need for both Houses to begin to move beyond the rather piecemeal and hand-to-mouth approach to financing and staffing their scrutiny functions that they have adopted in the past. In parallel to the clearer leadership we have proposed for the politicians in the two Houses, there needs to be clearer leadership of the permanent staff of each House, planned around a clear set of expectations. That leadership needs to be able to take a wider view of how to deliver on those plans, and to be able to co-ordinate the various resources available, both within the permanent staffs and outside, to do that in the most effective and efficient manner. **The House authorities should review the work of the clerk's department and levels of support to ensure that committees, and the scrutiny function more generally, are supported in the most effective way possible.**

Conclusion: Enforcing accountability

3.57 It should not be doubted that the current operation of select committees is central to the performance of the House of Commons, and in general the select committees work well. Our survey of MPs revealed that MPs thought the committees were far and away the most effective way in which Parliament held Government to account. Our findings (which are included in figure 4E) show that 83.8% regard select committees as an effective or very effective means of holding ministers to account, and in total 57.5% of MPs regarded the select committees as the most effective weapon in Parliament's armoury.[109]

3.58 The Commission's recommendations must be viewed in this context. However, the success of the committees relies on their keeping pace with Government so that the they make the best possible use of the information and performance indicators provided by departments. The Commission is concerned with the effectiveness of Parliament as a whole and that reform of the select committees fits into changes to other parts of the Commons and Lords. One of the committees' principal strengths is that they provide a less adversarial forum in which to draw out issues of political significance, however, such an atmosphere is not suitable for all forms of

---

[109] Appendix 4

accountability. The task, and what our reforms are intended to achieve, is to link the various parts of Parliament with each other (so that, for example, the work of the committees illuminates that of the chamber) and with the outside world (engaging with information from government departments, regulators and the public). The Commission believes that committee work should be an integral feature of every MP's activity and complement their work in other spheres, notably the chamber.

Principle 3 – Committees should play a more influential role within Parliament

The Commission believes that the system of departmental select committees provides the basis for a more effective system of scrutiny. However, the work of the committees needs to be made more systematic. The duties of the select committees should be more closely defined, their relationship with external scrutiny bodies made more formal and their input into the other areas of parliamentary activity increased.

Recommendations

Core duties and performance indicators

7. **Both Houses should maintain a central list of all those organisations obliged to report to Parliament. This list should be distributed to every committee, so that every departmental select committee is aware of the organisations which come under their jurisdiction. (para 3.24)**

8. **The select committees should be given a set of core duties and functions. To improve the coverage of issues, to utilise the work of the regulators and to give the committees a continuity to their work they should meet pre-agreed objectives over the course of a Parliament. These objectives would provide a set of criteria against which their performance can be judged. (para 3.25)**

9. **These objectives should be agreed with the reformed Liaison Committee, which would also be responsible for monitoring progress over the Parliament. These objectives might include; balancing inquiries between administration, finance and policy of their department; monitoring all departmental reports, business plans and performance indicators; conducting a regular cycle of work on activities of the regulators, executive agencies, quangos and other associated bodies within their department's purview; and review the progress of the department following the committee's previous reports. (para. 3.26)**

10. **Select committees should have a set of objectives and performance indicators by which their performance could be judged. This would provide a public measurement of their effectiveness. (para 3.28)**

Developing new methods of work

11. **The principal method of work for these enlarged committees should be through a series of sub-committees with specific remits for examining different aspects of departmental activity. The Commission believes that this would markedly improve the breadth and depth of scrutiny. (para. 3.31)**

12. The House of Commons should allow committees to experiment with the use of rapporteurs who would gather evidence and produce background papers for the whole committee. (para. 3.34)

Improving impact

13. The impact of committee reports will be determined by the assiduity with which their recommendations are monitored and followed up. Committees should publish a periodic review (two to three years after the original report) assessing how far their recommendations have been implemented. (para 3.40)

14. Government replies should conform to a set of minimum standards. These should include an undertaking that a reply should address each of the committees' specific recommendations and oblige Government to formally publish their response. (para 3.42)

Integrating committee work into parliamentary activity

15. There should be regular opportunities for short debates/questions on recently published reports during a peak period in the chamber, to which ministers should give the Government's preliminary response. (para 3.46)

16. The expertise of select committees should be deployed much more effectively in examination of legislation. Committees should play a greater role in the scrutiny of draft legislation. However, this relies on earlier publication by departments so that committees have sufficient time to examine draft bills. (para. 3.47–3.50)

17. In addition, one or two dual-purpose committees, conducting departmental inquiries and scrutinising legislation, should be established on a pilot basis and their performance evaluated by the re-organised Liaison Committee. (para 3.50)

Staffing and support

18. The recommendations for increasing select committee responsibilities also require a consequent increase in staffing and resources. (para 3.51) However, the resourcing of Parliament needs to be examined strategically. The provision of extra resources should be tied to a clarification of the committees' roles and their core tasks. Extra staff or secondments should be related to their agreed functions and duties. (para 3.55)

19. The House authorities should review the work of the clerk's department and levels of support to ensure that committees, and the scrutiny function more generally, are supported in the most effective way possible. (para 3.56)

Chapter Four

Restoring the centrality of the Commons' chamber

4.1 The floor of the House of Commons is the main public focus for activity at Westminster. It is the arena for the discussion and dissemination of the most important issues, and at times of extreme political tension, the chamber provides the most vivid images. The Government ultimately derives its authority from being able to carry a majority in the chamber. It is the public face of Parliament and the ultimate forum for holding ministers to account. But the Commission believes the chamber is in decline; judged in terms of the amount of public interest it generates, the extent to which it influences events or even attendance by MPs, it appears to be waning.

4.2 The chamber performs a unique function in holding ministers to account, highlighting issues and illuminating them for the public. Yet the structures and procedures of the chamber have not sufficiently adapted to accommodate the changes to the committee system, the role of MPs and the interests of the public. As a result it does not effectively complement other aspects of MPs' work. The chamber should be the plenary session of the House of Commons, in order to perform this function it should meet less often, and meet for a purpose.

4.3 The role of the chamber needs to be refined so that its activity is more likely to highlight the most important political issues. This requires changes to the hours that the chamber sits, the way that business is conducted, the content and subject matter of questions and debates, and the way this activity links with other parts of the MP's job.

Role of the chamber – the importance of party politics

4.4 The chamber's role in contributing to the scrutiny and calling to account of government has three main components, namely authorising Government actions, debating issues of political significance and calling ministers to account for their actions through questions and debates. The chamber's role is distinct in that it provides a broader oversight role than that of the committees which can engage in more detailed investigation. The fact that the Government must maintain a majority in the division lobbies means that it carries the ultimate sanction of accountability. Its role in illuminating issues for the public means the ministers should not only be accountable to MPs through the chamber but also be judged by public opinion. The chamber should be the summit of the process of parliamentary scrutiny, with MPs drawing on information gathered from other sources, and perhaps filtered by the committees, to question and seek clarification from government ministers.

4.5 The chamber is inevitably more partisan and party political than the committees. The structure of the chamber and the vast majority of its procedures are built around the assumption of two main parties. Party cohesion is fundamental to the working of

Parliament. Commons business is organised around a series of informal agreements between the political parties. These agreements, and by default Parliament, work only for as long as the parties can carry their MPs with them. An effective Parliament needs effective parties. Proposals to improve the quality of scrutiny and accountability cannot be based on the removal of political party influence from Parliament. Rather they must acknowledge its importance.

4.6   The clash of differing political opinions in the chamber should highlight the most significant features of an argument, in their starkest form. Party politics should add to the public understanding of policy matters, and allow the electorate to decide on the basis of the performance of the main parties.

4.7   However, the current quality of the party political debate falls short of what is required at Westminster. The principal audience for most contributions appears to be other MPs in the chamber rather than the wider public and as Betty Boothroyd noted in her farewell speech in the Commons, "engagement with the real issues is seen to be overshadowed by political point scoring simply for its own sake."[110] The Commission is concerned that too little of what goes on in the chamber reflects issues of public relevance. As we have stated throughout the report, accountability to Parliament is a task undertaken on behalf of the public. Parliament is strongest where it engages with and articulates issues of public interest in a manner that the public understands.

The chamber's failure to adapt

4.8   The quality of activity in the chamber is partly a result of its failure to adapt to changes elsewhere in Parliament and in the role of MPs themselves. The thrust of recent parliamentary reform has been to remove some of the chamber's traditional functions to other forums such as committees, or more recently, the parallel chamber in Westminster Hall. However, this siphoning off of tasks has not been matched by a clarification or even a reduction in the chamber's hours. It is not clear what the chamber should do with this extra time, it still meets as often, but its purpose is now less clear.

4.9   As figures 4A and 4B show, over the last 40 years neither the total number of sitting days nor sitting hours has fallen significantly. In figure 4A the peaks in the graph are sessions following election years and are therefore unusually long, (and the preceding session unusually short). But ignoring election years, the variation in the number of sitting days is limited.

---

[110] Rt Hon Betty Boothroyd MP, Speaker's resignation statement, HC debs, 26 July 2000, vol. 354, col. 1114

Figure 4A – Total number of sitting days per session, 1960–1999

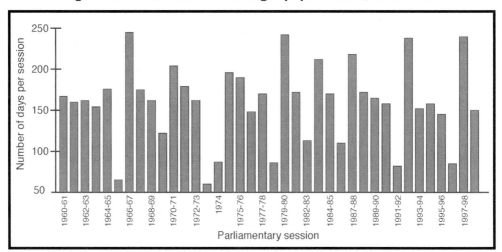

4.10 Figure 4B eliminates election years and takes a mid-term year from each of the Parliaments since 1960. Again it shows that there is no significant drop in the number of hours that the chamber sits for each year. But, over this same period the pressures on MPs to be active outside the chamber have increased. Some MPs serve on select committees, others serve on standing committees and research suggests that the amount of constituency work faced by the average MP has grown dramatically in recent years.[111] In addition there are opportunities to be active in backbench and all-party groups, and the introduction of Westminster Hall in 1999 has increased the amount of time overall for MPs to debate matters.

Figure 4B – Total sitting hours per session 1960–1999

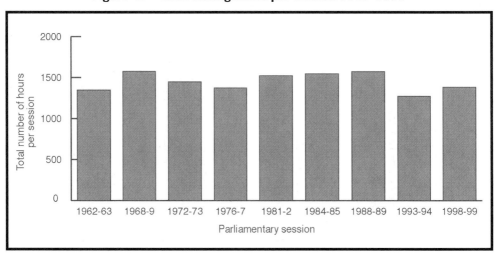

[111] See for example Norton, P., & Wood, D., (1994), *Back from Westminster*, Kentucky University Press; Power, G., (1998), *Representatives of the People?*, Fabian Society: London

4.11 This combination of factors has made the chamber simply one option among many for the active politician and in many respects it is the least appealing. The structure of debate in the chamber restricts backbenchers ability to make a meaningful contribution. The 2001 report of the Review Body on Senior Salaries included a generic job description for MPs which stated that "Members appear in the chamber to speak rather than to listen. It is a forum for making a case but for most of the time has only a marginal effect on major decisions."[112] One backbench Labour MP told the Commission although his opportunities to speak in the chamber were not formally limited he had been advised unofficially by the Speaker's office (who are ultimately responsible for the choice of speakers) to choose his subjects wisely as he would only get called four times in each parliamentary session. Philip Norton suggests that the introduction of the select committees in 1979 was in part a reaction to the frustration felt by many MPs who wanted to have some impact on public policy but had few opportunities in the chamber.[113]

Figure 4C – Attendance during debates March 2000[114]

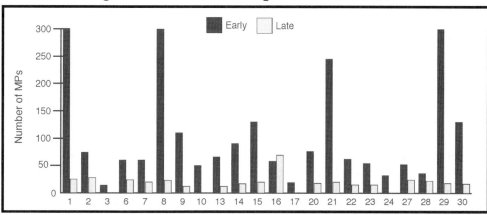

Figure 4D – Attendance during debates November–December 2000

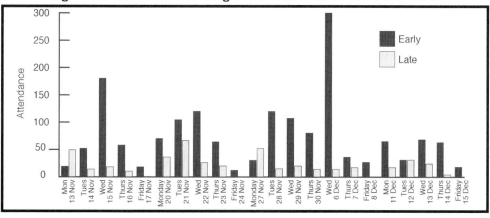

[112] Review Body on Senior Salaries, Report No. 48: *Review of parliamentary pay and allowances, Volume 2: Independent study on pay and allowances*, Cm 4997-II, p.32
[113] Norton, P., (1998), *Parliaments and Governments in Western Europe*, Frank Cass: London, p.30
[114] The number of MPs in the chamber were recorded at a peak period and a low period. They were recorded at 2.45pm and 8pm on Monday, Tuesday and Wednesday, 11.30am and 2pm on Thursday, and at 10am on Friday. Numbers over 300 were not recorded, the high points are therefore 300 plus.

Mechanisms for accountability in the chamber

4.12 The low levels of attendance may not therefore be surprising but they reflect the quality of much activity in the chamber. The principal means of being involved is through either debates or questions to ministers, but our poll of MPs revealed that none of these mechanisms are regarded in particularly high esteem. Although select committee hearings were regarded as effective or very effective by 83.8%, the chamber's mechanisms fared less well. The percentage of MPs who regarded them as 'effective' or 'very effective' for written questions were 50.8%, ministerial statements 45.2%, private notice questions 43%, departmental question time 25.1%, Opposition Day Debates 22.9% and only 7.8% for Prime Ministers Questions.

Figure 4E – Effectiveness of parliamentary mechanisms

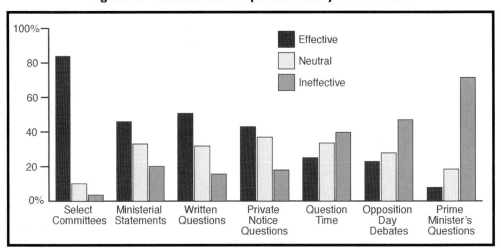

Debates

4.13 Given that the Government controls the timetable in the Chamber it is usually able to choose the territory on which it will debate. Debates initiated by the Opposition are therefore an important mechanism for scrutiny by forcing the Government to give an account of its activity. For the most part these opportunities lie in either adjournment debates or Opposition Days. Backbench adjournment debates allow MPs to raise almost any topic that is the responsibility of government. However, they are often concerned with the MPs' own constituency interests, are usually poorly attended and the only vote is on whether the House should adjourn. As such they cannot be used to reach any substantial decision.

4.14 The main tool of the Opposition parties is their ability to call debates on 20 days each year on a subject of their choosing. The topics are often broad departmental or policy areas, but a significant number seek to force the government to address more specific topical issues. The debates revolve around a substantive motion which is usually critical of the Government's policy. The results are predictable; the Opposition motion is rejected and the Government's amendments accepted and the quality of debate similarly formulaic.

4.15 Their main weakness is not that they are dominated by party politics, but the quality of the political debate they tend to engender. The debates allow the Opposition parties to raise contentious issues, test the arguments of ministers and occasionally illuminate a particular public problem. By exposing the key elements of government policy to sustained criticism, the Commons should highlight the strengths and weaknesses of that policy. However, the ritualistic nature of most contributions and the low quality of debate in general means that there is little public interest in Opposition Days. Their merit is purely for the benefit of those attending, "It is the debate which counts, and the general approach and commitment of the main speakers."[115] Speeches and interventions are aimed at parliamentary colleagues and party whips, designed to identify which MPs deserve promotion.

4.16 In addition MPs find it difficult to raise issues of concern to their constituents other than in sparsely attended adjournment debates. The procedures of the House mean that it is almost impossible for substantive topical debates to be raised on anything other than party political grounds. There is no equivalent of the 'short debate' or 'interpellation' used in other democracies, which require the attendance of a minister, and usually generate a packed plenary.

4.17 The introduction of Westminster Hall in October 1999 provided 134 opportunities (or 108 hours) for MPs to raise issues with ministers in the 1999–2000 session. There were also 13 debates on committee reports (39 hours).[116] This should not be derided as it provides a valuable new mechanism for raising issues. However, whilst individual MPs might welcome the opportunity to speak more often, the fact that the average attendance over the session was between 10 and 12, raises a question about their wider value.[117]

4.18 It may be that debates are no longer suitable for today's politics. In an era of soundbite politics and 24 hour news, the idea of debating a single issue for six hours is alien to most MPs and their electorate. The results are also questionable, as it is rare for such debates to bring a new clarity to a contentious political issue, and hardly surprising that so few MPs sit through the proceedings.

Questions and statements

Oral questions

4.19 In theory the purpose of PQs is to elicit information from Government. In practice, although the daily question time of Ministers can be informative, it is often motivated more by the desire for political point-scoring. Certainly PQs do not fulfil the same purpose they did at the end of the 19th century, as Norman Chester points out,

> "In 1901, and indeed for some years after, a Member could hand in a Question at the Table as late as 11pm or 11.30 on, say, Monday for answer the next afternoon. His Question would be certain to be reached. If he did not like the answer he could come out of the Chamber, think out one or two further Questions, hand them in and be certain of the Minister having to reply to him on the Thursday. If the Minister again failed to satisfy him he could put in another Question which would be reached on Friday, and so on, day after day if he so wished."[118]

[115] Griffith, J.A.G. & Ryle, M., (1988), *Parliament: Functions, Procedures and Practice*, Sweet & Maxwell: London, p. 342
[116] Modernisation Committee, (2000–2001), *Sittings in Westminster Hall: Report, Proceedings and Appendices of the Committee*, HC 906
[117] *ibid.*, para 14
[118] Chester, N., (1977), 'Questions in the House', in Walkland and Ryle, *The Commons in the Seventies*, Fontana, p. 155–6

4.20 This sort of repeated oral questioning is impossible today given the volume of Questions and the increase in the scope of Government. The desire to accommodate more PQs saw the introduction of the 'Order of Questions' which means that a department faces concerted questioning during Question Time, but only once a month.

4.21 Question Time has tended to become another part of the 'permanent election campaign' on the floor of the House. The process is heavily influenced by PPS's and whips who plant pre-arranged questions amongst backbenchers in the hope that these 'favourable' subjects will dominate. For their part the Opposition will often orchestrate questions around a particular policy failure. The apparent misuse of Question Time led Speaker Michael Martin to make a statement to the House on 14 February 2001, which upbraided both Government and Opposition,

> "The primary purpose of Question Time is to hold the Executive to account. *Erskine May* says that a question must either seek information or press for action, and that it must relate to matters for which Ministers are officially responsible. Questions are out of order if they relate to Opposition party policies rather than Government responsibilities . . . Answers should be confined to points contained in questions, giving only such explanation as renders an answer intelligible."[119]

4.22 The accountability value of question time hits its nadir during questions to the Prime Minister. Former PM John Major in evidence to the Committee on Public Administration in 2000 stated that PMQs was a 'bear garden' and "does not actually deal with the great important issues of government"[120] It is dominated by point scoring and the vast majority of questions on both sides of the House are planted by the whips. The high level of political management of questions is illustrated by the fact that in the first 21 PMQs in 1997 the Prime Minister's "standard reply to [planted] questions – 'My honourable friend is absolutely right' – was used 35 times."[121]

4.23 The use of statements and Private Notice Questions is more highly regarded by MPs because they provide the opportunity to question ministers on the most topical issues. Statements are used by ministers to respond to events and allow the Opposition and backbenchers around 30 minutes for questions on the subject. Private Notice Questions allow a similar questioning but are tabled by individual MPs and are permitted at the discretion of the Speaker and, in recent years, have been rare – in the 1998–9 session there were only 12.

Written questions

4.24 Written questions are used by MPs often genuinely seeking information. By using written Parliamentary Questions, Members can obtain information which they may use as the basis for a campaign, for further inquiries, or for exposing errors or inconsistencies in the activities of the executive. However, the 1998 Public Administration committee noted that,

---

[119] HC debs, 14 February 2001, vol. 341, col. 315
[120] Public Administration Committee (2000–2001), *The Ministerial Code: Improving the Rule Book*, HC 235
[121] Weir & Beetham, *op cit*, p. 432

"The effectiveness of the system, however, depends crucially on the acceptance by Ministers of the principle that they should be as open as possible in responding to questions. The report of the Scott Inquiry, on the Export of Defence Equipment and Dual-Use Goods to Iraq and Related Prosecutions, expressed concern about the failure of Ministers to discharge the Government's obligation to give Parliament and the public "as full information as possible", and not to deceive them about government policy and actions."[122]

4.25 The Scott Report had raised concerns about the approach adopted by civil servants in drafting replies to questions. It appears that some officials regarded it as a matter of professional pride that answers were so worded as to give away as little as possible. Sir Michael Quinlan, the former permanent secretary at the Ministry of Defence, in evidence to the Scott inquiry stated that the purpose of PQs was for the Opposition to

"give the Government a hard time", and for the Government "to avoid having a hard time" . . . "the Opposition will seek to extract information which they can use to portray the Government in a bad light; and they will, within conventions looser than those binding the Government, feel free thereafter to exploit the information, if necessary selectively and tendentiously, to that end. The Government, for its part will be reluctant to disclose information of a kind, or in a form, that will help the Opposition to do so."[123]

4.26 The Public Administration committee also raised concerns about the amount of questions that were either 'blocked' or that received 'holding answers'. Although there were good reasons for using both of these – not least the volume of questions now being asked of departments – the committee expressed concern at the extent of their use. Their report highlighted the implications of blocking answers, which not only mean that an answer is refused, but prevent others from asking questions on the same subjects, and recommended that departments explain more fully their reasons for using holding answers. In sum, these defects – the high level of political management, Whitehall's less than fulsome provision of information, the use of blocking and holding answers, and the fact that backbench MPs have no effective means of recourse if they are dissatisfied with an answer – weigh against effective scrutiny.

Reforming the chamber

4.27 **To improve the attendance and influence of the chamber its core tasks need to be refined and clarified. It should become the plenary session of the Parliament.** The Commission believes that the value of much of the chamber's activity needs to be re-assessed. There is scope for making much of the chamber's proceedings shorter, sharper and more to the point. Although it is important for the Commons to deal with subjects at length and in detail, it is not clear that six-hour debates make for rigorous analysis. They generate little public interest, and the lengthy contributions of some MPs combined with the limited opportunities for participation make them equally unattractive to other backbenchers. The content of many debates is dictated more by party politicking than scrutiny, and contributions are often more for the benefit of parliamentary colleagues than the public good.

---

[122] Public Administration Committee (1997–8), *Ministerial Accountability and Parliamentary Questions*, HC 820, para 1
[123] Quoted in Public Service Committee, (1995–6), *Ministerial Accountability and Responsibility*, HC 313-I, para 40

Shortening the hours of the chamber

4.28   The chamber remains the ultimate forum for holding ministers to account. However to improve its effectiveness in doing so the Commission believes that Parliament should become a more committee-based institution. The committees offer much greater opportunity for detailed scrutiny and accountability of Government. But they also offer the prospect of a more effective chamber working to complement the work of the committees. **In order to reflect the importance attached to the select committee system, and not take MPs away from the chamber, one day each week should be devoted to committee activity. To reflect the importance of this work other parliamentary business should be arranged around the committees so that the chamber would not meet on this day.**

4.29   Such recommendations have been debated in the past by the Procedure Committee, which has recommended experimenting with the timing of parliamentary business.[124] There have been numerous changes affecting the parliamentary timetable in the last thirty years such as the select committee system, morning sittings and the introduction of constituency Fridays, and logic would suggest that the 'committee day' should be either Tuesday or Wednesday. This recommendation would not only enhance the status of the committees, but also by rationing the time in the chamber would mean that it acts more as a plenary session for issues of importance. However, the Commission acknowledges that re-arranging the timing of the chamber relies heavily on how it deals with legislation, which is beyond the scope of this inquiry.

More statements, fewer debates

4.30   **MPs should have more opportunities for short debates on substantive issues.** A common feature of European legislatures is the 'interpellation' or 'short debate' where an opposition party (or an equivalent number of MPs) can call a debate on a topical issue. The system obliges a government minister to attend and provide an official statement on a matter of public concern. The debates are more substantial than adjournment debates in that they cover important topical issues and generate a high level of attendance. The closest equivalent in the Commons is probably Standing Order 24, which allows for emergency debates. However, the practice is very rarely used. In the 1998–9 session there were only three applications for a debate, none of which were successful.

4.31   The key is to provide opportunities for MPs to introduce topical and substantive issues, which allow a number of MPs to participate. In this vein, the Norton Commission recommended experimentation with 'unstarred questions', a practice used in the Lords allowing for 60 or 90-minute debates, and also 60 minute 'emergency debates'.[125] Both suggestions would improve the quality and topicality of debates in the chamber.

---

[124] For example, Procedure Committee, (1966–7), *Sixth Report*, HC 539; Procedure Committee, (Session 1977–8), *First Report*, HC 588-I
[125] Commission to Strengthen Parliament, *op cit.*, p.28

4.32 However, debates have a limited value in holding government to account and it may be more effective to extend existing arrangements in the Commons for questioning ministers and calling for ministerial statements. The first recommendation is that **opposition parties should be able to trade some of their Opposition Days for the chance to call for a statement on a topical issue**. At present Opposition parties have 20 days (or 120 hours) of debating time on issues of their choosing. A straight trade of hours for ministerial statements would probably be unacceptable to Government. Ministers are rarely present throughout Opposition Days, it would dramatically increase the amount of time they had to spend in the House, and the ability to question a minister for an hour is arguably more valuable than three hours of debate. It would need to be on a ratio therefore of, say, four statements for one full day's debate. The main opposition party would be able to trade a quarter of their time (five days) for twenty extra statements. This, in turn, would reduce the hours of the chamber.

4.33 Some of this extra time could be used for the second recommendation in this area – **that the Speaker should grant more Private Notice Questions**. Given that scrutiny is a task for all MPs and not just the opposition, PNQs have an advantage over Opposition Days. The current rules governing the use of Private Notice Questions mean that few are permitted and most go to frontbench MPs or Privy Councillors. The solution may be to use some of the extra hours, created by trading Opposition Day Debates for statements, for extra PNQs. The decision would still be at the discretion of the Speaker, and the practice relatively infrequent, but along with other changes they may be a more effective weapon for the backbench MP.

Public interest debates

4.34 The chamber should also complement other spheres of MP activity. A very high proportion of MPs regard the constituency as their most important role and, for Parliament and the Government, the constituency experience of Members is an important valve for alerting MPs to policy failure. MPs knew about the problems of the Child Support Agency and the Passport Agency long before they were debated in Parliament, but there were limited opportunities to raise issues on substantive motions. Adjournment debates tend to be sparsely attended and deal with parochial issues, whilst Opposition Days mean that important issues can be obscured by political point-scoring. There should be **specific provision for 'public interest debates'** motivated by policy failure or maladministration on a broad scale (as opposed to constituency-specific concerns).

4.35 MPs should have the opportunity to call a short debate and require a ministerial response on such issues where there is a clear case of policy failure. These would be similar to the emergency debates under SO 24, but they would be specifically linked to the concerns of constituents. The trigger for such debates would be a specific number of MPs (it is suggested between 150 and 200) drawn proportionately from all the parties. The cross party requirement would prevent their abuse by pressure groups or manipulation by the whips. The system would effectively allow Early Day Motions to force a debate, but given the number of signatures and the cross-party balance they would only happen in the rarest of cases.

Debates on committee reports

4.36   As we suggested in the previous chapter (see para 3.46) the chamber should also reflect some of the valuable work done by MPs in committees. The thrust of most parliamentary reform has been to turn Westminster into a more committee-based Parliament. The chamber should reflect the importance of this work. There should be a weekly opportunity to raise issues related to recent select committee reports. At present they tend to be debated only during adjournment debates and get little interest from those outside the committee.

Time limits and order of speakers

4.37   In addition, to provide greater incentives for MPs to attend the chamber there should be time limits on the length of debates and the contribution of individuals. The Speaker already has the power to impose such limits, but a standard time limit on every contribution would encourage a more effective debating style, ensure the participation of more MPs and make the discussions generally more accessible. Provisions would have to allow for 'injury time' where the speaker gives way for other's interjections. Following Lords practice there should also be an ordered list of speakers produced in advance so that MPs know whether they are likely to be able to participate.

Improving Questions and Answers

4.38   The existing system of questions is one of the more effective ways in which MPs can hold Government to account. They are well attended and allow many MPs to participate. Yet there remain problems in the topicality of many questions, the length of time between tabling questions and a response, and the quality of many answers.

Prime Minister's Questions (PMQs)

4.39   Prime Minister's Questions receives a great deal of criticism for its overly-adversarial style, and as such, the desire for accountability is often sacrificed for point-scoring. The format of PMQs fosters this approach. Open-ended questions mean that the PM cannot be certain which questions he will be asked, and although this keeps the PM on his toes, it tends not to provide detailed, thoughtful or substantial responses. The gladiatorial atmosphere means that the questions aim to embarrass, and the PM's reply is designed to worst his opponent.

4.40   The recommendations of the Procedure Committee in 1995[126] should be implemented. **Open-ended questions should be banned at Prime Minister's Questions (although the leaders of the main Opposition parties should retain this ability); instead Members should give notice of their intention to ask a question ten days in advance.** As now, a ballot would decide the MPs, **but MPs would table their (substantive) question by noon two days before PMQs.** Supplementaries would have to relate to the original question. This would improve the topicality of PMQs, and provide a greater obligation for the PM to provide a detailed response.

---

[126] Procedure Committee, (1994–5), Seventh Report, *Prime Minister's Questions*, HC 555, para 61

4.41 However, changes made to PMQs may not dramatically improve parliamentary oversight. PMQs is dominated by point-scoring between the political parties and too deeply embedded in the adversarial tussle for any reforms to entirely remove this element. Despite its serious deficiencies as a mechanism of scrutiny, PMQs has a value in distilling some of the key political issues for consumption by the public at large. For good or ill it provides the most memorable moments of political theatre and is more effective than any other parliamentary mechanism in providing a focus for the public. There are few other countries where the Prime Minister is regularly questioned on a weekly basis.

4.42 Although improvements should be made, the equally important task is to bolster the accountability of the emerging Prime Minister's department to the select committees. The centre of government is becoming increasingly important in determining policy across a range of departments. Although the Committee on Public Administration (CPA) is responsible for scrutinising the work of the Cabinet Office, much of the work of the Prime Minister and the No 10 policy unit goes unscrutinised. Attempts to get the Prime Minister to appear before the CPA at the end of the 1999–2000 session failed, and the CPA has recommended that the Prime Minister should appear before the Liaison Committee once or twice a year.[127] Such a proposal was supported by former Prime Minister John Major, who told the CPA, "it would be of advantage, I think, for the Prime Minister if he was to meet an equivalent of the Liaison Committee on a regular basis . . . that would be of use to the Prime Minister, I think it would be of use to Parliament and I think it would be of use to the public." [128] The Commission agrees with the CPA and recommends that **the Prime Minister should appear before a select committee on an annual basis to account for the work of Government. The most appropriate opportunity would be once a year to give evidence on the Government's Annual Report.**

Oral Questions

4.43 As the Norton Commission report notes, during departmental Question Time there is a tendency to try to get through as many questions as possible. The Commission argues that "the emphasis should be on depth rather than breadth, allowing the House to pursue a particular question in some detail."[129] The effect of syndicating questions by whips around particular policy issues has been to allow prolonged questioning, but the motivation for this is almost entirely party politics and not a quest for accountability.

4.44 Reform should aim to create a dialogue between the ministers and MPs, to allow a subject to be more fully investigated. Following the recommendations of the Norton Commission, and aiming to minimise the number of planted questions, **no more than ten questions should appear on the Order Paper for each Question Time and no duplicate questions should be allowed.** Each question would be pursued for five to eight minutes, with any MP able to ask a supplementary question on the subject.

---

[127] Public Administration Committee (2000–2001), *Minutes of Evidence*, HC 821-I
[128] *ibid*
[129] Commission to Strengthen Parliament, *op cit*, p. 27

4.45   The topicality of the questions also needs to be improved, but the two-day notice period for PMQs would not be suitable for Question Time given the greater number of questions and the level of detail which will be expected from ministers. As such, **the period of notice should be reduced from ten working days to five**.

Written Questions

4.46   Concerns about the system of written questions revolve almost entirely around the quality of answers from departments. The Committee on Public Administration (CPA), and its predecessor the Public Service Committee, raised their concerns about the standard of ministerial replies to questions. The committees questioned the use of blocking and holding replies, and the lack of recourse open to MPs if they are not content with the answer. Official guidance given to civil servants answering PQs stresses that departments should be as open as possible. Yet refusals to answer questions, although helpfully published in the Table Office's 'pattern of answering', are frequently not fully explained by departments. Evidence to the CPA from David Clark MP, then Chancellor of the Duchy of Lancaster, suggested that the Freedom of Information Act might be an easier way to get information than a parliamentary question.[130] This combined with the availability of information on the internet, means that the common argument of disproportionate cost becomes less convincing. **In cases where the Government does not produce a response to a written question the reasons for not answering must be made clearer. A denial of information should be accompanied by a reference to the relevant section of the Code of Practice on Open Government or the Freedom of Information Act.**

Conclusion: The importance of the chamber

4.47   One of the underlying themes of the report is that Parliament should become a more committee-based institution. However, the Commission believes that by strengthening the committees, the work of the chamber will achieve greater focus and will itself be more effective in holding ministers to account. The chamber remains the ultimate forum in Parliament and our recommendations seek to restore the chamber to its central position. The reforms therefore aim to clarify its purpose in relation to Government and thus improve the quality of contributions on the floor. In her farewell speech as Speaker Betty Boothroyd commented that the chamber was the "chief forum of the nation – today, tomorrow, and I hope forever."[131] The Commission endorses these sentiments without reservation and we hope that our recommendations will help to achieve the former Speaker's wish.

Principle 4 – Restoring the centrality of the Commons' chamber

The floor of the House of Commons is the main public focus for activity at Westminster. However, attendance by MPs and the extent to which it dominates political debate has declined.

---

[130]   Public Administration Committee, (1997–8), *Your Right to Know: the Government's Proposals for a Freedom of Information Act*, HC 398-II
[131]   HC debs 26 July 2000, vol 340, col. 1114

Recommendations

20. To improve the attendance and influence of the chamber its core tasks need to be refined and clarified. It should become the plenary session of the Parliament. (para 4.27)

21. In order to reflect the importance attached to the select committee system, and not take MPs away from the chamber, one day each week should be devoted to committee activity. To reflect the importance of this work other parliamentary business should be arranged around the committees so that the chamber would not meet on this day. (para 4.28)

22. In general, the chamber should have fewer lengthy debates. Opportunities for MPs to initiate short debates on substantive issues should be increased. Opposition parties should be able to trade some of their Opposition Days for the chance to call for a statement on a topical issue. (paras 4.30–4.32)

23. In addition, the Speaker should grant a greater number of Private Notice Questions each session. (para 4.33)

24. MPs should have the ability to call for 'public interest debates' on issues of public concern on a cross-party basis. (para 4.34)

25. Prime Minister's Questions (PMQs) displays many of the worst aspects of Westminster. Open-ended questions should be banned at PMQs (although the leaders of the main opposition parties should retain this ability); instead Members should give notice of their intention to ask a question ten days in advance and should table their (substantive) question by noon two days before PMQs. (para 4.40)

26. However, even a reformed PMQs is unlikely to ensure the necessary scrutiny of the Prime Minister's expanding role and office. The Prime Minister should appear before a select committee on an annual basis to account for the work of the Government. The most appropriate opportunity would be once a year to give evidence on the Government's Annual Report. (para 4.42)

27. Question time for other departments and ministers should also be reformed to improve its topicality, substance and relevance. No more than ten questions should appear on the Order Paper for each Question Time and no duplicate questions should be allowed. The period of notice for oral questions should be reduced from ten working days to five. (paras 4.44–4.45)

28. In cases where the Government does not produce a response to a written question the reasons for not answering must be made clearer. A denial of information should be accompanied by a reference to the relevant section of the Code of Practice on Open Government or the Freedom of Information Act. (para 4.46)

Chapter Five

Parliament and financial scrutiny

5.1 Parliament, and in particular the Commons, has a unique constitutional role in the authorisation and scrutiny of government expenditure. This chapter considers two main elements of financial scrutiny. First, we examine the Commons' authorisation of future Government spending. Through the system of Estimates the Commons must give its approval prior to spending; however, MPs have limited ability to challenge Government priorities and the process tends to be politically-charged.

5.2 Second, the chapter assesses parliamentary scrutiny once money has been spent. In this area Parliament's scrutiny is more systematic and thorough, due in large part to the work of the National Audit Office and the Public Accounts Committee. However, improvements could be made to both processes, giving the system a greater flexibility and providing committees with a greater role.

Authorising Government spending

5.3 The main opportunities for scrutinising future government expenditure are through "Estimates Days" where spending plans are debated on the floor of the Commons. Until 1982 there were 19 "Supply Days" each year (designed to provide Parliament with the opportunity to debate and give authorisation to government expenditure).[132] However these days became increasingly used for debates on issues chosen by the Opposition and this reality was officially recognised by renaming them Opposition Days and introducing instead three specific "Estimates Days." The subject for debate in these Estimates Days is chosen by the Liaison Committee, the intention being that they should be used for debating select committee reports on particular Estimates. The possibility exists that a committee chair can table a motion to reduce an Estimate, which could be then be voted on. In fact, as has been widely recognised, the committee reports chosen for debate frequently bear only a tenuous relationship with the Estimate concerned. Therefore what was intended to be 19 Supply Days, designated specifically to scrutinise the Estimates, has ended up as three days discussing select committee reports, with only passing reference to the Estimates.

5.4 The Government regards getting its spending proposals through the House of Commons, in the form already decided in the Treasury and Cabinet, as essential to its programme and its credibility. Parliament has no ability to vary the contents of the Estimates (by proposing virement between budget heads) and its only sanction is to reject the Estimates in their entirety. With the Government enjoying a majority in the Commons, this 'nuclear option' is unlikely, and the limited options mean that, for the most part, the Government takes Parliament's approval for granted. As a result, neither the chamber nor select committees give finance a high priority. The current system of Estimates means that the House of Commons must vote on large sums of money which have not been subject to any detailed scrutiny.

---

[132] Further information about financial procedures is shown in Appendix 6

Reforming the Estimates

5.5   The 1999 Procedure Committee Report considered changes to allow the House greater powers in these areas, such as the ability to propose increases or transfers within budget totals,

> 'The principle of the financial initiative of the crown rightly precludes motions recommending increases to the Estimates themselves. However, we consider that when motions are directed to future plans, motions recommending that 'in the opinion of the House' increases in expenditure or transfers between certain budgets are desirable, should be permissible.'[133]

5.6   The Government rejected such changes,[134] but we believe that the above proposal has considerable merit. For example, under this proposal the House would not be able to increase or decrease the spending total for an individual department but could propose changes to the allocations within the total (say, to give greater support to rail rather than road schemes or vice versa). It would not add to government spending nor threaten its revenue settlement nor even change agreed departmental allocations. It would however give the House some say in the overall settlement where effectively it has none.

5.7   The process, even if unsuccessful, would give meaning to the debate and any potential division. Even if changes were not made, (and it is understandable that the Government would seek to prevent changes it did not like), the mere proposals to change the sub-heads, and the subsequent debate, would focus the House on the particular totals within the Estimates. It would also involve government explanation of its position, more thorough debate and perhaps more media coverage. **The Estimates procedures should be changed to allow Parliament to debate and vote for transfers within overall departmental budgets. This would help focus the attention of MPs and ministers, and hopefully the media and the public, on the scrutiny of spending plans.**

Estimates and select committees

5.8   Changes to the nature of Estimates debates by themselves are not sufficient. As we have noted in chapter four, the process of debating matters in the Commons does not guarantee effective scrutiny. The Commission believes that select committees should play a greater role in financial scrutiny. Although Standing Orders establishing the departmental select committees gave powers to examine the expenditure (as well as the administration and policy) of the relevant government departments and associated public bodies, the Commission's research confirmed the low priority given to finance. Only around a third of select committee inquiries considered any form of expenditure issue, and only 9.1 per cent examined the Estimates.[135]

---

[133] Procedure Committee, (1998–99), *The Procedure for Debate on the Government's Expenditure Plans*, HC 295, para. 27
[134] The Government's reply was printed as: Procedure Committee, First Special Report, Session 1999–2000, *Government Response to the Sixth Report of Session 1998–99: Procedure for Debate on the Government's Expenditure Plans*, HC 388
[135] Appendix 5

5.9   At present there is little incentive to pursue financial issues and chapter three highlighted the problems that committee chairs have in focusing their members on such issues (see para 3.11). Part of the problem is the limited influence of such reports, as by the time a committee had received the Estimates, inquired and reported, it would probably be too late to make any difference. Understandably, the greater likelihood of influencing policy or administration will condition a committee's activity.

5.10   The Procedure Committee made a number of important recommendations to involve select committees in the Estimates process,

> 'Given that, almost without exception, committees do in fact undertake some examination of their department's annual report, we do not believe that a formal referral of Estimates to committees would present them with too great a burden.

> We propose that a Standing Order should provide that, when laid, the Main Estimates should automatically be referred to the relevant select committee, together with the relevant departmental plan and, later in the year, the departmental report.

> There is no point in referring the Estimates if committees are not required to report back to the House, however briefly. We recommend that committees should, at the minimum, produce a short report to the effect that "the Committee has examined the Departmental plans and the Estimates and has no comment to make".'[136]

5.11   Again, the Government rejected the Procedure Committee's proposals.[137] The Commission believes that select committees should play a greater role in financial accountability of Government. Improved scrutiny of the Estimates by select committees is an important element in improving Parliament's performance overall.

Resource accounting and budgeting

5.12   The introduction of Resource Accounting and Budgeting has provided the potential for more systematic scrutiny. It is hoped that Resource Accounts and Estimates will be accompanied by considerable amounts of extra information tied to policy objectives included in the Estimates, in departmental plans and in departmental annual reports for the previous year. The chair of the Liaison Committee and former Public Accounts Committee chair, Rt. Hon Robert Sheldon MP expressed the hope that resource accounting might lead to more effective scrutiny by committees,

> "There is now a great momentum in the country and the House for more informed and better decision making – no question about it. Resource accounting is expected to lead finally to a proper assessment of how we decide on the Government's detailed expenditure plans."[138]

---

[136] Procedure Committee, (1998–99), *The Procedure for Debate on the Government's Expenditure Plans*, HC 295, paras 45–47
[137] Procedure Committee, (1999–2000), HC 388
[138] HC debs, 9 November 2000, vol 341, col 478

5.13 However the extra transparency and more meaningful figures could turn out to be irrelevant if MPs, and the House as a whole, fails to respond positively. The Procedure Committee expressed its concern that committees need to take greater account of this extra information as "they will give far more detail of the Government's plans than the Estimates themselves."[139]

5.14 Given the existing weaknesses of the Estimates process and overall select committee performance in this area, it seems quite possible that this concern is well founded. Resource Accounting and Budgeting is a complex process and unless MPs, and Commons' staff, are well trained and supported, there is the distinct possibility that the opportunities for greater scrutiny will not be seized. The key to making best use of the benefits of resource accounting is the motivation of MPs, and the priorities they set for themselves, in the chamber and in committee. Improved accounts, more meaningful and open information, training and support resources all ultimately count for very little if MPs do not engage in the process.

Looking elsewhere for inspiration: The Scottish Parliament budget procedures

5.15 One option is to integrate the committees more fully into the budget process. In some other countries, for example New Zealand and India, Parliaments prioritise pre-budget inquiries, budget proposals are formally submitted to committees and influence can be brought to bear before the budget is a done deal. The Scottish Parliament budget process provides a useful comparison for Westminster.

5.16 The Scottish Parliament budget procedures were devised by the Financial Issues Advisory Group (FIAG) of the Consultative Steering Group[140] and enshrined in the Public Finance and Accountability (Scotland) Act 2000. Parliament has the opportunity to comment on the Executive's spending plans at several points prior to the budget being agreed. There are a number of distinctive features including the involvement of the subject committees and the role of the Finance Committee in shaping the executive's budget. There are three main stages in the process. Outlined below is the timetable of the stages for the 2001/2002 budget, which took place in 2000/2001.

---

[139] Procedure Committee, (1998–99), *The Procedure for Debate on the Government's Expenditure Plans*, HC 295, para 23

[140] For further information on the Scottish Parliament budget procedures, see The Scottish Parliament Information Centre Sheet, The Annual Budget Process, 22/11/00, Series 00/07.

Figure 5A – Scottish Parliament budget process 2000–2001

UK budget process	Scotland budget process	Scottish process – commentary
Spring: UK budget	March/April: Publication of Annual Expenditure Report ▼ Finance Committee oversees consultation process ▼ April/May: Subject Committees examine relevant chapter. Each reports to Finance Committee ▼	**Stage 1: April–June 2000** This year's expenditure report, *Investing in You* comprised a detailed breakdown of the Executive's spending plans. Each chapter covered the expenditure of particular portfolios. Subject committees are responsible for commenting on the relationship between expenditure plans and policy priorities in the relevant spending area (this may also involve consultation with outside bodies and interested individuals).
End year flexibility announcement made (end June)	June: Finance Committee Reports to Parliament. Parliament debates this report	Each Committee decided on the most appropriate way to approach the process. These responses were co-ordinated by the Finance Committee, which reported to the Parliament. In 2000, the Report was debated by the Parliament on 28 June.
July: Comprehensive spending review (2 years)	Mid September: Executive publishes draft budget and spending plans ▼ Subject Committee examine and report to Finance Committee ▼ Finance Committee considers the draft budget and may propose alternative ▼	In the light of the Parliament's input (and comment from other interested bodies), the Executive prepared its draft budget. **Stage 2: Sep–Dec 2000** The year's spending plans *(Making a Difference for Scotland)* were published in September 2000. Again, each subject committee reported to the Finance Committee on relevant parts of the package, to identify whether the stage 1 recommendations were acted upon by the Executive.
October: in-year changes Oct–Nov: UK pre-budget report	December (1st wk): Finance Committee report. Mid December: Parliament debates report	At this stage the Finance Committee has the option of putting forward an alternative budget with the proviso that this must keep within the over all spending limit set by the Executive's draft budget. In any event, the Finance Committee will produce a Report by the beginning of December 2000 which will then be debated by the Parliament before Christmas Recess.
	January: Executive produces proposals (having considered Parliament's recommendations) ▼ Parliament debates budget Bill ▼ Executive amendments and parliamentary vote	**Stage 3: Jan–Feb 2001** The Budget (Scotland) Bill was introduced in January 2001. Only a member of the Executive may move amendments. Parliament has a vote to accept or reject it. If accepted, it authorises expenditure for financial year 2001/02.

Financial audit and accountability of Government expenditure

The proper and productive use of public money is an indispensable element of any modern, well-managed and fully accountable democratic state. It is essential that, where Government and the prime instrument of scrutiny, Parliament, interact, there exists a common understanding of how, and on what terms, public money can be used.[141]

Holding to Account, The Review of Audit and Accountability for Central Government
Lord Sharman of Redlynch (chair)

5.17 Whilst Parliament's performance in scrutinising spending plans and forward expenditure is weak, it has proved more effective in calling Government to account once money has been spent. The National Audit Office and Public Accounts Committee mean that there are well-resourced structures in place to audit public expenditure, assess value-for-money outcomes and make recommendations for improvement. However, the Commission believes that such activity could be broadened and should be tied more closely to the work of other parliamentary committees.

The Public Accounts Committee and the National Audit Office

5.18 The Public Accounts Committee (PAC) is the most high-profile vehicle for parliamentary scrutiny of expenditure, its strength deriving in large part from its connection with the National Audit Office (NAO). The NAO has around 800 staff responsible for auditing and providing value for money surveys of government spending. Although the NAO has a remit to investigate any area of expenditure, it cannot question the merits of the policy objectives of any department or authority. Its reports are submitted to the PAC which can query the priorities of Government. The PAC then conducts around 50 inquiries each year on the basis of the NAO's work.

5.19 The existence of the PAC and NAO provides permanent oversight and has a deterrent effect on ministerial activity. However, the PAC has limitations. Even though the PAC already works at maximum capacity, publishes about 50 reports a year and meets twice a week for 25 weeks a year, it is only able to take a limited look at government expenditure, and pick up only a proportion of the NAO's work. The enormous scope of government means that even with the resources of the NAO, the PAC is necessarily highly selective in the inquiries it undertakes. The range of government activity means that neither the NAO nor PAC can track all the money spent by Government.

---

[141] *Holding Government to Account: Review of Audit and Accountability for Central Government,* Report by Lord Sharman of Redlynch, February 2001

An alternative approach: Finance and Audit Sub-Committee

5.20 Members of the PAC cannot be expected to become experts on the enormous range of subjects into which they inquire. They are likely to be less well informed on a given subject than a member of the relevant departmental select committee. Reforms should encourage and enable departmental select committees to play a greater role in the scrutiny of finance. **Each departmental select committee should pilot and evaluate a new form of committee, a Finance and Audit Sub-Committee. The sub-committee should consider, for example, Estimates and departmental allocations, audit and value-for-money inquiries, Public Service Agreements, performance indicators and outcomes.**

Resources for financial scrutiny

5.21 Select committees and new sub-committees must improve their capacity for carrying out effective financial scrutiny. To do this they will need an analytical capacity as well as enhanced research facilities and access to financial expertise. There appear to be two ways of providing this support either by a new research and support function or by using existing capacity as far as possible.

5.22 We have already commented on the vast amounts of analytical and investigative material that are readily available but apparently not digested or used by select committees. For example, much of the audit and analytical work produced by the NAO is not fully used by Parliament. The NAO performs specific audit functions of public sector bodies, but it is not the appropriate body to provide support functions on issues of Estimates, scrutiny of government expenditure, analysis of expenditure outcomes, performance targets and the like. However, much of the NAO's work could and should be better utilised by the departmental committees which can bring their subject-specific expertise and experience to the policy content of an NAO report in a way that the generalist and time constrained PAC is often unable to do.

5.23 **We do not suggest that the NAO should provide a servicing function for specific committees, but their reports and expertise should be shared more equitably among the other committees of the House of Commons. Select committees and their sub-committees should use the NAO and PAC reports as the basis for more detailed examination of Government finance.**

5.24 This will be a new and significant function for select committees and **a Parliamentary Finance Office should be established to provide high quality research, information, access to specialist advice and expertise, and support for the collection and analysis of evidence and report drafting.** The Parliamentary Finance Office (PFO) would have certain functions in common with the economic and finance support functions currently provided by the Commons' Library. However whereas the Library at present provides services for all Members, with a concentration on individual cases, the PFO would be solely designated to the scrutiny function, primarily for the select committees.

5.25   There would of course be budgetary implications in establishing a new office but there is no doubt that scrutiny support functions are presently under-resourced. As the Liaison Committee noted in *Shifting the Balance*, 'No-one could accuse select committees of being profligate in their staffing.'[142] If the scrutiny function is to be effective, adequate resources should be deployed and the necessary budget provided.

Parliament and the Audit Commission

5.26   Regardless of these changes Parliament is weakened by the fact that there are certain areas that the NAO and PAC cannot investigate. The Audit Commission rather than the NAO, audits many of the most important public services, including health, the police service and many local authority functions. These huge areas are outside Parliament's direct audit remit. The departmental select committee on Environment, Transport, and Regional Affairs (ETRA) published a report on the Audit Commission in June 2000[143] which stated that it was, "generally highly regarded, due in large part to its independence from central government."[144] The Report cited a proposal by the PAC chair, Rt. Hon David Davis MP, that a new select committee should be established to consider and report on the work of the Audit Commission, in much the same way as the PAC relates to the NAO.

5.27   The ETRA committee however did not see that there was a strong case for establishing a separate select committee to oversee the Audit Commission.[145] Arguing that services provided by local authorities should be accountable to local electorates, it considered that Parliament should not, even indirectly, attempt to hold such authorities to account.[146]

5.28   We do not share the ETRA committee's analysis and conclusion. Many of the services currently under the remit of the Audit Commission (most notably health and police services) are not directly provided by locally elected authorities, and a high proportion of all local revenues come from centrally raised taxation. The absence of formal links between Parliament and the Audit Commission means that the quality and detail of financial oversight in certain crucial areas is variable. The Audit Commission is in a position to provide an overview of performance across local/health/police authorities and make good practice recommendations. **Parliament should make greater use of the Audit Commission's work. To improve parliamentary oversight in areas of public expenditure such as the police and the health service, the Audit Commission should formally report to Commons departmental select committees.**

5.29   To ensure that best uses are made of its evidence the Audit Commission should report to the departmental committees relevant to its work. Therefore, National Health Service reports should be submitted to the Health Committee, police service reports to the Home Affairs Committee and local government reports to the Environment Committee.

---

[142]   Liaison Committee, (1999–2000), HC 300
[143]   Environment Transport and Regional Affairs Committee, (1999–2000), *Audit Commission*, HC174-I.
[144]   *ibid.*, paras 68–70
[145]   *ibid.* para 74
[146]   *ibid.* para 75

Conclusion: The Sharman Report – holding to account

5.30 Similar conclusions were reached by the Government-initiated Review of Audit and Accountability, chaired by Lord Sharman, which reported in February 2001.[147] Many of the report's recommendations related to improvements in the government's internal audit and financial control. The report also recommended that audit procedures for Non-Departmental Public Bodies should be strengthened and that the statutory access of the NAO should be formalised so that almost all public money was within its remit. Looking particularly at the role of Parliament, the report recommended that,

- the Public Accounts Committee could provide further powerful support to improvements in financial management by continuing to examine themes across central government as a whole (such as risk management, corporate governance, developments in performance measurement and fraud).

- further use could be made of the work of the NAO, for example by providing the Comptroller and Auditor General with resources to brief the departmental select committees annually on key financial issues, although it was mindful not to 'undermine the key relationship between the NAO and PAC or drawing the C&AG and his staff into questioning policy matters.'

- the PAC and departments should take a 'flexible' approach in dealing with 'joined-up' matters; for example, allowing one Accounting Officer to represent others or with the PAC holding several hearings on a subject.

- the NAO and Audit Commission should co-ordinate with the Office of National Statistics and the Statistics Commission and other relevant bodies to provide Parliament with information about the performance of government departments and external validation of departmental information.

5.31 The Commission welcomes the recommendations of the Sharman report as it reinforces many of our conclusions. We hope that the Government will use it as the basis for reforming the way in which Parliament and Government deal with finance. The Commission believes that the scrutiny of finance is central to Parliament's ability to hold Government accountable and reforms should reflect this importance.

Principle 5 – Financial scrutiny should be central to accountability

Parliament, and in particular the Commons, has a unique constitutional role in the authorisation and scrutiny of Government expenditure. At present the Commons fails to perform this role in either a systematic or effective manner.

Recommendations

29. **The Estimates procedures should be changed to allow Parliament to debate and vote for transfers within overall departmental budgets. This would help focus the attention of MPs and ministers, and hopefully the media and the public, on the scrutiny of spending plans. (para 5.7)**

---

[147] *Holding to Account: Review of Audit and Accountability for Central Government,* Report by Lord Sharman of Redlynch, February 2001

30. Each departmental select committee should pilot and evaluate a new form of committee, a Finance and Audit Sub-Committee. The sub-committee should consider, for example, Estimates and departmental allocations, audit and value-for-money inquiries, Public Service Agreements, performance indicators and outcomes. (para 5.20)

31. We do not suggest that the NAO should provide a servicing function for specific committees, but their reports and expertise should be shared more equitably among the other committees of the House of Commons. Select committees and their sub-committees should use the NAO and PAC reports as the basis for more detailed examination of Government finance. (para 5.23)

32. A Parliamentary Finance Office should be established to give high quality support to the committees. The office would provide research, information, access to specialist advice and expertise, and support in the analysis of evidence and drafting of reports. (para 5.24)

33. Parliament should make greater use of the Audit Commission's work. To improve parliamentary oversight in areas of public expenditure such as the police and the health service, the Audit Commission should formally report to Commons departmental select committees. (para 5.28)

Chapter Six

Scrutiny, accountability and the second chamber

'Given the Government's enormous power in our system, it seems to us important to have a second chamber able and willing to complement the House of Commons in its essential work of scrutinising the executive and holding the government to account.'[148]

A House for the Future
Royal Commission on the Reform of the House of Lords

6.1 The Commission has focused most of its attention on the House of Commons. The fact that, at the time of writing, the Lords is in transition, means that the Commission can only outline tentative and less specific recommendations than those for the Commons. We did not wish to speculate or add to the numerous proposals for Lords reform, but instead have used the Wakeham Commission's report as the basis for our work.

6.2 The Commission nevertheless believes that the Lords plays an important role in complementing the work of the Commons and holding Government to account. The Commission believes that the Lords can add real value through its different base of expertise and the greater independence of its members. The Lords should play a significant role in scrutinising cross-departmental initiatives and examine issues of ethical, constitutional and social issues for which the Commons has insufficient time. However, the effectiveness of Parliament as a whole requires a greater co-operation and co-ordination of the activity of the two Houses.

The distinct role of the second chamber

'The House of Commons, because it is directly elected by the whole people, is the ultimate repository of democratic authority in the United Kingdom. It alone . . . can call the Prime Minister and the Government fully to account.'

We are concerned that the House of Commons often finds it difficult to balance its twin responsibilities of sustaining a government in office and at the same time holding it effectively to account.

A revitalised second chamber could enhance the ability of Parliament as a whole to scrutinise the executive and act as a check upon it.'[149]

A House for the Future
Royal Commission on the Reform of the House of Lords

6.3 While the fully elected Commons may have the greater legitimacy in ensuring the accountability of government, it also has other functions, notably making and sustaining the Government which, as we have shown, means that there are conflicting pressures on MPs, in their loyalty to party, in their support or opposition of the Government and in their role as impartial scrutineer of its actions. Such conflicts often hamper the quality of scrutiny in the Commons. In contrast, the second chamber is generally less partisan and its members are able to exercise a less partial form of scrutiny than their Commons counterparts.

---

[148] *A House for the Future*, Royal Commission on the Reform of the House of Lords, chaired by Rt. Hon Lord Wakeham DL, January 2000, para 3.6
[149] *ibid* (para 3.10)

6.4   The fact that the Government does not have a majority in the second chamber contributes to a less adversarial approach, as cross-party support is required to take decisions. The maintenance of Government does not rely on a majority in the Lords and, as such, no divisions can be regarded as votes of confidence. Party discipline is less strong in the second chamber and the atmosphere means that, up to now, the chamber has been almost entirely self-regulating. There is no Speaker to enforce order and no procedure for guillotining business. There are few formal restrictions on the ability of members to raise issues of concern. In general, these traits allow for a broader and more spontaneous questioning of ministers, often in greater depth than is possible in the Commons.

6.5   It is clear, however, that reforms to the second chamber will affect some of the traditional procedures. There are early signs that a greater role is being played by the whips attempting to enforce party discipline, a feature which is likely to grow with the election of a proportion of the second chamber. The election of members may also make them less willing to take up unpopular or controversial issues, such as euthanasia or cases of life imprisonment. The Wakeham Commission's recommendation that members should be elected for non-renewable fifteen year terms might prevent such developments. However, at the time of writing it is unclear how the Government intends to proceed. Crucially, though, all the political parties are committed to maintaining a second chamber where no party has an overall majority.

6.6   The new second chamber should reflect its existing strengths and reforms should deliberately build on these advantages. Scrutiny committees operate in very different contexts in the two Houses. The party balance means that the Government does not dominate Lords committees as it does in the Commons. As the Government also has no majority in the chamber itself, the chamber could refer matters of its choosing to committees, although up to now it has rarely done so against the wishes or approval of Government. The potential exists to develop a different dynamic to the Commons, opening up new and innovative means of scrutinising Government. The next stages of reform provide a rare opportunity to devise and consolidate a specifically second chamber form of scrutiny and accountability.

Scrutiny in the Lords

6.9   The Lords already performs a significant and frequently effective scrutiny role, quite independent of the Commons, although it receives media coverage. Peers, like MPs, have opportunities to question the Government, and thereby scrutinise the Executive and hold it to account. Since the 1960s the number of written questions in the Lords has increased 20-fold (albeit from a very low starting point). More significantly for accountability, each day in the Lords four oral questions are asked of Ministers. These are called "Starred Questions" and take up about 15 per cent of the time in the chamber. Starred Questions can be on any topic within government responsibility and are tabled first come first served. Each week, two of the questions a week are 'Topical Questions', drawn by ballot 48 hours in advance. There is a time limit of 30 minutes for the four questions each day (allowing much longer for each question than in the Commons) and any Peer may ask supplementary questions. This system of starred questions allows peers to raise topical questions in a manner denied to the Commons. The topicality and random nature of the questions provide useful lessons for the Commons.

6.10   The ability of the Lords to question senior ministers has, however, declined over the course of the twentieth century as the number of Cabinet ministers from that chamber has been significantly reduced.[150] In recent years there have been exceptions to the overall trend as some Lords ministers have held very high-profile, controversial briefs; for example, Lord Macdonald of Tradeston and Lord Falconer of Thoroton, with responsibility for transport and the Millennium Dome respectively. Additionally most departments of state have a minister below cabinet rank sitting in the Lords. In total, members of the Lords thus represent a small but significant proportion of the Government.

6.11   As most members of the Cabinet and of the Government sit in the Commons, it is in the Commons that the primary role of questioning Ministers is likely to take place. The Wakeham Commission nevertheless believed that an opportunity to tap into the expertise of the Lords was wasted because Peers in the Chamber were unable to question Commons Ministers. Lords can question Commons Ministers in committees, in the same way as Commons select committees question Lords Ministers. However, most members of the second chamber do not regularly question most members of the Government.

6.12   The Royal Commission did not wish to change the long standing convention that members of one chamber should not speak in the other but believed that parliamentary scrutiny as a whole would be enhanced if Commons Ministers could make statements to and answer questions from members of the second chamber. They suggested that this should take place in a special committee away from the Lords' chamber.[151] The Grand Committee in the Lords could provide the basis for such a procedure.

6.13   To ensure topicality under such a new procedure, it was suggested there should be no fixed rota of Ministers nor any advance notice of questions. Instead Ministers responsible for current issues might be invited to appear before the Committee at a few days notice to take questions and explain their position. It was envisaged that rather than 'ambulance chasing' [of the latest crisis or headline], the new procedure would be a way to explore issues of longer-term significance. In fact, although the principle of enabling members of the second chamber to question Commons ministers is important, the Royal Commission's proposal to issue invitations at short notice seems likely to result in just the sort of 'ambulance chasing' it wishes to avoid. A more measured approach would be achieved if Commons Ministers were invited to answer questions on an agreed, with-notice basis. Ministers should be invited to make statements and answer questions in a committee of the whole of the second chamber on specific issues within their responsibility on a long-term rota basis.

---

[150] Since 1964 only seven peers have sat in the Cabinet (other than the Lord Chancellor and Leader of the Lords who are ex officio members of the Lords).
[151] op cit., paras 8.7–8

6.14 The right of Members of the Commons to question those Ministers who sit in the Lords is also an issue. It is already commonplace for Lords Ministers to account for their department to the relevant Commons' select committee. Parliamentary scrutiny would be more comprehensive and thorough if Lords Ministers were able to be questioned by the Commons as a whole, in addition to scrutiny by select committee. This could take place away from the Chamber, for example in Westminster Hall.

6.15 **Parliamentary scrutiny would be strengthened if all government Ministers were able to make statements to and be questioned in both Houses. We do not seek to challenge the long standing convention that members of one chamber should not speak in the other. Instead, alternative forums away from the chamber of each House should be instigated to allow Ministers of the other House to be questioned. In the Lords a version of the Grand Committee procedure could be used to provide such a forum to question Commons Ministers. In the Commons, the Westminster Hall procedure would be appropriate.**

Lords Committees: existing good practice

6.16 The Lords does not have departmental select committees on the Commons model. Instead, the Lords has two longstanding committees on the European Union and on Science and Technology. In addition the Lords expanded its committee work in the 2000–2001 session, with the establishment of two new permanent committees to consider the constitution and economic affairs. The Lords also continues its tradition of setting up *ad hoc* committees on particular topics: in 2000–2001 new *ad hoc* committees on Stem Cell Research and Animals in Scientific Procedures were set up. The Lords is also working with the Commons in establishing a joint committee to consider human rights. The Royal Commission recommended a committee to consider the implications and progress of the devolution settlement, although this has not as yet been formally agreed and the subject matter could fall within the remit of the new constitution committee.

6.17 Wakeham strongly endorsed the existing specialist committee work undertaken by the Lords. The Royal Commission believed that further specialist committee work should attempt to complement the work of the Commons, in particular by inquiring into cross departmental issues. In evidence to the Commission, Damien Welfare, former special adviser to the Leader of the Lords, considered the second chamber more inclined to take a cross-cutting approach, with a greater capacity to stand back and take the 'long view'.[152] The Science and Technology Committee in the Lords is a good example of a cross-cutting committee. It was established after a similar Commons committee was abolished in 1979 and frequently looks at issues which cut across departmental boundaries and is able to draw on considerable expertise within the House and outside, where it has a high reputation. Some recent inquiries have attracted major coverage; for example *Air Travel and Health*[153] and *Complementary and Alternative Medicine*.[154]

---

[152] Appendix 2, Evidence 34
[153] Science and Technology Committee, (1999–2000), Fifth Report, HL121
[154] Science and Technology Committee, (1999–2000), Sixth Report, HL123

6.18 It is arguable that all political issues are cross-cutting in that they are likely to touch on the affairs of more than one department. However, the emphasis of the Labour administration on 'joining-up' government has given it a greater impetus and potentially provides the Lords with an important strategic role. The example of ONE (see figure 6A), designed to improve access to benefits, shows the complexity of accountability. Although in this case the Commons initiated its own inquiry through the Education and Employment and Social Security Committees, the Lords, by establishing a cross-cutting committee could complement the work of the Commons and provide a strategic overview.

Figure 6A: Cross-cutting issues in practice — ONE

An integrated 'One Stop Shop', a single gateway for claiming social security benefits, has many merits. Rather than having to make multiple claims for the various benefits to which they may be entitled, claimants need make just one claim with one disclosure of circumstances. The costs to the state of multiple claims should be significantly reduced. Furthermore, if claiming, and reclaiming, benefit is considered straightforward, claimants might be more likely to take temporary or potentially insecure work; confident that they will be able to receive benefit easily should they need it.

The Labour Government has attempted to deal with the issue with the establishment of ONE. This initiative has brought together the Department for Education and Employment (DFEE), the Department of Social Security (DSS), the Employment Service (ES), the Benefit Agency (BA) and local authorities, who administer Housing Benefit and Council Tax Benefit on behalf of the Department of Social Security.

There are complex lines of responsibility, communication and liaison between all these organisations, all the more so when national, regional, area and district levels are also involved. Project Management Groups at regional level bring together BA, ES and local authorities to manage the project in each region. At national level, the two departments, DFEE and DSS, are responsible to Parliament and the two agencies, ES and BA, are responsible to the departments. While all contributing departments and organisations remained accountable for the resources they put in, it was crucial to judge the success of the initiative as a whole, and not just on its component parts. The Commons responded positively and the two select committees involved, Education and Employment and Social Security, held a joint inquiry and published a joint report.[155]

6.19 **It is not desirable to have a set of second chamber committees shadowing government departments as they would duplicate much of the work of Commons committees. The second chamber should continue its distinctive approach by addressing cross-departmental and 'joined-up' issues to complement the work of the departmental select committees in the Commons.** The Science and Technology Committee is one effective existing example. Others might include, for example, access to benefits, rural affairs, environmental protection, equal opportunities and social exclusion. The new committees on the constitution and economic affairs should see their work as primarily cross-cutting.

---

[155] Joint Report by the Social Security and Education Committees, (1998–99), *The One Service Pilots*, HC 412

6.20 In addition, some of the most successful committees in the Lords are the *ad hoc* committees on specific topics appointed for specific periods; for example, the committee on relations between central and local government, which led to the report *"Rebuilding Trust"*.[156] Such committees consider particular inquiries and dissolve on completion. There is currently less opportunity for such flexibility in the Commons. Such committees provide a useful model for enhancing the scrutiny function, in both the Lords and Commons and in the Lords in particular greater use of such committees, for a specified purpose, would provide a complementary function to the permanent committees of the two Houses. **The second chamber should continue to establish *ad hoc* committees to consider specific issues and developments, such as those recently appointed to consider Animals in Scientific Procedures and Stem Cell Research. Such an approach would bring greater flexibility and responsiveness to Parliament's committee system and would allow the second chamber to respond to gaps in the Commons work.**

European Union scrutiny

6.21 The scrutiny of European Union issues is an example of very highly effective scrutiny work undertaken by the Lords. It is also the best example of the two Houses working in a complementary and mutually beneficial manner. The Lords' European Union Committee operates with six sub-committees involving some 70 peers and carries out detailed scrutiny of proposed European Union legislation. Its predecessor Committee, the European Communities Committee, was established on the UK's accession to the European Economic Community in 1972 to scrutinise proposals coming from Brussels.

6.22 It takes a different approach to that of the Commons European Scrutiny Committee which rapidly sifts all proposals under the consideration in the Council of Ministers (usually about 400 a year). Instead the Lords European Committee identifies about 30–40 items for in-depth study and analysis. The issues considered in the Lords are usually those which raise issues of policy or principle rather than the detailed programme or administrative issues which are more frequently covered by the Commons Committee.

6.23 These arrangements are supplemented by the European Scrutiny Reserve, a resolution of the House of Commons that UK Ministers should not enter into any new commitment in the Council of Ministers until the Commons scrutiny has been completed (apart from in exceptional circumstances). A similar resolution applies to the House of Lords. Wakeham believed that the current system of Lords European scrutiny should be maintained and that in order to improve and strengthen the process, additional staff and other resources should be made available. It was also proposed that the system could be strengthened by inviting Commons ministers to make statements and answer questions to a second chamber committee after meetings of the Council of Ministers. **The two different approaches taken by the separate Houses in the field of European Union scrutiny complement each other extremely well. This approach should be used as a model for future complementary, division of scrutiny functions between the two Houses.**

---

[156] (1995–96), HL Paper 97

Conclusion: Complementary and co-ordinated scrutiny

6.24 Wakeham described the current systems taken by the two Houses as 'complementary and mutually reinforcing.'[157] Reform should play to their respective strengths and avoid duplication of inquiries. On a practical basis, similar inquiries would place demands on joint witnesses and respective House resources. On a broader level, it is difficult to see what reports on the same subjects from the two Houses would achieve. If their reports came to similar conclusions, they could be accused of wasteful duplication. If they came to different conclusions, the Government might be tempted to play off one against the other.

6.25 A complementary approach relies on both Houses adopting mechanisms for co-ordination and closer working. At present, the working relationship between Lords and Commons is virtually non-existent. **The two Houses, their members and staff need to co-ordinate more closely to increase their effectiveness and to prevent unnecessary duplication and overlap.**

Principle 6 – The House of Lords should complement the Commons

The Lords plays an important role in complementing the work of the Commons and holding Government to account, but the effectiveness of Parliament as a whole requires greater co-operation and co-ordination of the activity of the two Houses.

Recommendations

34. Parliamentary scrutiny would be strengthened if all government ministers were able to make statements to and be questioned in both Houses. We do not seek to challenge the long standing convention that members of one chamber should not speak in the other. Instead, alternative forums away from the chamber of each House should be instigated to allow Ministers of the other House to be questioned. In the Lords a version of the Grand Committee procedure could be used to provide such a forum to question Commons Ministers. In the Commons, the Westminster Hall procedure would be appropriate. (para 6.15)

35. It is not desirable to have a set of second chamber committees shadowing government departments as they would duplicate much of the work of Commons committees. The second chamber should continue its distinctive approach by addressing cross-departmental and 'joined-up' issues to complement the work of the departmental select committees in the Commons in areas such as rural affairs, environmental protection, equal opportunities and social exclusion. (para 6.19)

---

[157] *ibid*, para 8.12

36. The second chamber should continue to establish *ad hoc* committees to consider specific issues and developments, such as those recently appointed to consider Animals in Scientific Procedures and Stem Cell Research. Such an approach would bring greater flexibility and responsiveness to Parliament's committee system and would allow the second chamber to respond to gaps in the Commons work. (para 6.20)

37. The two different approaches taken by the separate Houses in the field of European Union scrutiny complement each other extremely well. This approach should be used as a model for future complementary, division of scrutiny functions between the two Houses. (para 6.23)

38. The two Houses, their members and staff need to co-ordinate more closely to increase their effectiveness and to prevent unnecessary duplication and overlap. (para 6.25)

Chapter Seven

Two-way Communication: Parliament and the outside world

'The acid test of success will depend on the perception of the media and the population, as to whether Parliament is effectively scrutinising the executive.'[158]

Ofwat, Evidence to the Commission

7.1 Parliament holds Government to account on behalf of the public. In order to retain its legitimacy Parliament must not only be more effective, it must convince the public that it is more effective. Parliament's task is to engage more fully with the public interest, highlighting and explaining issues. Parliament is strongest where it articulates and mobilises public opinion. To do this it must communicate more effectively with the voters.

7.2 There are three main areas in which Parliament's communication with the electorate is poor. In the first place, the style and procedures of the Commons are alien to most voters. Parliamentary debates are conducted in a manner that is, on occasion, difficult to understand. The Commons looks, for the most part, arcane and old-fashioned. Secondly, Parliament, and specifically, the Commons, has been slow to adapt the developments in the media as tools for communicating with the public. TV broadcasting of the Commons began only in 1989, and Parliament's resources for dealing with the media are still not sufficient to guarantee the effective dissemination of its work. Thirdly, there are limited means by which the public can convey their concerns to Parliament as an institution. Whereas the constituency link provides a useful channel for individual concerns, Parliament's consultation with the electorate is weak and it is often slow to react to issues.

7.3 The Commission believes that Parliament's deficiencies in these areas seriously undermine its ability to hold Government to account. The main forum for public debate of political issues is the TV studio rather than the chamber of the Commons. The Commission believes that if Parliament is to be effective the public must regard it as relevant and topical. To do this it must adapt more quickly than it has done in the past.

The public impression of Parliament

7.4 Despite extensive media coverage of politics it is rare for Parliament to lead the day's news bulletins. With the exception of Prime Minister's Questions, coverage of parliamentary proceedings is very limited. As a result most people tend to derive their understanding of Parliament and politicians from the jousting at PMQs. Evidence suggests that, overall, the public is not impressed.

---

[158] Appendix 2, Evidence

7.5   Research by Dr Stephen Coleman[159] into the televising of the Commons showed that the effect of PMQs was that the public saw Parliament "more as a theatrical performance, and sometimes a spectacular verbal duel, than a representative legislature."[160] He cited MPs and broadcasters who concurred with that view. Claire Ward MP described the coverage as "A load of people shouting at each other without any real substance or outcome."[161]

7.6   The media, relying as it does on confrontation for most of its political stories, perhaps inevitably, focuses on the more gladiatorial aspects of what goes on at Westminster. However, the structure and content of parliamentary activity outside of PMQs does not encourage journalists to broaden their scope. The fact that debates can last six or seven hours does little to generate wider public interest. Although it is important for the Commons to deal with subjects at length and in detail, it is not clear that such debates make for rigorous analysis.

7.7   Similarly, the hours of the Commons mean that most of its activity misses newspaper and broadcast deadlines. The Commons starts business late in the day, and finishes even later. The early evening, when many substantive debates are reaching their peak and when many of the committees do their work, is unlikely to generate anything other than the slightest coverage. This is to say nothing of the debates which run to midnight. Press conferences to publicise a Government initiative are uniformly held mid-morning so as to catch the lunchtime bulletins and evening newspapers, and so, ideally, dominate the bulletins for the rest of the day. Parliament's approach to media coverage is poor by comparison.

7.8   Although the Commission believes that parliamentary reform should not solely be dictated by the needs of the media, Westminster must update its proceedings. Opinion poll research[162] shows that 59% think that 'Parliamentary procedures seem to be old-fashioned and outdated'. Additionally 43% agree that 'Much of what is said in Parliament is difficult to understand' compared with 27% who disagree. Parliamentary debates, revolving around lengthy speeches, are seen as archaic. Rightly or wrongly, the public is unused to simply listening to people speak, without any other aids or information, and it is regarded by many people as an outdated and ineffective form of communication.

Parliament and the media

7.9   The inflexibility and verbosity of much of what goes on in the chamber has meant that the TV and radio studios have taken over as the principal means of political debate. As Dr Ralph Negrine stated in evidence to the Commission, 'The media have taken the view that Parliament as a source or location of news is of lesser importance than it may have been either thirty or even ten years ago.'[163] The media studios provide

[159] Coleman, S., (1999), *Electronic Media, Parliament and the People*, Dr Stephen Coleman , Hansard Society: London
[160] *ibid*, p. 10
[161] *ibid*, p. 10
[162] *ibid*, p. 17
[163] Appendix 2, Evidence 22

a much more manageable arena, they present the issues for the public clearly, with the necessary background information, and allow politicians to talk directly to the electorate. Unless steps are taken to improve Parliament's use of the media, it will continue to decline as a forum for debating and communicating issues of national importance.

Ministerial announcements

7.10   Concern has been expressed by many, not least by former Speaker Betty Boothroyd, about the tendency of ministers to announce policy through the media rather than in the chamber. This is despite the fact that the Ministerial Code stipulates that when Parliament is in session 'Ministers will want to bear in mind the desire of Parliament that the most important announcements of government should be made, in the first instance, in Parliament.'[164] In reality, Parliament may be formally told of the policy only after the media has run the story and any parliamentary reaction may be ignored, or considered peripheral to the main story. Several former ministers put this into perspective, telling us that ministers chose to make statements to the media precisely because those interviews were easier to manage than the floor of the Commons.[165]

7.11   Whilst most MPs accept this trend as inevitable many are concerned about its implications for accountability. At a select committee hearing Rt Hon Stephen Byers MP, Secretary of State for Trade and Industry, was criticised for attempting to manipulate the news. The committee chair, Martin O'Neill MP, complained that the minister's desire to generate weekend coverage deprived Parliament of any chance to digest government policy.[166] Betty Boothroyd, former Speaker of the House, has also reprimanded government ministers for revealing new initiatives before the House has had a chance to discuss them.[167] By the time MPs get to question ministers the most salient political issues have already been discussed, and with the politics sucked out of an issue the parliamentary debate provides little that is newsworthy.

Publicity and dissemination

7.12   However, Parliament has more than contributed to this situation. Whereas the Government machine, the political parties and many individual MPs, are attuned to media requirements, Parliament is not. Our survey of MPs revealed the importance attached to media appearances by politicians. Asked how important they regarded appearing on TV or radio to their role as an MP, 40.8% thought it was very or quite important, whilst a quarter of MPs felt it was quite or very unimportant. Even so, 72% of politicians spend between one and five hours every week on media work.[168]

7.13   Despite some recent improvements Parliament as an institution still does not effectively publicise or disseminate its work in any co-ordinated fashion.

---

[164] Cabinet Office, (1997), *Ministerial Code – A Code of Conduct and evidence on proceedings for ministers*
[165] Appendix 3
[166] *Times* 16 February 2000
[167] For example, the former Speaker upbraided sports minister Kate Hoey on 5 April 2000 for announcing policy initiatives on the *Today* programme. HC Debs 5 April 2000, vol. 347, col. 975
[168] See appendix 4

7.14 For example, increasing numbers of people have access to Parliament on digital, cable or satellite television but there is little publicity for these programmes. It is unlikely that they will ever be rating toppers but there will be a small proportion interested in certain debates or select committee hearings. And although they may be aware of the timing of some debates, BBC Parliament screens various select committee hearings over the weekend with no advance warning.

7.15 Evidence submitted to the Commission suggested there was much scope to improve coverage and forewarning of select committee inquiries and reports. As we noted in chapter 3, the chair of one committee told us his only power was that of embarrassing the Government occasionally. Whilst the committees do not have any formal power to change Government policy they can shame ministers into addressing issues raised in their reports. Having that impact, though, requires media coverage.

7.16 The problem for the committees is that there is little or no co-ordination of their press activity. It is left to individual select committees to make their own press contacts. Age Concern believed that Parliament does not publicise itself effectively, particularly in the case of select committees and their reports, stating that "publicity is not always effectively handled by the committees themselves".[169] The Commission's meeting with the Liaison Committee bore out this impression. Several chairs told us that they had not known when other committees were publishing their reports. As a result it was common for different committees to publish on the same day, thus reducing the coverage and impact of their findings.

7.17 The appointment of a communications adviser to the Commons in the summer of 2000 is a positive development. However, this appointment is put into context when it is realised that Whitehall departments have 1,083 full time staff working on media relations, publicity campaigns and advance planning of ministers' announcements.[170]

7.18 But at a more basic level the Commons must improve the accessibility of its publications. Whereas Government publications have been overhauled in recent years to make them readable, Parliament's publications still look like outdated mathematics textbooks. It is unlikely you would encounter publications in this format outside of Westminster. Unless information is made more comprehensible and attractive it should not come as a surprise when few people use it.

7.19 The one area where there have been important developments in recent years is in Parliament's use of the internet. Parliament was ahead of many others in seeing the value of the web and has a website which means that select committee reports and evidence, library papers, and Hansard are now far more accessible. The internet allows far easier access to parliamentary material than has ever previously existed.

---

[169] Appendix 2, Evidence 1
[170] *Information and Press Officers' Directory*, Central Office of Information, (2001)

Responding to issues of public concern

7.20 The biggest task facing Parliament is convincing the public that the proceedings are topical and relevant. In this respect the content and structure of proceedings works against topicality. There is a limited interest in many debates because of their highly-specialised nature and the sheer length of many debates means that few people are willing to sit through the entire discussion, especially when the outcome will be inconclusive. This, of course, might not matter – Parliament should deal with technical issues which are of limited interest. However, there is a question as to whether these issues should be discussed in the main chamber. The rows of empty green benches are not a convincing advert for the centrality of Parliament and it may be that many debates could be moved from the chamber into Westminster Hall, so that the floor of the House is reserved for those issues of most importance, likely to generate maximum interest.

7.21 A potentially bigger problem is that Opposition parties and backbenchers have limited opportunities to initiate debates on relevant and substantive issues. The case of the Passport Agency highlights the problem, which is explained in more detail in the next chapter. Despite problems emerging as early as February, Parliament did not discuss the issue properly until the end of June by which time the situation was reaching crisis point. There are of course other ways of raising such an issue in Parliament. But no backbencher initiated an adjournment debate on the Passport Agency in that period. The case highlights the limited opportunities for MPs to raise topical issues in a meaningful way.

7.22 The lack of topicality does not apply solely to debates, the topicality of questions are also limited because they have to be tabled two weeks in advance. Parliament's ability to respond to issues of public concern appeared to reach its nadir in the autumn of 2000. As Tony Benn stated in the debate on Parliament's return from summer recess at the end of that October, "We have been in recess since July, and during that time there has been a fuel crisis, a Danish no vote, the collapse of the Euro and a war in the middle east, but what is our business tomorrow? The Insolvency Bill *[Lords]*. It ought to be called the Bankruptcy Bill *[Commons]*, because we play no role."[171]

7.23 The choice of whether to recall Parliament lay with the Government and there was little that any MP could do to influence their decision. But as the case of the Passport Agency shows, even when Parliament is sitting, MPs have very few ways of translating public concerns into parliamentary action.

7.24 The Commission believes that the way that Parliament communicates and consults with the public needs to be radically updated. Its style and proceedings need to bear more relation to everyday conversation, its relationship with the media needs to be more systematic and its response to issues of public concern needs to be swifter and more comprehensive.

---

[171] HC debs, 23 October 2000, vol. 330, col.12

Updating parliamentary proceedings

7.25 Our recommendations in chapter 4 cover some aspects of improving the sharpness of debates in the Commons, such as the ability to trade Opposition Day Debates for ministerial statements. The Commission believes that there should be less time spent debating and more time devoted to more rigorous questioning of ministers.

Changing the hours of the Commons

7.26 Historically, **the House of Commons has been notoriously slow in adapting to the requirements of the press (especially compared with the House of Lords) and despite the objections of some parliamentarians, this is a problem for Parliament, not the broadcasters**. There are though precedents for altering Commons procedure to improve coverage. The introduction of standing orders in 1902 moved Question Time to earlier in the day so that, according to Balfour, then Leader of the House, proceedings "may be reported in the newspapers that have currency in the country."[172] The House needs a similar shift now. Government announcements are trailed in the press and on the *Today* programme, so that by the time the minister makes a statement the House is already aware of its content. **The Commission believes that the House should sit earlier in the day and allow for morning statements from ministers.**

7.27 Most press conferences tend to take place at around 10.30 in the morning. By opening the chamber at 10.30, ministerial announcements could be made at the start of the day. The House would need to be informed the previous day that the Government intended to make such an announcement. This would not differ greatly from the current system where the vast majority of statements are indicated to journalists at the Monday morning lobby briefing.

7.28 The system would be likely to ensure greater coverage of the statement, by providing TV pictures for the news bulletins, but also improve coverage of the opposition's point of view. The present system of ministerial announcements at 3.30, followed by a press briefing at 4.30 means that the opposition's view is rarely covered in much detail. It is very unlikely that such a change would prevent the trailing of government initiatives, but it would lower the incentives, give Parliament a greater role and mean that the chamber became the focal point for political activity.

7.29 The morning sittings would also allow the House to finish earlier in the day and improve the chances of the media covering other parliamentary activity. In the past objections to morning sittings were that they would prevent MPs from getting on with constituency or committee work, and ministers from work in their departments. However, if the chamber sat for one less day a week such problems would be alleviated (see recommendation 21). Alternatively, committee work could be re-arranged so that committees sat in the early evening or in recess. For most ministers, the pressures of their work means that most attend the chamber only when they are obliged.

---

[172] Seymour-Ure, C., (1979), 'Parliament and mass communications in the twentieth century', in S.A. Walkland (ed), *The House of Commons in the Twentieth Century*, Clarendon Press: Oxford, p. 533

7.30 The Commission hopes that this recommendation would provide incentives for ministers to make announcements in the House rather than the TV studio, but we acknowledge that this would not entirely alleviate the problem. **The Commission recommends that if a policy announcement is not accompanied by a statement to the House the Speaker should grant a PNQ, allowing MPs to question the minister on the policy.**

Publicising Parliament

7.31 Obviously Parliament is hampered by the fact that business is announced only one week in advance and provisional business two weeks in advance. The Government's attempts to programme business in the Commons might make proceedings more predictable, but even without programming Parliament should make more of an effort to publicise forthcoming activity, at least to interest groups.

Greater use of the internet

7.32 The Commission acknowledges that recently committees have started e-mailing interested parties about their forthcoming work. This is a welcome development, however the Commission believes that Parliament should make greater use of the internet, and use it innovatively.

7.33 Various members of the Liaison Committee suggested to the Commission that every select committee oral evidence session should be recorded on video as it is impossible to know which ones will be interesting.[173] Currently meetings to be recorded are chosen in advance; as a result, rather predictable ones may be chosen but surprisingly exciting or important ones can be missed. **To improve the interest in, and coverage of, select committee hearings, every oral evidence session should be recorded on video.**

7.34 However, even if they were videoed it cannot be guaranteed that individuals or organisations would be aware of where or when they would be shown on BBC Parliament. **The footage of hearings should be kept for a limited period and stored on the individual select committee's page of the Parliament website.** Every interested organisation would be able to check the website, and if necessary, download committee hearings.

A designated press office

7.35 Parliament needs its own press office. The Commons and Lords have designated communications advisers to provide expertise on relationships with the media. A cross-departmental group on information to the public has also been formed in the Commons.

7.36 But given the size of Government, the size of the job that Parliament is expected to do and the amount of information that is generated by Westminster and Whitehall it is absurd that Parliament's press activity is not better co-ordinated. **The Commission believes that Parliament should establish a press office for Parliament. The office would be responsible for co-ordinating the press activity of the committees so that reports were not published on the same day, would highlight to journalists forthcoming issues to be debated and promote Parliament as an institution to the media.**

---

[173] Appendix 3

Layout of reports

7.37 While the internet has transformed dissemination, attention should still be paid to the longer established methods of communication. Indeed in the rush to embrace new technologies, improvements to the longer established methods appear to have been ignored. For example, select committee reports are difficult to read and look outdated. Hansard's daily record is little better. The Liaison Committee Report, *Shifting the Balance*, criticised the poor layout of committee reports and suggested changes.[174] The committee chair Rt Hon Robert Sheldon MP stated that the poor design was "an absurd situation and relegates us to the also-rans in the publicity stakes".[175]

7.38 **The Commission believes that there should be a comprehensive reform of the layout and design of select committee reports.**

Systematic consultation

7.39 At our meetings with the Liaison Committee, and others, it has been said that select committees tend to receive evidence from the same groups, such as professional, 'representative' bodies, pressure groups and academics. A number of written submissions have made similar points. For example, according to RADAR, little effort is made to collect information from, or disseminate it to, disabled people,

> "Particular thought needs to be given to the involvement of groups who have traditionally been farthest from the exercise of power and decision making . . . .
> RADAR believes that consultation papers should be available on request in all formats
> – Braille, audio-tape, sign-language video . . . The price of ordinary print copies is often prohibitive [for those on low incomes]"[176]

7.40 The Equal Opportunities Commission believed that the widest range of interest groups should be consulted, with particular reference to those with access difficulties, for example linguistic barriers, those in remote areas. They suggested greater use of video conferencing and the internet.[177] A report produced by the Hansard Society, *New Media and Social Inclusion*, looked specifically at the ways that excluded groups could be brought into consultation processes through the internet.[178] The report described how the All-Party Parliamentary Group on Domestic Violence successfully used the internet to hear the views of women who had experienced domestic violence, a group who would usually be considered extremely difficult to consult. Subsequently on-line consultation was used by the Social Security Select Committee to hear directly the views of low-income claimants.

7.41 **The internet provides the opportunity for committees to consult much more widely with the public. The internet must be used more creatively during inquiries so that they go beyond the 'usual suspects'. Committees should use the internet as part of their effort to ensure that all interested parties are invited to contribute and are notified of future select committee work.**

---

[174] HC 300
[175] HC debs, 9 November 2000, vol. 341 col. 479
[176] Appendix 2, Evidence 28
[177] Appendix 2, Evidence 6
[178] Coleman, S and Norman, (2000), *New Media and Social Inclusion*, Hansard Society: London

Publication of an annual report

7.42 Parliament should also make greater effort to publicise its activity as a whole, through an annual report. Such a report is now published by the Government, and also by the Edinburgh Parliament. There are various mechanisms currently in use in Westminster – the Lords publishes an annual report, and the Commons Sessional Returns, but these tend to have a specialist audience and are often difficult to follow and hard to obtain. The annual report would provide a sharper focus for parliamentary activity and, importantly, allow members of the public to judge its performance. **Both Houses of Parliament should produce Annual Reports on their work which set out their activity and achievements during the year. They should be publicised properly and made easily accessible to the public through the Stationery Office and the internet.**

Responding to public concern

Recall of Parliament

7.43 As the petrol crisis of autumn 2000 showed, Parliament is hamstrung at times of crisis by the fact that only the Government can recall Parliament. The Commission believes that Parliament as an institution must be able to respond to issues as they arise. If Parliament is to be an effective forum at times of crisis, and retain its significance to political debate, there must be an alternative mechanism for the recall of Parliament.

7.44 **The Commission believes that the Speaker of the Commons should have the ability to recall Parliament at times of emergency.** The recall would have to be instigated by a Member of Parliament and the Speaker would adjudicate claims for recall, along similar lines to those for the choice of Private Notice Questions. The Speaker would therefore consult with the leaders of the political parties before taking the decision. It is envisaged that a recall would occur only when an urgent development affecting the national interest had to be discussed by Parliament.

Greater use of petitions

7.45 One method of engaging more systematically with the public interest is to make petitions a more significant feature of the work of Parliament. At present they are governed by strict rules about wording and there is little sense that petitions to Parliament result in any concrete action on the part of MPs. Although there are approximately 80–100 petitions submitted to Parliament each year[179], between January 1999 and January 2001, 492 petitions of over 200 signatures were presented to 10 Downing Street.[180]

---

[179] The number of petitions presented in recent years is as follows, the figures in brackets are the number that received an 'observation' or response from the relevant government department; 1997–8: 99 petitions (55), 1998–9: 99 petitions (37), 1999–2000: 87 petitions (54).

[180] Petitions of under 200 signatures are not kept by 10 Downing Street, but are forwarded to the relevant department.

7.46   This is in contrast to the Scottish Parliament where the Public Petitions Committee plays a pivotal role between the public and the Executive. All petitions go to the committee which then assesses the merits of each submission by consulting with the Executive, MPs and, if necessary, taking evidence from individuals and organisations. The Commission filters out petitions where action is already being taken or where the case is weak. Where there is a case to be answered the committee refers petitions on for further consideration. In the 1999–2000 session of the Parliament the committee referred 92 petitions (57.5%) on to the relevant subject committee for further consideration, 17 (10.6%) to the Scottish Executive and 4 (2.6%) to a UK Government minister for a response.[181]

7.47   Even where the Petitions Committee, the subject committee, or the Executive decides no action should be taken, the fact that it was discussed in Parliament is significant. That Parliament addressed and responded to the issue is important to members of the public and it also offers a valuable means for MSPs to remain in touch with issues of public concern.

7.48   **The House of Commons should re-establish a Petitions Committee which would play a significant role in mediating between issues of public concern and select committees. The committee should be structured along lines similar to the Scottish Parliament's committee and should draw the attention of MPs to issues where it feels there is public concern. By channelling such petitions through the relevant departmental select committee, greater pressure would be placed on the Government to respond to public concerns.**

Principle 7 – Parliament must communicate better with the public

Parliament is strongest where it engages with and articulates issues of public concern. If Parliament is to be effective the public must regard it as relevant and topical, but to do this it must adapt more quickly than it has done in the past.

Recommendations

39.   **The House of Commons has been slow to adapt to the needs of the media. Whereas the Government machine, the political parties and most individual MPs, are attuned to the needs of the media, Parliament is not. To improve media coverage the Commons should sit earlier in the day and allow for morning statements from ministers. (para 7.26)**

40.   **In recent years concern has grown at the number of policy announcements made outside Parliament. Mid-morning statements might reduce this tendency, but where a policy announcement is not accompanied by a statement to the House the Speaker should grant a Private Notice Question, allowing MPs to question the minister directly on the policy. (para 7.30)**

41.   **To improve the interest in, and coverage of, select committee hearings, every oral evidence session should be recorded on video. This footage could be kept for a limited period and stored on the individual select committee's page of the Parliament website, allowing the public to access the evidence. (paras 7.33–7.34)**

---

[181] The Scottish Parliament, (2000), *Scottish Parliament Statistics 2000*, Stationery Office: London, pp. 38–9

42. Although both the Commons and Lords have information officers both Houses need a designated press office. The press offices would be responsible for co-ordinating the press activity of the committees, highlight to journalists forthcoming issues and promote Parliament as an institution to the media. (para 7.36)

43. Parliamentary publications are poorly designed and presented. The layout and design of committee reports, in particular, should be comprehensively reformed. (paras 7.37–7.38)

44. The internet provides the opportunity for committees to consult much more widely with the public. The internet must be used more creatively during inquiries so that they go beyond the 'usual suspects'. Committees should use the internet as part of their effort to ensure that all interested parties are invited to contribute and are notified of future select committee work. (para 7.41)

45. Both Houses of Parliament should produce Annual Reports on their work which set out their activity and achievements during the year. They should be publicised properly and made easily accessible to the public through the Stationery Office and the internet. (para 7.42)

46. At present, only the Government can recall Parliament if an emergency develops during a recess. The Speaker of the Commons should, after having consulted the main political parties, have the ability to recall Parliament at times of emergency. (para 7.44)

47. The House of Commons should re-establish a Petitions Committee which would play a significant role in mediating between issues of public concern and select committees. The committee should be structured along lines similar to the Scottish Parliament's committee and should draw the attention of MPs to issues where it feels there is public concern. By channelling such petitions through the relevant departmental select committee, greater pressure would be placed on the Government to respond to public concerns. (para 7.48)

Chapter Eight

Parliament at the apex

8.1 Parliament has a unique role in holding ministers to account on behalf of the public. However, as this report has shown, Parliament displays numerous shortcomings in its monitoring of government. The Commission has argued that Parliament's role is not to attempt to scrutinise systematically every aspect of government itself. Government is too large and complex for Parliament to do the job alone. Its role, and the role of individual politicians, needs to be refined and clarified according to the context in which it operates. Alongside the growth of government there have developed numerous other interrogatory and scrutiny bodies who are better equipped, in terms of resources and expertise, to monitor government.

8.2 As a result, one of the most significant characteristics of modern government is the wealth of information available on its performance. The creation of executive agencies, utility regulators, inspectors and ombudsmen has meant that Parliament now has a greater number of facts and figures than ever on which to draw in the pursuit of accountability. Through the scrutiny work, annual reports and performance assessments of such independent bodies there exists an array of indicators by which government can be judged.

8.3 However, the effectiveness of such work relies on it being used for a purpose. By challenging ministers on the basis of independent analysis it not only strengthens Parliament's case but also gives added value to the original work. Parliament needs to use the work of these other bodies in a more rigorous and systematic fashion, and provide a framework for their scrutiny of government.

8.4 This chapter examines how Parliament currently uses the available information by reference to a number of case studies. The first part of the chapter examines Parliament's relationship with executive agencies. Using the Public Trust Office, the Child Support Agency and the Passport Agency as examples we assess how effectively Parliament adapted to, and utilised, their work. The second part of the chapter looks at growth of extra-parliamentary scrutiny and examines the implications for Parliament of the independent regulators and the increasing use of judicial review.

8.5 The chapter highlights the strengths and weaknesses of the current system. It draws on the recommendations of the report, showing what the Commission's proposals are designed to achieve and how they might work in practice. The underlying message of this chapter, and the report as a whole is that Parliament must adapt, and adapt swiftly.

Parliament and executive agencies

8.6   It is estimated that three-quarters of central government activity is now undertaken by executive agencies.[182] The process of giving civil service functions to arms-length agencies was a result of the *Next Steps* programme in the late 1980s and early 1990s, and it has transformed the provision of government services.[183] Although executive agencies remain formally part of their original department and operate within 'framework agreements' established by the ministry, they are headed by a chief executive who has a large degree of autonomy and is responsible for the day to day performance of the service.

8.7   The size and scope of their activity, as well as the removal of direct responsibility from the Government department has raised concerns about the accountability of these new agencies to Parliament. Lord Nolan, at the Second Radcliffe Lecture in 1996 voiced his concerns,

> ". . . if accountability is only through Ministers, in respect of an agency with hundreds of offices and thousands of clients, the chain is too long, the person who should be answerable – perhaps at local level – remains shielded from public view, and true accountability is weakened . . . The right people have to be accountable . . . Eventually, the framework of accountability will have to change, to follow the new management and organisational structure."[184]

8.8   However, the accountability of agencies is not solely through ministers. Parliament has the capacity to scrutinise the activity of the agencies and their chief executives directly through the work of select committees. The publication of framework documents, targets and annual reports has increased the amount of information upon which committees can base their investigations. An official review in 1995 argued that agencies clarified the roles and functions of chief executives, agency and departmental officials, and therefore 'facilitated accountability.'[185] The Public Service Committee made a similar argument in 1996, commenting,

> '. . . the formal delegation of responsibility to agency Chief Executives can offer better accountability because it makes more transparent the relationship between Minister and civil servant . . . With the information it now has available in the Framework Document and elsewhere, it ought to be possible for Parliament and the public to examine the relationship between Ministers and some civil servants to decide to whom should be attributed praise or blame.'[186]

8.9   However, the accountability of the agencies relies ultimately on the performance of Parliament. They can only be made accountable if MPs and committees use the information that agencies produce in a more systematic fashion. As the following case studies show, in practice, the performance of the committees in relation to agencies has been haphazard. Where some committees regularly review the activities of the agencies within their ambit, others are less thorough. In many areas Parliament has failed to detect agency problems early enough and once problems have been diagnosed MPs have not been fully effective in ensuring that remedial action is implemented. Parliament needs to adapt its structures so that it engages more effectively with the work of the agencies.

---

[182] Weir, S., & Beetham, D., *op cit*, p. 194

[183] The Efficiency Unit report *'Improving Management in Government: the Next Steps'*, published by the Cabinet in February 1988, laid the basis for agencies. Its main recommendation was that agencies should be created to 'carry out the executive functions of Government within a policy and resources framework set up by a department.' The agencies vary considerably in terms of size and scope ; the largest are major enterprises such as the Benefits Agency, HM Prisons Service and the Employment Service.

[184] Lord Nolan, Radcliffe Lectures, Warwick University, November/December 1996

[185] *Prior Options Review*, 1995

[186] Public Service Committee, (1995–96), *Ministerial Accountability and Responsibility*, HC 313-I, para 88

Administrative failure, ineffective scrutiny – the case of the Public Trust Office

8.10   The Public Trust Office (PTO) was established in 1987. Its Mental Health Sector had responsibility for the management of the private assets and financial affairs of people with mental incapacity when they had no one able or willing to act as receiver. The appointment of receiverships is made by the Court of Protection, which oversees around 22,000 public and private receiverships. The PTO was responsible for around 2,500 'public trustee receiverships', to act directly on a patient's behalf and obliged to account for all their transactions. In return the PTO charged each patient a fee for their monitoring and receivership work.

8.11   The PTO was thus responsible for the financial affairs of some of the most vulnerable people in society. In 1994 the National Audit Office investigated the operation of the agency, ranging over 400 case files and interviewing patients, receivers and carers. The NAO found serious deficiencies in the service being provided for patients. This was followed four months later by the Public Accounts Committee which reinforced the findings of the original NAO report. Both reports highlighted a backlog of accounts and investments awaiting review, as well as numerous instances of fraud, inefficiency and incompetence. The PAC questioned the role of the PTO in keeping receivers informed and the high fees that the PTO was charging for such an unsatisfactory service.

Figure 8a – Case study: the Public Trust Office

1987	January: Public Trust Office established. In 1994 the PTO became an executive agency within the Lord Chancellor's Department.
1994	March: National Audit Office publishes its report *Looking after the Financial Affairs of People with Mental Incapacity*.[187] The report found a significant backlog in the case files of patients and that money was not being accounted for properly.
1994	July: Public Accounts Committee publishes its report on the same subject.[188] The committee reinforced the NAO's findings and expressed its concern at the backlog of cases, the frauds being committed against patients accounts and the high fees patients were charged by the PTO.
1994	October: Public Trust Office responded to the PAC report stating it was taking action to remedy the deficiencies.[189]
1999	February: National Audit Office returned to the case five years after its original report publishing *Protecting the Financial Welfare of People with Mental Incapacity*.[190] The NAO found a marked deterioration in the service.
1999	September: Public Accounts Committee publishes its report *Public Trust Office: Protecting the Financial Welfare of People with Mental Incapacity*.[191] The report was highly critical of the PTO and the deterioration since their previous report. PAC chair David Davis stated that the PTO had displayed an "unacceptable level of performance"[192]
1999	November: Lord Chancellor's Department and the Public Trust Office stated "we accept the Committee's overall conclusions as well as the specific areas for improvement which the Committee has identified" which "demand a fundamental programme of change".[193]
2000	December: Lord Chancellor's Department announced that as of April 2001 the PTO would cease to exist and its functions would be performed by a new organisation the Public Guardianship Office.

[187]   National Audit Office, (Session 1993–94), *Looking after the Financial Affairs of People with Mental Incapacity*, HC 258
[188]   Public Accounts Committee, (1993–94), *Looking after the Financial Affairs of People with Mental Incapacity, p. v–vii*
[189]   Treasury Minute on the thirty-ninth report from the Committee of Public Accounts 1993–94 – *Looking after the Financial Affairs of People with Mental Incapacity*
[190]   National Audit Office, (1998–99), *Protecting the Financial Welfare of People with Mental Incapacity*, HC 206
[191]   Public Accounts Committee, (1998–99) *Public Trust Office: Protecting the Financial Welfare of People with Mental Incapacity*, HC 278
[192]   BBC online, "Patients' cash badly managed", 1 September 1999
[193]   Treasury Minute on the thirty-fifth report from the Committee of Public Accounts 1993–94 – *Looking after the Financial Affairs of People with Mental Incapacity*

8.12   The reports made a series of recommendations to reduce the backlog and to ensure that receivers were regularly informed and advised. In October 1994 the Public Trust Office responded, stating that it had "taken action on each of the Committee's conclusions and recommendations to ensure that opportunities to improve the service offered by the PTO are not missed".[194]

8.13   In February 1999, the NAO investigated the PTO again. Far from improving, the NAO found that the five years since its previous report had been marked by a serious deterioration of the service. The NAO noted that in almost 40% of cases, the PTO had failed to obtain accounts from receivers explaining how they had used patients' money.[195] When accounts were received, the report stated that only 25% were reviewed within the target time of four weeks – a deterioration since the previous report when 85% were dealt with on time.[196]

8.14   The subsequent PAC report in September 1999 stated that "there has been a serious deterioration in the Public Trust Office's performance in several key areas since our predecessors' 1994 report which has not been addressed through the Lord Chancellor's Department's oversight and monitoring."[197] The chair of the committee Rt Hon David Davis MP in an annual Commons debate on the work of the PAC expressed the seriousness of their concerns,

> "The Committee first considered the issue in 1994 and, as a consequence, published one of its most critical reports of the decade. Revisiting the subject this year, we found that the improvements that we had been promised had not been delivered and that, worse still, in some important areas performance had deteriorated markedly. That fell far short of what patients have a right to expect . . . Patients have been failed at every turn."[198]

8.15   In November 1999, the Lord Chancellor's Department and the Public Trust Office responded, stating "we accept the Committee's overall conclusions as well as the specific areas for improvement which the Committee has identified . . . [these] demand a fundamental programme of change".[199] A subsequent review recommended that the Public Trust Office's operations should be performed by other parts of the Lord Chancellor's Department, specifically the Court Service and the Official Solicitor's Office.[200]

8.16   The Government's subsequent actions revealed the depth of the problems at the PTO. The Lord Chancellor's Department announced in December 2000 that, as of 2 April 2001, the PTO would cease to exist. Its functions would be taken over by a

---

[194]   *ibid*

[195]   National Audit Office, *Protecting the Financial Welfare of People with Mental Incapacity*, (1998–99), HC 206, p.1

[196]   *ibid*, p.25

[197]   Public Accounts Committee, (1998–9), HC 278

[198]   HC debs, 25 November 1999, Vol. 339, Col. 789

[199]   Treasury Minute on the thirty-fifth report from the Committee of Public Accounts 1998–99 – Public Trust Office: *Protecting the Financial Welfare of People with Mental Incapacity*

[200]   Lord Chancellor's Department, (2000), *Making Changes – The Future of the Public Trust Office*, para 201

new organisation, the Public Guardianship Office (PGO) and its investments functions would be radically overhauled to improve management of clients' funds. Initially the PGO would be part of the Court of Protection but ministers would consider whether it should be a candidate for agency status.

Improving select committee coverage and follow-up

8.17   The case of the Public Trust Office highlights serious deficiencies in the quality of accountability exercised over this particular agency. Although Parliament, through the NAO and the PAC, was able to identify serious problems, it failed to ensure that their recommendations were acted upon. As a result, the quality of the service affecting the financial affairs of people who were already amongst the most disadvantaged, was allowed to deteriorate unacceptably over the course of five years without any further intervention.

8.18   Clearly, the bulk of the responsibility must lie with the Government, the Lord Chancellor's Department as the agency's sponsoring department, and the chief executive of the PTO. However, Parliament failed to monitor the situation and, perhaps knowing that there would be little continuing oversight, neither the LCD nor the PTO felt pressure to act upon the reports' findings. Regardless of the strength of evidence, argument and recommendations, years elapsed before the situation was rectified. The fact that the PTO had to be abolished reflects the extent of the problems that were being faced by 1999. And, despite significant changes in service provision, it is not clear that Parliament was able to identify and hold to account those responsible for the deterioration.

8.19   There seems little point in spending significant sums on the NAO and the PAC if no action is taken after they report and no mechanisms are in place to ensure that their work is followed up. As this report has argued, if Parliament is to be effective committees must follow up their recommendations and publish a periodic review within two to three years of the original report (recommendation 13).

8.20   The case also highlights the need for the departmental select committees to work more closely with the PAC and NAO. The Home Affairs committee, under whose jurisdiction the PTO came, did not broach the subject between 1994 and 1999. Had they done so, they may have exerted the necessary pressure to ensure that matters were rectified before they reached crisis point. Select committees should use the reports of the NAO and PAC as the basis for more detailed policy investigations (recommendations 30 & 31).

8.21   Most significantly though the case highlights the extent to which agencies can easily slip through the net of parliamentary scrutiny. Select committees must have as part of their core duties an obligation to track and monitor the work of the agencies and non-departmental public bodies which are the responsibility of their department (recommendations 8 & 9).

Policy failure compounded by maladministration – the Child Support Agency

8.22 The Child Support Agency (CSA) was established in 1993 to ensure that parents made sufficient financial contributions for the maintenance of their child's welfare. The CSA would adjudicate and enforce rulings on the amount that each parent should make to their child's upkeep. The principle behind the legislation introducing the CSA was supported by all the political parties and the Bill passed through Parliament with little scrutiny and few amendments.

8.23 The problems which occurred when the agency began its work in 1993 were compounded by administrative shortcomings. The sheer number of cases and the number of decisions being challenged by parents meant that the agency was struggling to cope. The volume of work further weakened the agency's ability to deal with the cases swiftly and efficiently. The failings were evident at a number of levels and in its early years the agency failed to meet its targets for arrangement of maintenance, customer service and administrative performance.[201]

8.24 In contrast to the case of the Public Trust Office the CSA became a significant feature of every MP's work and as a result it could not avoid parliamentary scrutiny. The sheer volume of cases meant that most MPs were having to deal with constituents who were in difficulty with the CSA. It appears that for many MPs CSA cases were the single most time-consuming element of their constituency work.[202] As our survey of MPs shows, by the summer of 2000 over 70% of MPs were still spending between one and five hours each week on CSA casework, with a further 10% spending between six and fifteen hours.[203]

8.25 This level of concern could not be ignored by Parliament, and the CSA was the subject of successive inquiries by a variety of select committees, Opposition Day Debates, Adjournment Debates and parliamentary questions. The Social Security Select Committee alone produced five reports on the CSA in just over three years. During their investigations the committee took regular oral evidence from ministers, CSA chief executives, senior officials, pressure groups and those personally affected by the CSA. The committee received in excess of 12,000 letters and submissions from the public in a two year period. This level of concern meant that the committee monitored the CSA's developments very closely, it received monthly written evidence from the CSA (including detailed figures on its performance) and took evidence on the CSA's business plans and annual reports.[204]

---

[201] Child Support Agency, (1994–5), *Annual Report and Accounts*, HC 596
[202] See Power, G., (1998), *Representatives of the People?*, Fabian Society: London
[203] Appendix 4
[204] HC 50 (1995–96)

Figure 8b – Case study: The Child Support Agency

1993   Child Support Agency established to ensure that parents made a financial contribution for the welfare of their child.

1994   Social Security Select Committee publishes two reports highlighting deficiencies of the CSA, *The Operation of the Child Support Act* (March), *The Operation of the Child Support Act; Proposals for Change* (October)[205]

1995   January: Ombudsman lays first report on the CSA before Parliament.[206]

1995   January: Government publishes White Paper *Improving Child Support* and amending legislation subsequently introduced which became the *Child Support Act 1995*

1995   March: Select Committee on the Parliamentary Commissioner for Administration publishes report responding to Ombudsman's concerns.[207]

1995   November: Public Accounts Committee publishes its report on the finances of the CSA.[208]

1996   January: Social Security Select Committee publishes third report on the CSA, *The Performance and Operation of the Child Support Agency*[209]

1996   March: Ombudsman lays second report on the CSA before Parliament.[210]

1996   June: Social Security Select Committee publishes fourth report on CSA, *Child Support; Good Cause and the Benefit Penalty*[211]

1997   March: Public Accounts Committee publishes second report on finances of CSA[212]

1997   March: Social Security Select Committee publishes fifth report on CSA, *Child Support*[213]

1997   April: CSA Independent Case Examiner introduced to assess cases of maladministration.

1997   July: Labour Government publishes Green Paper on CSA reform

1999   July: Government publishes White Paper *A new contract for welfare, Children's Rights and Parents' Responsibilities*[214]

8.26   The inquiries of the social security select committee were buttressed by the work of the Ombudsman and the Committee on the Parliamentary Commissioner for Administration (PCA) to which the Ombudsman reported. The extent of the CSA's problems were reflected in the fact that by the end of 1994 complaints against the agency accounted for more than one third of the total of all complaints being referred to the Ombudsman. So acute was the situation that the Ombudsman took the unusual step of writing to all MPs asking them not to refer further CSA cases unless they contained novel features or were resulting in financial loss.[215]

---

[205] Select Committee on Social Security, (Session 1993–4), *The Operation of the Child Support Act*, HC 69: Select Committee on Social Security, (Session 1993–4), *The Operation of the Child Support Act: Proposals for Change*, HC 470

[206] Parliamentary Commissioner for Administration, (1994–5), *Investigations of Complaints Against the Child Support Agency*, HC 135

[207] Select Committee on the Parliamentary Commissioner for Administration, (1994–5), *Child Support Agency*, HC 199

[208] Public Accounts Committee, (Session 1995–6), *Department of Social Security: Appropriation Funds – Child Support Agency*, HC31

[209] Social Security Select Committee, (Session 1995–6), *The Performance and Operation of the Child Support Agency*, HC 50

[210] Parliamentary Commissioner for Administration, (1995–6), *Investigations of Complaints Against the Child Support Agency*, HC 20

[211] Social Security Select Committee, (1995–6), *Child Support; Good Cause and the Benefit Penalty*, HC 440

[212] Public Accounts Committee, (1997–8), *Child Support Agency: Client Funds Accounts*, HC 313

[213] Social Security Select Committee, (1996–97), *Child Support*, HC 282

[214] Cm 4349, July 1999

[215] Social Security Committee, (1998–99), *Tenth Report: The 1999 Child Support White Paper*, HC 798

8.27 As well reporting on individual cases the Ombudsman used his powers to lay two special reports to Parliament, in January 1995 and March 1996 summarising what his investigations into individual complaints had found.[216] In March 1995 the PCA also published a report based on the ombudsman's finding and concluded that the committee were "in no doubt that maladministration within the CSA cannot be divorced from the responsibility of ministers for the framework within which it operated."[217] In addition the Public Accounts Committee published two reports in the period on the CSA's finances.[218]

8.28 The Government had to respond to these problems and in 1995 introduced legislation to amend the working of the CSA. This was undoubtedly partly a response to parliamentary pressure from individual MPs and committees, and the Government acknowledged the merit of many of the committees' recommendations.[219]

8.29 Despite these reforms the CSA remained a problem beyond the 1997 election and the Labour government introduced further changes designed to overhaul the agency. The Social Security Select Committee conducted an inquiry into the Government's White Paper, *A New Contract for Welfare: Children's Rights and Parents Responsibilities*, taking evidence from a range of interested parties, including the Ombudsman to ensure that the lessons were brought to bear on future legislation.[220] It also took evidence from the CSA Independent Case Examiner, a post created in 1997, partly as result of an earlier recommendation by the PCA. Legislation introducing major changes to child support was passed in 2000 with an implementation date of 2002.

Effective oversight – parliamentary pressure channelling public concern

8.30 The experience of the CSA showed how the departmental select committee, the Ombudsman (and its parliamentary committee) and the Public Accounts Committee (PAC) can work effectively together. Whilst the Ombudsman dealt with cases of maladministration and the PAC with finance, the Social Security Select Committee could effectively bring together the various strands of their work, and channel public concern into specific policy recommendations. The considerable evidence accrued by the committees was used in debates, parliamentary questions and media coverage of the CSA. Many of the committees' recommendations were accepted by Government and they undoubtedly shaped the content of subsequent legislation.

8.31 The case highlights the effectiveness of Parliament where its engages with and articulates issues of public concern (principle 7). The value of constituency casework was evident throughout, in that individual MPs of all parties were well aware of the hardship of many constituents and many became expert in the technicalities of child support. In addition, scrutiny may have been easier for select committees because of its agency status. The CSA was required to publish performance targets, framework

---

[216] (1994–5), HC 135; (1995–6), HC 20
[217] Select committee on the Parliamentary Commissioner for Administration, (1994–95), *Third Report; The Child Support Agency*, HC 199, para 27
[218] Session (1995–6), HC 31. Session (1997–8), HC 313
[219] See Government Replies 1993–94, Cm 2469, Cm 2743.
[220] Social Security Select Committee, (1998–99), *Tenth Report: The 1999 Child Support White Paper*, HC 798, para 26

agreements, staffing and resource requirements in a business plan and account for its performance in an annual report. In short, it was much more transparent than the equivalent maintenance-collecting section of the DSS, the Liable Relatives Unit, which the CSA replaced. The committees were able to draw effectively on a vast amount of information and expertise.

8.32 However, the CSA was an unusual case and Parliament's response atypical. It would have been difficult for Parliament to ignore, and the apparent success of Parliament should be put into context by the fact that it took approximately five years for the original mistakes to be properly rectified. Although the various parts of Parliament complemented one another, the case emphasises the need for a formalised relationship between agencies and select committees, between the ombudsman and Parliament and between the committees and the chamber (principle 3, recommendations 10 & 15). In addition, the case highlights the value of select committee consultation and ensuring that evidence is taken from a wide variety of sources. There is scope for further improvement, and the Commission has made a number of recommendations to enhance public interest, processes of consultation and the ability of the public to feed their concerns into Parliament (recommendations 41, 42, 43, 44, & 47).

8.33 In some respects lessons still need to be learned with respect to scrutiny of legislation. Although the experience of the CSA was a significant factor in the Labour Government's desire to introduce more draft Bills for scrutiny, the Social Security Select Committee was not able to consider the Draft Bill to reform child support. This was despite a commitment from the previous Secretary of State for Social Security that such a bill would 'certainly' be made available to them.[221] The expertise built up by the members of select committees should be deployed much more effectively in the examination of legislation (recommendations 16 & 17) at an early stage.

Parliament's limited response to mismanagement at the Passport Agency

8.34 From its inception in 1991 until the summer of 1999 the Passport Agency had an unremarkable history. One of many agencies within the Home Office, it had performed its core tasks adequately and been given its Charter Mark in 1992. However, administrative and policy changes introduced by the department meant that the agency reached crisis point during 1999 affecting the service to thousands of individuals.

8.35 The problems began with a Home Office decision to introduce a new computer system into two of the Passport Agency's offices. Added to this, the Government announced in April 1998 that from October that year, children under 16 would need to carry separate passports when travelling abroad. The agency, however, failed to anticipate the number of applications they would have to process and received almost 800,000 in the first six months of 1999. The increased demand coincided with an underestimation of how long it would take to train staff in the new system.

---

[221] *ibid.*, para 124

8.36 In February 1999 the Passport Agency decided to prioritise applications by dates of travel, and by March the delays in processing were beginning to attract media attention, leading to increased numbers of applications and congestion in the system.[222] By June 1999, about 565,000 applications were awaiting processing. Between May and July 1999, the Home Office and Agency introduced emergency measures including free two year extensions to passports and extra staff at passport offices.

Figure 8c – Case Study: The Passport Agency

1991	Passport Agency established.
1998	October: New computer system introduced to the Agency
1998	April: Government announces that from October 1998 all children will need passports. In the first six months of 1999 the Passport Agency received almost 800,000 applications for child passports.
1999	February: agency chief executive informs ministers of problems in processing passports.
1999	March: Business recovery plan approved by Home Office minister Mike O'Brien MP and Home Secretary Jack Straw MP.
1999	April: Leader of the House Margaret Beckett MP is asked about the delay in passports and acknowledges the great difficulties being experienced by the Passport Agency "and their serious effect on the service available to people."
1999	May: Ministers begin to receive questions from MPs on the delay in processing passport applications
1999	29 June: First Commons debate, Opposition day (Conservatives) 'Delay in the Issue of Passports'
1999	July: Permanent under-secretary and Principal Finance Officer (Home Office) appear before Home Affairs Select Committee, questioned on Passport Agency and other issues.
1999	July: Agency loses its Charter Mark (held by the Agency since 1992).
1999	October: National Audit Office publishes report 'The Passport Delays of Summer 1999'
1999	December: Jack Straw MP makes a statement to the House of Commons to explain imminent rise in passport fees.
2000	June: Public Accounts Committee publishes 'The Passport Delays of Summer 1999'
2000	June: Government response to PAC report: "We accept the recommendations. The Passport Agency is already implementing most of them."

8.37 Despite these early warnings Parliament's response was slow and muted. The problems were acknowledged in Parliament in April when, during business questions Margaret Beckett MP, Leader of the House of Commons, told MPs that "I think that the whole House . . . will be aware of how great are the difficulties being experienced by the Passport Agency and their serious effect on the service available to people."[223]

---

[222] Maximum processing times in the Agency's 6 regional offices ranged between 25 and 50 days, compared to the Agency's target of 10 working days.
[223] HC debs, 29 April 1999, vol. 330, col. 487

8.38 The first questions to the Home Office began in May, but Parliament did not debate the issue properly until the Conservatives held an Opposition Day Debate at the end of June. This was a full two months after the matter was originally raised, and by which time the situation was reaching crisis point. By June there was clearly a political value in the Conservatives raising the issue, but the debate did not provide a new perspective on the agency's problems nor did it provide any constructive recommendations for its solution. In the intervening period there had been no select committee hearing and not even an adjournment debate.

8.39 The impact of these problems was to be borne by the taxpayer – the cost of additional measures taken by the Agency in an effort to maintain services during the year from October 1998 was £12.6 million[224] and the cost of adult passports rose by £7 to £28, and the cost of children's passports went up by £3.80 to £14.80.

8.40 Whilst the National Audit Office published its report in October 1999, the Public Accounts Committee did not pick up the issue until June of 2000. It highlighted that the Agency did not have adequate risk management and contingency plans in place and had failed to communicate effectively with the public, and made a variety of recommendations on this basis. By this time, the Government stated in its response of the same month, the vast majority of recommendations were already being implemented.

Improving the responsiveness of Parliament

8.41 The Passport Agency highlights the shortcomings of Parliament in acting as an early warning system for policy and administrative failure. Although the warning signs of problems at the Passport Agency were evident early on in 1999, Parliament did not address them fully until the following summer when the Public Accounts Committee published its report. Important though such reports are, the case reinforces the point that departmental select committees should not simply conduct *post hoc* investigations after crises have been resolved, they should maintain a watching brief over the activities of the agencies and bodies within their department and report regularly on their performance (recommendations 8, 9 & 10). In this case the Home Affairs Select Committee did not engage with the issue at all, save for one hearing in July 1999, which also covered a range of other subjects. The extent to which MPs secured accountability or redress in this case is not clear.

8.42 Parliament's slow response time was also reflected in the chamber. Although Opposition Day Debates provide a useful political function, this was a case of poor administration on the part of the Home Office and the Passport Agency. The suitability of such debates to deal with administrative matters is highly questionable, and the role of the chamber needs to be clarified in the light of such instances (recommendations 20 & 21). A more productive exercise might have involved the Opposition trading some of their debating time for a statement from the Home Secretary, granting of a Private Notice Question or reforms to improve the topicality of question time (recommendations 22, 23 & 27).

---

[224] Public Accounts Committee, (1999–2000), 'The Passport Delays of Summer 1999', HC 208, para 7

8.43 The case also highlights the limits on MPs in calling substantive debates on anything other than party political grounds. Although adjournment debates serve some purpose, in this case the fact that no MP used them highlights their limited value. This was a predominantly non-party issue, and MPs of all parties were having to deal with constituency cases. Yet there is no mechanism for a 'public interest debate' moved by a significant number of MPs across party boundaries which might produce a fuller chamber and a more constructive debate (recommendation 24).

Quangos and Non-Departmental Public Bodies

8.44 A related but separate category of organisation which has presented similar problems of scrutiny to executive agencies is the quango or non-departmental public body (NDPB). These have played an increasingly important role in government, particularly in the fields of health, housing, education, and social care in the last 25 years.[225] These bodies vary enormously in structure, remit and powers and have altered the delivery of government services through a combination of local government, special purpose bodies, the voluntary sector and the private sector. Their defining features are that they are removed from the mainstream political channels and are often created without any reference to Parliament. More significant for parliamentary accountability, there are no formal requirements for their reporting to Parliament, and although they spend billions of pounds of public money much remains outside direct scrutiny of the Comptroller and Auditor General.

8.45 An inquiry by the Public Administration Committee found that most select committees' chairs believed it was difficult, perhaps impossible, to monitor closely NDPBs in their department under existing structures, resources and staffing. The common complaints were the lack of time and resources.[226]

Figure 8d – Case study: The Housing Corporation

The Housing Corporation is a non-departmental public body, sponsored by the Department of the Environment, Transport and the Regions, whose role is to fund and regulate Registered Social Landlords (RSLs) in England. The Corporation's Board, appointed by the Secretary of State for the Environment, Transport and the Regions, advises ministers on housing policy and implementation. As well as distributing public money to RSLs, the Housing Corporation has a regulatory role to ensure that taxpayers money is safeguarded.[227]

The Corporation reports annually to Parliament through the Secretary of State for the Environment, Transport and the Regions on the use of the funding allocated to it. It is subject to scrutiny by the National Audit Office and can be called before the House of Commons Public Accounts Committee and the Parliamentary Commissioner for Administration. The Corporation also publishes performance standards covering finance, lettings, tenant involvement, development and management.

However despite the size of the organisation and the information available the Corporation has not been subject to any direct parliamentary scrutiny by the departmental Environment, Transport and Regions select committee since 1992–3, although the Corporation has given evidence to Commons committees on subjects such as rural housing.[228]

---

[225] Figures compiled by Democratic Audit had put the total executive quango count at 5,573 in 1994 and 5,681 in 1997, the biggest single categories being housing associations, grant maintained schools and further education corporations.

[226] Public Administration Committee, (1998–9), *Quangos*, HC 209-I

[227] £20 billion has been invested since RSLs were set up in 1964

[228] HC 32-I (1999–2000)

8.46 The Public Administration Committee made a series of recommendations to improve the quality of scrutiny such as select committee 'confirmation hearings' of appointments, extending the scope of the NAO to audit all executive NDPBs and the standard circulation of notes from ministerial meetings with NDPBs to the relevant select committee.[229]

8.47 However, as the committee acknowledged increased responsibilities require increased staffing and resources. As this report has advocated, the resources of the committees need to be assessed strategically so that additional resources are tied to a clarification of committees' roles and core tasks (recommendations 18 & 19).

8.48 However, in the first place committees need to be clearer about their responsibilities. Parliament must compile a central list of all the bodies obliged to report to both Houses and distribute to the committees the list of organisations under their jurisdiction (recommendation 7). In addition the committees should pilot new methods of working to improve their coverage, the obligation to report regularly could be made easier by making greater use of sub-committees and possibly rapporteurs (recommendations 11 & 12).

Extra-parliamentary scrutiny

8.49 As the executive has changed and grown so a host of external mechanisms have evolved to monitor the activity of government, service delivery and, most recently, the public utilities. In some respects the 'extra-parliamentary' scrutiny of the various regulators, inspectors and commissioners has challenged the traditional role of Parliament, providing new and more extensive scrutiny beyond the capacity of Westminster.

8.50 The Parliamentary Commissioner for Administration provides an example of how Parliament is strengthened by the investigative work of an independent office. The Ombudsman's work investigating individual cases of maladministration often illuminates much broader issues of policy and practice. The above example of the CSA showed how the work of the Ombudsman and its parliamentary committee effectively complemented the work of the Social Security Select Committee.

8.51 The Ombudsman is officially tied to Parliament through a parliamentary committee and thus in theory it should be easier for politicians to build on its work. There are though a range of organisations which provide technical information on the quality of government and increase the opportunities for improved accountability. The Government-initiated *Review of Audit and Accountability for Central Government*[230] stressed the potential benefits of greater use by Parliament of the available external evidence. Suggesting greater co-ordination of the work of the NAO, Audit Commission, the Office of National Statistics and the Statistics Commission its theme was that there already exists considerable, high quality evidence from a range of external mechanisms. Holding Government to account requires Parliament, and specifically its committees, to engage with and utilise their evidence in a more systematic manner.

---

[229] HC 209-I, (1998–9), para 43
[230] *Holding Government to Account: Review of Audit and Accountability for Central Government*, Report by Lord Sharman of Redlynch, February 2001

Regulators and Inspectorates

8.52 There was a significant growth in the number of independent regulators and commissions during the 1990s. Many were established by statute to regulate former public utilities such as electricity, telecommunications and water following their privatisation. Others, such as Ofsted or the Postal Services Commission, conduct regulatory or supervisory functions over government controlled public services.

Figure 8e – Utility regulators and public service regulators

Utility regulators
OFTEL   (Office of Telecommunications)
OFGEM   (combined Office of Gas and Electricity Regulation)
OFWAT   (Office of Water Regulation)
ORR   (Office of the Rail Regulator)
OFREG   (Office for the Regulation of Electricity and Gas – Northern Ireland)

Other UK regulators
Civil Aviation Authority (CAA)
Data Protection Commission
Drinking Water Inspectorate
Electoral Commission
Financial Services Authority (FSA)
Food Standards Authority (FSA)
Health and Safety Executive
Independent Television Commission (ITC)
Law Commission
National Lottery Commission
Office for Standards in Education (Ofsted)
Office of the International Rail Regulator
Occupational Pensions Regulatory Authority (OPRA)
Postal Services Commission (Postcomm)
Press Complaints Commission
Radio Authority
Securities and Investments Board

8.53 Parliament's relationship to these bodies is sometimes difficult to define and the quality of parliamentary accountability has two dimensions. The first is the extent to which the regulators are accountable to Parliament, so that their internal administration and activity is scrutinised by politicians. The second is the extent to which Parliament uses the technical investigations of these bodies as the basis on which to hold Government to account.

8.54 In the first instance, despite their close relationship with Government there are few formal links between the regulators and Parliament, scrutiny is still variable and there are no annual debates of even the most major regulators. A Hansard Society Commission on the regulation of privatised utilities showed that the relationship of these new bodies with Westminster was tenuous and poorly-defined, stating,

> "Parliament has very few specific powers directly over the operation of the regulatory system, particularly over the industry regulators. Its two main specific powers are to vote appropriations to pay for the industry regulatory bodies and to overturn ministerial decisions which are in the form of Orders (for instance, the designation of public telecommunications operators) by passing a Resolution in the House of Commons. In addition, it can use its general scrutiny powers, notably via the National Audit Office and select committees."[231]

---

[231] Hansard Society, (1996) *The Report of the Commission on the Regulation of Privatised Utilities, Chaired by John Flemming FBA*, Hansard Society/European Policy Forum, London p. 30

8.55 As was noted in chapter one, evidence to the Commission from a number of regulators highlighted the sporadic and unsystematic scrutiny of Parliament. In some areas Parliament is adapting as the case study of the Financial Services Authority (figure 8f) shows. But such developments are rare and the danger for Parliament as noted by David Edmonds, Oftel's Director General, was that "accountability to other bodies, especially stakeholders, is increasingly seen as important and this acts to ensure efficient and effective regulatory action."[232] In other words, for so long as Parliament's oversight is patchy and other mechanisms remain in place, the role of MPs and Peers will be further marginalised.

Figure 8f – Case study: The Financial Services Authority

The issues surrounding regulator accountability were central in the establishment of the Financial Services Authority. The Financial Services and Markets Act 2000 recast financial regulation in the UK, creating the Financial Services Authority (FSA) solely responsible for regulating the finance industry. The original bill was published in draft and examined by the Treasury Select Committee which highlighted the need for the FSA to be accountable and efficient. In response the Treasury acknowledged these concerns, and stressed that it was "fully committed to ensuring that the FSA operates in a fair, open and accountable way"[233] and promised to make several amendments to the Bill before its introduction.

Although these amendments placed various public obligations on the FSA, they did not include accountability to Parliament. The accountability of the body was thus also an issue for the joint committee, chaired by Lord Burns, which scrutinised the draft bill. Its first report stated that, "Proper Parliamentary accountability is essential. We believe that this can best be achieved by asking a parliamentary committee to review the FSA's annual report and to take regular evidence from a broad range of consumers and practitioners"[234]

This recommendation was welcomed by the Government and has since been put into practice – the FSA published its Annual Report for 1999–2000 in July 2000, and the FSA's first annual meeting was held on 20 July 2000. On 7 November 2000, Howard Davies, chair of the FSA, and 3 of his staff, appeared before the Treasury select committee for questioning on the annual report.

8.56 The second, and more significant dimension to regulator accountability is the extent to which Parliament uses the technical investigations as the basis for its pursuit of accountability. The regulators provide alternative and more direct forms of accountability for individuals mistreated by the privatised utilities or other public services. However, whilst the regulators deal with cases of individual mistreatment, their ability to secure strategic solutions to industry-wide problems is improved if Parliament builds on their scrutiny. Parliament's task is two-fold, to maintain its relevance in the public mind by drawing out the lessons from the work of the regulators and giving greater worth to their investigations by using it as the basis for holding Government to account.

8.57 In practice though, the departmental committees do not engage systematically enough with the work of regulators and commissioners. A sizeable proportion of evidence to the Commission emphasised such problems, but the submission from Elizabeth France, the Data Protection Commissioner, was particularly telling. The Commissioner is obliged to report to both Houses of Parliament annually on the work of the Office of the Data Protection Commissioner (ODPC). It is responsible for spending almost £5 million of public money each year.

---

[232] Appendix 2, Evidence 24
[233] HM Treasury, 'Financial Services and Markets Bill: Progress Report', page 4, para 1b
[234] Joint Committee on Financial Services and Markets, (1998– 9), *Draft Financial and Markets Bill*, HC328, para. 121

8.58 During the 1990s and the genesis of the Freedom of Information Act 2000 issues of data protection were a significant feature of government activity. John Major's government introduced a Code of Practice on Open Government in 1994 which touched on issues of data protection. The Labour Government introduced a Data Protection Act in 1998 which was originally published in draft form in 1997. The Government was heavily criticised at one stage because the early drafts of its Freedom of Information Bill directly contradicted provisions in the Data Protection Bill then going through Parliament. Other policy proposals and pieces of legislation such as social security fraud had a direct bearing on data protection.

8.59 Despite the salience of the issues since the creation of the ODPC in 1984 the Commissioner has given evidence to the Home Affairs select committee on only two occasions.

8.60 There are many other examples of Parliament's failure to engage with outside expertise and numerous missed opportunities which would enhance the status of the committees. Formalising the relationship between committees and regulators, by obliging them to report regularly on their work would not only improve the coverage and quality of scrutiny but would also strengthen their work. In addition, allocation of time in the chamber for select committee reports on such issues would further integrate the external investigations with the work of Parliament (recommendations 8, 9, 10 & 15).

The growth of judicial review

8.61 Since the late 1970s judges have played an increasingly influential role in challenging ministerial decisions. In part the growth of judicial review reflects a desire on the part of individuals and organisations for a more direct form of redress, and cases have tended to fall into one of three categories – crime, immigration or housing – but in recent years there has been a dramatic increase in the number of planning applications challenged in the courts.

8.62 A series of high-profile cases in the early to mid-1990s, most notably, Pergau Dam in 1995, where Foreign Secretary Douglas Hurd was found to have unlawfully used £234 million of government money to fund a project in Malaysia, were followed by cases such as the restriction on asylum seekers' benefits in 1996 and the judgement on performance related pay for teachers in 2000. The publicity given to these cases emphasised the power of the courts in challenging government activity and, at the same time, implicitly questioned the relative inability of MPs to gain accountability from ministers through Parliament. The Commission was told in a private meeting with former Ministers that the trend reflected the fact that the power of Parliament was being usurped by the courts. However, the ex-ministers also remarked on MPs' lack of desire to reverse such developments.[235]

---

[235] Appendix 3

Figure 8g – Case study: Teachers' Pay Award

On 14 July 2000 the High Court declared illegal the proposed performance related pay scheme for teachers. The National Union of Teachers had argued that the Secretary of State for Education, David Blunkett MP, did not have the power to set the standards by which teachers applying for performance-related pay should be judged.[236]

In his ruling on the case, Mr Justice Jackson said he would not allow Mr Blunkett to "foist" such a major reform of pay and conditions on the teaching profession. He stated that Mr Blunkett had acted "in a manner not authorised by Parliament", had bypassed the independent School Teachers Review Body, which advises him on pay, as well as the Welsh Assembly and as such had "evaded proper scrutiny". The judge rejected the argument that Mr Blunkett had "inherent powers" as a minister of the Crown to take administrative action in support of policies to promote education.

In response Schools Minister Estelle Morris MP made an emergency statement to the Commons, at the request of the Conservatives, on 17 July 2000. She said Mr Blunkett had believed it was not necessary to refer the standards to the review body because "they are about standards of teaching, not about pay structures and scales". She announced that the government would follow a formal consultation process on introducing performance-related pay for teachers in England and Wales, following the court ruling that it had acted illegally. Following the completion of the formal consultation process, performance related pay was introduced in the first half of 2001, backdated to September 2000.

8.63 How far MPs wish to enhance the power of Parliament is a moot point, but the fact remains that there are no parliamentary mechanisms to monitor or follow up court cases overturning ministerial decisions or assess their implications in any systematic fashion. There is no formal mechanism for Parliament to challenge the Government when it fails to follow proper procedure. As the teachers' pay award case shows, even though a Secretary of State unlawfully by-passed Parliament, MPs were unable to remedy the situation. It took outside bodies, in this case the trade unions, to resort to the courts and force the minister to go through the proper procedures.

8.64 Parliament cannot, of course, control or force the courts to account to Parliament in the same way that it should with agencies, NDPBs and regulators. It should though monitor and evaluate judicial decisions in such cases. The departmental select committees should record instances of ministerial decisions overturned in the courts and the reasons given. Reforms should mean that Parliament plays a role in improving the quality of policy making and ensure that mistakes are not repeated.

---

[236] Approximately 197,000 teachers in England applied for the new pay scale, which if successful, would give them an immediate pay rise of £2,000 and access to a higher pay scale.

Conclusion: Putting Parliament at the apex

8.65 The effectiveness of Parliament relies on it adapting to the environment in which it operates. It cannot expect to scrutinise the whole range of Government activity, but it does not have to. The expertise and resources available to external bodies, combined with the amount of information produced by executive agencies, as well as bodies such as the Ombudsman and NAO, should make Parliament's core task of making Government accountable much easier than it has been in the past.

8.66 This though requires that Parliament uses the available information effectively. It needs to be more systematic and rigorous in its relations with external organisations, agencies and, indeed the public. To achieve accountability Parliament must reform its structures, its procedures and its ethos.

8.67 The Commission is well aware that parliamentary reform has traditionally been a slow process. The success of reforms often relies on balancing the aspirations and objectives of MPs and ministers, frontbenchers and backbenchers, Government and Opposition. Reforms should, as far as possible, seek to meet the needs of these different groups. However, it has often been the case that the perceived difficulties of reform have prevented a creative and long-term approach to the role of Parliament. This has, in turn, lengthened the time it has taken to implement change.

8.68 *The Challenge for Parliament* has set out seven principles as the basis on which Parliament should be improved. It has sought to combine a strategic approach to the role of Parliament with a series of smaller recommendations designed to improve the working of Westminster. We have not provided a detailed blueprint, but hope to provide the principles which will govern future reform, so that Parliament effectively adapts to the context in which it operates, but also, crucially, retains and clarifies its core roles.

8.69 The Commission acknowledges that our proposals are not all-encompassing, they will not be quickly or easily implemented. However, our proposals reflect the concern with which we view the current position of Parliament. If Parliament is to retain its central role in scrutinising and holding Government to account, it must perform that role more effectively. It must adapt, and it must adapt quickly.

Conclusions and recommendations

Principle 1 – Parliament at the apex

If Parliament is to improve its effectiveness, reform must be based on underlying principles which improve Parliament's relationship with the public and outside bodies. Parliament needs to be at the apex of the network of regulatory bodies and alternative scrutiny mechanisms. (para 1.53)

Principle 2 – Parliament must develop a culture of scrutiny

The task of holding Government to account should be central to the parliamentary work of every MP but, in practice it is often defined in party political terms. Reforms should seek to enable MPs to balance their party role with their parliamentary role in the pursuit of the public interest. The Commission believes this should be achieved mainly through the system of select committees.

1. To develop a culture of scrutiny and allow all MPs to pursue their scrutiny function every backbench MP should be expected to serve on a select committee. (para 2.29)

2. The high turnover of MPs on committees is partly a result of the large number of MPs on the payroll vote. This should be reduced, so that all but the very largest government departments are limited to one PPS. (para 2.33)

3. Reforms should also seek to improve the attractiveness of committee service and create a parliamentary career path for ambitious MPs. Key posts on select committees should be paid and MPs chairing committees should receive a salary equivalent to that of a minister. (para 2.34)

4. The Commons should build on current practice and provide continuing training for MPs related to their work on committees, parliamentary procedure and subject specialist policy areas. (para 2.39)

5. Fostering a culture of scrutiny requires greater leadership and co-ordination of parliamentary activity. Parliament needs a steering committee or bureau which formally organises parliamentary business. (paras 2.47–2.49)

6. In addition, the Liaison Committee should be restructured and re-named to provide a greater degree of leadership and co-ordination for parliamentary activity. The committee should be reduced in size and elect its own executive body of six MPs. It should play a greater role in determining the membership of the committees and oversee their work. (paras 2.50–2.56)

Principle 3 – Committees should play a more influential role within Parliament

The Commission believes that the system of departmental select committees provides the basis for a more effective system of scrutiny. However, the work of the committees needs to be made more systematic. The duties of the select committees should be more closely defined, their relationship with external scrutiny bodies made more formal and their input into the other areas of parliamentary activity increased.

Core duties and performance indicators

7. Both Houses should maintain a central list of all those organisations obliged to report to Parliament. This list should be distributed to every committee, so that every departmental select committee is aware of the organisations which come under their jurisdiction. (para 3.24)

8. The select committees should be given a set of core duties and functions. To improve the coverage of issues, to utilise the work of the regulators and to give the committees a continuity to their work they should meet pre-agreed objectives over the course of a Parliament. These objectives would provide a set of criteria against which their performance can be judged. (para 3.25)

9. These objectives should be agreed with the reformed Liaison Committee, which would also be responsible for monitoring progress over the Parliament. These objectives might include; balancing inquiries between administration, finance and policy of their department; monitoring all departmental reports, business plans and performance indicators; conducting a regular cycle of work on activities of the regulators, executive agencies, quangos and other associated bodies within their department's purview; and review the progress of the department following the committee's previous reports. (para 3.26)

10. Select committees should have a set of objectives and performance indicators by which their performance could be judged. This would provide a public measurement of their effectiveness. (para 3.28)

Developing new methods of work

11. The principal method of work for these enlarged committees should be through a series of sub-committees with specific remits for examining different aspects of departmental activity. The Commission believes that this would markedly improve the breadth and depth of scrutiny. (para 3.31)

12. The House of Commons should allow committees to experiment with the use of rapporteurs who would gather evidence and produce background papers for the whole committee. (para 3.34)

Improving impact

13. The impact of committee reports will be determined by the assiduity with which their recommendations are monitored and followed up. Committees should publish a periodic review (two to three years after the original report) assessing how far their recommendations have been implemented. (para 3.40)

14. Government replies should conform to a set of minimum standards. These should include an undertaking that a reply should address each of the committees' specific recommendations and oblige Government to formally publish their response. (para 3.42)

Integrating committee work into parliamentary activity

15. There should be regular opportunities for short debates/questions on recently published reports during a peak period in the chamber, to which ministers should give the Government's preliminary response. (para 3.46)

16. The expertise of select committees should be deployed much more effectively in examination of legislation. Committees should play a greater role in the scrutiny of draft legislation. However, this relies on earlier publication by departments so that committees have sufficient time to examine draft bills. (paras 3.47–3.50)

17. In addition, one or two dual-purpose committees, conducting departmental inquiries and scrutinising legislation, should be established on a pilot basis and their performance evaluated by a re-organised Liaison Committee. (para 3.50)

Staffing and support

18. The recommendations for increasing select committee responsibilities also require a consequent increase in staffing and resources. (para 3.51) However, the resourcing of Parliament needs to be examined strategically. The provision of extra resources should be tied to a clarification of the committees' roles and their core tasks. Extra staff or secondments should be related to their agreed functions and duties. (para 3.55)

19. The House authorities should review the work of the clerk's department and levels of support to ensure that committees, and the scrutiny function more generally, are supported in the most effective way possible. (para 3.56)

Principle 4 – Restoring the centrality of the Commons' chamber

The floor of the House of Commons is the main public focus for activity at Westminster. However, attendance by MPs and the extent to which it dominates political debate has declined.

20. To improve the attendance and influence of the chamber its core tasks need to be refined and clarified. It should become the plenary session of the Parliament. (para 4.27)

21. In order to reflect the importance attached to the select committee system, and not take MPs away from the chamber, one day each week should be devoted to committee activity. To reflect the importance of this work other parliamentary business should be arranged around the committees so that the chamber would not meet on this day. (para 4.28)

Improving topicality and effectiveness

22. In general, the chamber should have fewer lengthy debates. Opportunities for MPs to initiate short debates on substantive issues should be increased. Opposition parties should be able to trade some of their Opposition Days for the chance to call for a statement on a topical issue. (paras 4.30–4.32)

23. In addition, the Speaker should grant a greater number of Private Notice Questions each session. (para 4.33)

24. MPs should have the ability to call for 'public interest debates' on issues of public concern on a cross-party basis. (para 4.34)

25. Prime Minister's Questions (PMQs) displays many of the worst aspects of Westminster. Open-ended questions should be banned at PMQs (although the leaders of the main opposition parties should retain this ability); instead Members should give notice of their intention to ask a question ten days in advance and should table their (substantive) question by noon two days before PMQs. (para 4.40)

26. However, even a reformed PMQs is unlikely to ensure the necessary scrutiny of the Prime Minister's expanding role and office. The Prime Minister should appear before a select committee on an annual basis to account for the work of the Government. The most appropriate opportunity would be once a year to give evidence on the Government's Annual Report. (para 4.42)

27. Question time for other departments and ministers should also be reformed to improve its topicality, substance and relevance. No more than ten questions should appear on the Order Paper for each Question Time and no duplicate questions should be allowed. The period of notice for oral questions should be reduced from ten working days to five. (paras 4.44–4.45)

28. In cases where the Government does not produce a response to a written question the reasons for not answering must be made clearer. A denial of information should be accompanied by a reference to the relevant section of the Code of Practice on Open Government or the Freedom of Information Act. (para 4.46)

Principle 5 – Financial scrutiny should be central to accountability

Parliament, and in particular the Commons, has a unique constitutional role in the authorisation and scrutiny of Government expenditure. At present the Commons fails to perform this role in either a systematic or effective manner.

29. The Estimates procedures should be changed to allow Parliament to debate and vote for transfers within overall departmental budgets. This would help focus the attention of MPs and ministers, and hopefully the media and the public, on the scrutiny of spending plans. (para 5.7)

30. Each departmental select committee should pilot and evaluate a new form of committee, a Finance and Audit Sub-Committee. The sub-committee should consider, for example, Estimates and departmental allocations, audit and value-for-money inquiries, Public Service Agreements, performance indicators and outcomes. (para 5.20)

31. We do not suggest that the NAO should provide a servicing function for specific committees, but their reports and expertise should be shared more equitably among the other committees of the House of Commons. Select committees and their sub-committees should use the NAO and PAC reports as the basis for more detailed examination of Government finance. (para 5.23)

32. A Parliamentary Finance Office should be established to give high quality support to the committees. The office would provide research, information, access to specialist advice and expertise, and support in the analysis of evidence and drafting of reports. (para 5.24)

33. Parliament should make greater use of the Audit Commission's work. To improve parliamentary oversight in areas of public expenditure such as the police and the health service, the Audit Commission should formally report to Commons departmental select committees. (para 5.28)

Principle 6 – The House of Lords should complement the Commons

The Lords plays an important role in complementing the work of the Commons and holding Government to account, but the effectiveness of Parliament as a whole requires greater co-operation and co-ordination of the activity of the two Houses.

34. Parliamentary scrutiny would be strengthened if all government ministers were able to make statements to and be questioned in both Houses. We do not seek to challenge the long standing convention that members of one chamber should not speak in the other. Instead, alternative forums away from the chamber of each House should be instigated to allow Ministers of the other House to be questioned. In the Lords a version of the Grand Committee procedure could be used to provide such a forum to question Commons Ministers. In the Commons, the Westminster Hall procedure would be appropriate. (para 6.15)

35. It is not desirable to have a set of second chamber committees shadowing government departments as they would duplicate much of the work of Commons committees. The second chamber should continue its distinctive approach by addressing cross-departmental and 'joined-up' issues to complement the work of the departmental select committees in the Commons in areas such as rural affairs, environmental protection, equal opportunities and social exclusion. (para 6.19)

36. The second chamber should continue to establish *ad hoc* committees to consider specific issues and developments, such as those recently appointed to consider Animals in Scientific Procedures and Stem Cell Research. Such an approach would bring greater flexibility and responsiveness to Parliament's committee system and would allow the second chamber to respond to gaps in the Commons work. (para 6.20)

37. The two different approaches taken by the separate Houses in the field of European Union scrutiny complement each other extremely well. This approach should be used as a model for future complementary, division of scrutiny functions between the two Houses. (para 6.23)

38. The two Houses, their members and staff need to co-ordinate more closely to increase their effectiveness and to prevent unnecessary duplication and overlap. (para 6.25)

Principle 7 – Parliament must communicate better with the public

Parliament is strongest where it engages with and articulates issues of public concern. If Parliament is to be effective the public must regard it as relevant and topical, but to do this it must adapt more quickly than it has done in the past.

39. The House of Commons has been slow to adapt to the needs of the media. Whereas the Government machine, the political parties and most individual MPs, are attuned to the needs of the media, Parliament is not. To improve media coverage the Commons should sit earlier in the day and allow for morning statements from ministers. (para 7.26)

40. In recent years concern has grown at the number of policy announcements made outside Parliament. Mid-morning statements might reduce this tendency, but where a policy announcement is not accompanied by a statement to the House the Speaker should grant a Private Notice Question, allowing MPs to question the minister directly on the policy. (para 7.30)

41. To improve the interest in, and coverage of, select committee hearings, every oral evidence session should be recorded on video. This footage could be kept for a limited period and stored on the individual select committee's page of the Parliament website, allowing the public to access the evidence. (paras 7.33–7.34)

42. Although both the Commons and Lords have information officers both Houses need a designated press office. The press offices would be responsible for co-ordinating the press activity of the committees, highlight to journalists forthcoming issues and promote Parliament as an institution to the media. (para 7.36)

43. Parliamentary publications are poorly designed and presented. The layout and design of committee reports, in particular, should be comprehensively reformed. (para 7.37–7.38)

44. The internet provides the opportunity for committees to consult much more widely with the public. The internet must be used more creatively during inquiries so that they go beyond the 'usual suspects'. Committees should use the internet as part of their effort to ensure that all interested parties are invited to contribute and are notified of future select committee work. (para 7.41)

45. **Both Houses of Parliament should produce Annual Reports on their work which set out their activity and achievements during the year. They should be publicised properly and made easily accessible to the public through the Stationery Office and the internet. (para 7.42)**

46. **At present, only the Government can recall Parliament if an emergency develops during a recess. The Speaker of the Commons should, after having consulted the main political parties, have the ability to recall Parliament at times of emergency. (para 7.44)**

47. **The House of Commons should re-establish a Petitions Committee which would play a significant role in mediating between issues of public concern and select committees. The committee should be structured along lines similar to the Scottish Parliament's committee and should draw the attention of MPs to issues where it feels there is public concern. By channelling such petitions through the relevant departmental select committee, greater pressure would be placed on the Government to respond to public concerns. (para 7.48)**

Appendix I

The theory and practice of parliamentary accountability

Parliament performs a unique role in any parliamentary democracy. It provides the principal means by which the Government is held to account for its activities. Governments are directly accountable to the people at general elections. Between elections Parliament should aim to ensure that Government is run efficiently and effectively by providing oversight of its activity, call ministers to account for their actions, and where necessary, seek remedial action. It is a task undertaken on behalf of the public, with the principal objective of good government.

Defining the role of Parliament

Definitions of Parliament's role and function are many and varied. These in part reflect the variety of activities that Parliament is expected to perform. Most analyses tend to start with the definition provided by Bagehot in his *The English Constitution* of 1867, where he set out the following five functions; choosing and maintaining or dismissing the Government and guiding it; expressing the mind of the people; teaching the nation; informing the Government of grievances and complaints; passing legislation.

Bagehot, in common with other nineteenth century constitutional analysts, was attempting to provide a workable theory for the constitution as well as describing the situation at the time, and as such their writing was as much prescriptive as it was descriptive.[1] As Bagehot himself acknowledged Parliament should reflect the society in which it operates and its activity should evolve over time.[2] Attempts to revise and update Bagehot's functions, and reflect Parliament's changing role tend to include its tasks in approving Government finance, the representation of constituency and party interests, the redress of grievances and the articulation of public concern.[3] However, the evolving nature of Parliament, combined with the lack of strict definitions means that, as Bagehot illustrated, to a large extent Parliament is defined by what Parliament does.

The modern role and function of Parliament in relation to Government can be separated into two broad areas. The first of these is the legislative function. Parliament is responsible for scrutinising, amending and passing legislation. The Government relies on Parliament giving its assent to bills in order for them to become law. In 1992 the Hansard Society published the report of its commission on the legislative process chaired by Lord Rippon of Hexham.[4] The commission identified problems at almost every stage of the legislative process and made a series of recommendations for its improvement.

---

[1] For a discussion see Woodhouse, D., (1994), *Ministers and Parliament*, OUP: Oxford, chapter 1
[2] St. John Stevas, N., (editor), (1965) *Bagehot's Historical Essays*, Doubleday: London, p. 317
[3] See for example Norton, P., (2000), *Strengthening Parliament: The report of the Commission to Strengthen Parliament*, Conservative Party; Beyme, K. von, (2000), *Parliamentary Democracy: Democratization, Destabilization, Reconsolidation 17891–1999*, Macmillan: Basingstoke; Crick, B, (1970), *The reform of Parliament*, Weidenfeld and Nicholson: London; Tyrie, A., (2000), *Mr Blair's Poodle: An Agenda for Reviving the House of Commons*, Centre for Policy Studies: London
[4] Hansard Society, (1992), *Making the Law: Report of the Hansard Society Commission on the Legislative Process*, Hansard Society: London

The second broad area of parliamentary activity is the accountability or (in the language of political science) the 'control' function, which is the focus of this Commission's work. That is, the extent to which Parliament holds the Government collectively, and its ministers individually, to account for their actions. There has been increasing concern in recent years about the effectiveness of Parliament's performance in this area.

Accountability: The 'control' function of Parliament

Parliament's task, in terms of scrutinising and holding Government to account, is to ensure effective and efficient government on behalf of the electorate. Parliament should act to examine and, where necessary, influence Government activity. It is part of the machinery of government and provides the essential, legitimising link between Government and governed. It can be summed up as government through, not by Parliament.[5] As Bernard Crick puts it, "Parliamentary control of the executive – rightly conceived – is not the enemy of effective government, but its primary condition."[6]

However, Parliament's ability to achieve good government is integrally linked with the strength of the political parties at Westminster. The adversarial relationship between the governing and opposition parties in the House of Commons has tended to promote the idea that Parliament and Government are separate entities. To the public, the most obvious and public illustration of the way in which Parliament holds Government to account is through the party battle inside Westminster. Debates on the floor of the House, questions to ministers and, specifically, Prime Minister's questions are the principal features of this view of politics. The contributions of politicians from all sides tend to give the impression that Parliament's job is to obstruct, rather than to enhance effective government.

The reality is more complex than this. Griffith and Ryle note that underlying all parliamentary business there are two confrontations.[7] The first is the party political battle between Government and Opposition parties, which is reflected in the very shape of the chamber. The second is that between those MPs who are members of the Government and all other Members of Parliament. In theory, all MPs who are not part of the Executive have a responsibility to scrutinise and hold Government to account. Members of Parliament can pursue issues through a variety of means, depending on their role and position in relation to the Government. For example, Government backbenchers will often use the private meetings of the parliamentary party or personal contacts with ministers to raise an issue of concern.[8]

Although the select committees provide a notable forum for MPs to pursue accountability on a cross-party basis it is the party political battle that tends to dominate proceedings in the Commons. MPs tend to conceive their role more in party political rather than parliamentary terms and the party confrontation is often regarded as synonymous with

[5] See for example, Crick, B, (1970), *The reform of Parliament*, Weidenfeld and Nicholson: London, chapter 1; Griffith, J. A.G., & Ryle, M., (1989), *Parliament: Functions, Practice and Procedures*, Sweet and Maxwell: London, p. 10

[6] Crick, *op cit*, p. 259

[7] Griffith, J. A. G., & Ryle, M., (1989), *Parliament: Functions, Practice and Procedures*, Sweet and Maxwell: London, pp. 13–15

[8] See for example, King, A., (1976), "Modes of Executive-Legislative Relations: Great Britain, France and West Germany", *Legislative Studies Quarterly*, Vol. 1, No. 1

parliamentary accountability. To some extent this is inevitable; Parliament's role stems in the first instance from the fact that the Government derives its authority by maintaining the confidence of the House of Commons. Parliamentary democracy can be said to require that Parliament is able to dismiss a Government.

In practice, such dismissals are rare in Britain (only three times have Governments been defeated on votes of no confidence – twice in 1924 and again in 1979). The power is contingent on the strength of the parties in the Commons and, except in the most unusual circumstances, the Government will always be able to rely on its majority to avoid defeat. Indeed, it is a theoretical and practical weakness of our constitution that for the control and accountability of Government we rely mainly upon an elected House in which a majority see it as their principal function to maintain the Government in power. Nevertheless, that the Government must maintain the support of the House is a fundamental constitutional principle.

However, the lack of sanction historically available to MPs highlights the position of Parliament in relation to Government. Scrutiny and accountability relies ultimately on the convention of ministerial responsibility, that ministers, individually and collectively, have a duty to give an account to Parliament for their actions. Although MPs can demand the production of papers or punish ministers for contempt, effective accountability relies on ministers being willing to recognise and participate in that convention. By the same token, the extent to which Parliament has succeeded in influencing or controlling the Executive has relied on the doctrine of ministerial responsibility.

The doctrine of ministerial responsibility: Parliamentary control in practice

The growth of departmental government in the latter part of the nineteenth century saw a general acceptance develop that ministers individually would be held to account by Parliament for the activity of their department, and collectively the Government would be held to account for its policy and implementation. The doctrine gained force during the twentieth century and the emphasis for Parliament moved from collective responsibility to individual ministerial responsibility. In 1918, for example, the Haldane Committee, responsible for reviewing the structure and shape of government, supported the principle that the minister should have sole responsibility for the administration of his department.

The theory reached its height in the mid-1950s with the case of Crichel Down. Sir Edward Bridges, Permanent Secretary to the Treasury at the time, set out the classical idea of ministerial accountability as follows,

> "It is upon Ministers, and not upon civil servants that the powers of Government have been conferred: and it is Ministers – who are Members of one or other House of Parliament, whose dismissal from office Parliament can bring about if it so chooses – who are answerable to Parliament for the exercise of those powers. Save in special cases, not relevant in this context, civil servants have no powers of their own. They can take no decisions or do anything, except in so far as they act on behalf of Ministers, and subject to the directions and control of Ministers."

> . . . "the fact that Ministers alone exercise the ultimate powers of executive government and that they can be and are called to account both for their own acts and for those done on their behalf is our best safeguard against the abuse of those powers."[9]

---

[9] Quoted in Public Service Committee, (1995–6), *Ministerial Accountability and Responsibility*, HC 313-I, para 8

The resulting resignation of the Minister for Agriculture, Thomas Dugdale, appeared to give force to the theory that a) ministers are directly responsible for the activities of their civil servants and b) the principal means of holding that minister to account was Parliament's ability to force them out of office.

In practice, neither of these elements has held true.[10] The theory is based on the assumption that ministers are directly involved in the work of their departments. This may have been possible in the early 19th century, but not by the end of that century, and it has certainly not been the case since the expansion of the welfare state. Modern Government is so complex, and a minister's functions so various, that most of the work of each department is carried out with little reference to the minister. An inquiry by the Commons Treasury and Civil Service Committee (TCSC) in the mid 1980s found that "ministers are accountable for the Government's policies and their own actions or those carried out by civil servants on their specific instructions but not for actions carried out by officials of which they are unaware".[11]

The second element, that Parliament can force a minister to resign, is also not borne out by events. Ministers under siege over a matter of policy can almost always expect the support of their cabinet colleagues, through the acceptance of collective responsibility, and in the Commons the Government can rely on sheer force of numbers. It is up to MPs on the Government's benches to decide whether a minister will be forced from office, rather than Parliament as a whole. As a result their judgement is more to do with party political concerns, namely, is the retention of an errant minister likely to have an effect on the opinion polls? As such, a personal indiscretion, involving money or sex, which generates headlines in the tabloids is more likely to see the minister losing the support of his colleagues than a technical matter of policy.

The resignation of ministers is, according to Professor Samuel Finer, writing in the 1950s, often arbitrary, unfair and adds little to the pursuit of accountability.

> "whether a Minister is forced to resign depends on three factors, on himself, his Prime Minister, and his party. . . . For a resignation to occur all three factors have to be just so: the minister compliant, the Prime Minister firm, the party clamorous. This conjuncture is rare, and is in fact fortuitous. Above all, it is indiscriminate – which Ministers escape and which do not is decided neither by the circumstances of the offence nor its gravity."[12]

In summary, the traditional interpretation of the doctrine of ministerial responsibility is too simplistic a model of accountability. In the first instance, it tends to equate ministerial resignation with accountability. Citing the resignations of Leon Brittan and Edwina Currie during the 1980s Diana Woodhouse argues that a swift resignation can be used by Government as a way of avoiding a potentially embarrassing explanation to Parliament.[13] Resignation, rather than adding to accountability, can occasionally detract from it.

---

[10] For more detailed analyses see Nicholson, I.F., 'Another view of Crichel Down, in Marshall, G., Ed., (1989), *Ministerial Responsibility*, Oxford University Press: Oxford, chapter 15; Marshall, G., 'Individual responsibility: Some post-war examples', in Marshall, G., Ed., (1989), *Ministerial Responsibility*, Oxford University Press: Oxford, chapter 17. Woodhouse, D., (1997), 'Ministerial Responsibility: Something Old, Something New', *Public Law*, Summer

[11] Treasury and Civil Service Committee (1985–6), *Civil servants and ministers*, HC 92, para 3.16

[12] Finer, S. E., (1956), 'The Individual Responsibility of Ministers', *Public Administration*, Vol. 34

[13] Brittan resigned in the aftermath of the Westland Affair, following the leaking of an official letter from the Attorney General by his officials. He offered no explanation of his role. His resignation letter stated, "Since your statement in the House yesterday, it has become clear to me that I no longer command the full support of my colleagues. In the circumstances, my continued membership of your government would be a source of weakness rather than strength . . . it is for this reason that I have tendered my resignation."

The focus on resignation has also tended to distort understandings of what parliamentary control should achieve. The doctrine confused means and ends, so that one of the means of securing accountability (the threat of ministerial resignation) became an end in itself. The party political tussle over the fate of a particular minister often deflected attention from Parliament's broader role in improving the quality of government.

The doctrine also reduces a very complex concept to a series of basic assumptions. Ministerial accountability to Parliament can take a number of forms, the vast majority of which fall far short of resignation. At the most basic level this could involve the minister in; redirecting a letter to the relevant person or agency; reporting information to MPs; explaining the reasons for certain decisions; or promising Parliament that remedial action will be taken to deal with specific problems.[14] Only the most extreme form, which has been termed 'sacrificial responsibility', would require a minister to resign.[15] The spate of resignations during the 1980s and 1990s highlighted the flaws in the doctrine and the shortcomings of Parliament in its attempts to secure accountability. As a result, the doctrine has been subject to a number of revisions in the last decade.

Changes to the doctrine of ministerial responsibility

The Treasury and Civil Service Committee's (TCSC) 1994 report into the role of the civil service stated that ministerial responsibility rested on two elements – "clarity about who can be held to account when things go wrong and confidence that Parliament is able to gain the accurate information required to hold the Executive to account and to ascertain where responsibility lies."[16] However, it was apparent that Parliament's ability to do either was severely restricted by the way in which Governments interpreted ministerial responsibility.

The first element – clarity about the location of responsibility – goes to the heart of the debate about how far ministers can be held responsible for the activities of their civil servants. The ambiguities surrounding this issue were evident by the mid-1980s. They were further distorted by ministers seeking to narrow the application of the convention, who drew distinctions between 'policy' and 'operations' at one level, and at another between 'accountability' and 'responsibility'.

The first distinction, between policy (the responsibility of the minister) and 'administration' or 'operations' (the remit of civil servants) was used by three Home Secretaries to avoid direct responsibility for prison escapes. The first was James Prior in 1983, following a breakout from the Maze Prison. It was then used in 1991 by Kenneth Baker following the Brixton Prison escape, and again by Michael Howard in 1995 after the debacle at Whitemoor Prison. However, the distinction does not acknowledge the fact that ministers regularly intervene in 'administrative' matters, and the official report into the escape from Whitemoor highlighted the difficulty in determining the definition of an operational matter as opposed to a policy matter, which in turn led to "confusion as to where responsibility lies."[17]

---

[14] For a detailed analysis of different forms of responsibility to Parliament see Woodhouse, D., (1994), *Ministers and Parliament*, Oxford University Press: Oxford, Chapter 2

[15] *ibid*, p. 34–8

[16] Report of the Treasury and Civil Service Committee (1993–4), *The Role of the Civil Service*, HC 27-I, para 132

[17] *The Escape from Whitemoor Prison*, Cm 2741, quoted in Woodhouse, D., (1997), *op cit*, p. 269

The distinction between responsibility and accountability increases the potential for confusion. A Cabinet Office memorandum to the TCSC enquiry explained that responsibility implied direct involvement and ownership of an issue, whereas accountability related to the formal structures for reporting. As such, "a minister is accountable for all the actions and activities in his department, but is not responsible for all the actions in the sense of being blameworthy."[18]

This separation of concepts was rejected by the Commons Public Service Committee as a sound basis for Parliament to secure accountability. Reporting on their investigation into ministerial responsibility in 1996 the committee argued that,

> "It is not possible absolutely to distinguish an area in which a Minister is personally responsible, and liable to take the blame, from one in which he is constitutionally accountable. Ministerial responsibility is not composed of two elements with a clear break between the two. Ministers have an obligation to Parliament which consists of ensuring that government explains its actions."[19]

However, the then Government affirmed its commitment to this distinction in its response to the Committee's report.[20]

In both areas the Government was able to interpret elements of the convention on ministerial responsibility to restrict its application and justify its response. This obviously presents problems for Parliament, particularly in respect of the other element of the TCSC's requirements for ministerial responsibility – 'confidence that Parliament is able to gain the accurate information required to hold the Executive to account'. The extent to which Parliament fell short of this requirement was illustrated vividly by Lord Justice Scott's report into Arms-to-Iraq.[21]

The report stated that it is the obligation of ministers to give information and explanation to Parliament and this lies at the heart of ministerial accountability. However the report listed seven examples of "apparent failure by ministers to discharge that obligation."[22] Moreover, the report highlighted the fact that ministers could quite easily withhold information from Parliament and yet still fall within the guidelines on 'Questions of Procedure for Ministers' which effectively stated, in short, that not telling the whole truth is not the same as lying.

This, as Scott suggests, is a problem for Parliament and the public in the proper scrutiny of Government,

> "Without the provision of full information it is not possible for Parliament, or for that matter the public, to hold the executive fully to account. It follows, in my opinion, that the withholding of information by an accountable minister should never be based on reasons of convenience or for avoidance of political embarrassment and should always require special and strong justification."[23]

---

[18] Treasury and Civil Service Committee (1993–4), *The Role of the Civil Service*, HC 27-II, Cabinet Office memorandum

[19] Public Service Committee, (1995–6), *Ministerial Accountability and Responsibility*, HC 313-I, para 21

[20] Public Service Committee, (1995–6), *First special report: Government Response to the Second Report from the Committee on Ministerial Accountability and Responsibility*, HC 67

[21] Lord Chief Justice Scott, chair, (1995–6) *Report of the Inquiry into the Export of Defence Equipment and Dual-Use Goods to Iraq and Related Prosecutions*, HC 115

[22] *ibid*, K8.1

[23] *ibid*, D4.42

The performances of Government ministers and Parliament collectively during the 1980s and 1990s highlighted the flaws in the provisions, interpretation and application of the doctrine of ministerial responsibility. It was not possible for Parliament to guarantee either element of the TCSC's definition. The problems surrounding the doctrine were summarised best by the Public Service Committee. It stated,

"There have always been elements of ambiguity and confusion in the convention of individual Ministerial responsibility. The first of these involves its status. There is no comprehensive or authoritative statement of it which has the binding force, and it cannot be enforced by legal (as opposed to political sanctions). As a result, the way in which it is used in practice tends to be variable and inconsistent, and it has often been as useful politically to obscure the convention as to clarify it. Second, that inconsistency has helped to ensure that it has never been very clear what precisely individual Ministerial responsibility *means*: what a Minister has to do in order to discharge his responsibility through Parliament. Third, it has never been entirely clear, either, how far a Minister's formal responsibility for the actions of officials subordinate to him extends."[24]

One of the recommendations of the Public Service Committee report was a parliamentary resolution on ministerial accountability. Designed to clarify elements of the doctrine on ministerial responsibility, and following the findings of Scott and the Public Service Committee, it attempted to place a greater emphasis on ministers to be open and honest in the provision of information to Parliament. Although there was disagreement between the committee and Government on the wording of point 4 relating to civil servants (with neither side getting quite what they wanted) Parliament passed the following resolution on 17 March 1997.

1. The following principles should govern the conduct of Ministers of the Crown in relation to Parliament:
2. Ministers have a duty to Parliament to account and to be held to account, for the policies, decisions and actions of their departments and Next Steps Agencies;
3. It is of paramount importance that Ministers give accurate and truthful information to Parliament, correcting any inadvertent error at the earliest opportunity. Ministers who knowingly mislead Parliament will be expected to offer their resignation to the Prime Minister;
4. Ministers should be as open as possible with Parliament, refusing to provide information only when disclosure would not be in the public interest, which should be decided in accordance with relevant statute and the Government's Code of Practice on Access to Government Information;
5. Similarly, Ministers should require civil servants who give evidence before Parliamentary Committees on their behalf and under their directions to be as helpful as possible in providing accurate and truthful and full information in accordance with the duties and responsibilities of civil servants as set out in the Civil Service Code.

The passage of the resolution marked a shift in the definition of ministerial accountability to Parliament. It went some way to clarifying the duties of ministers, and was incorporated into the ministerial code in May 1997.[25] It reflected the political realities of Parliament's position *vis-à-vis* Government in that there was less emphasis on resignation and more on clarification and explanation. The PSC report had formally recognised that so long as ministers' colleagues were prepared to defend them, the chances of Parliament obtaining their removal were minimal.[26] Instead it argued that there had been too much emphasis placed on ministerial resignation and that "Proper and rigorous scrutiny and accountability may be more important to Parliament's ability to correct error than forcing resignations."[27]

---

[24] Public Service Committee, (1995–6), *Ministerial Accountability and Responsibility*, HC 313-I, para. 2
[25] Formerly *Questions of Procedures for Ministers*
[26] Public Service Committee, (1995–6), *op cit*, para 25
[27] *ibid*, para 26

The Commission's vision of parliamentary accountability

The effectiveness of the code of conduct relies, ultimately, on Parliament's ability to enforce it. The working through of the code thus requires Parliament not only to secure explanation from ministers, but also to be able to influence Government activity so that amendatory action is taken. This might take a variety of forms, ranging from a ministerial commitment to review an administrative error or direct remedial action, through to an enforced resignation in extreme circumstances. However, in the past MPs have placed too much emphasis on resignation, and not enough on explanation and correction. Accountability requires both elements, as Diana Woodhouse, in evidence to the Commission has argued,

> "Parliament's ability to secure information and explanations from ministers is clearly vital if it is to be effective in ensuring accountable government, but 'giving an account' cannot be separated from 'holding to account', which may require resignation. These elements of ministerial responsibility are part of the same process and are inextricably linked."[28]

Enforcement of sanctions has predominantly been linked with resignation, pursued through the party political battle at Westminster. However, Parliament's ability to impose sanctions is weakest where it relies on party politics. If accountability is conceived solely in party political terms, as part of the struggle between the party of Government and the parties of Opposition, the Government will always win out by virtue of its greater strength in the House of Commons.

In some respects this is inevitable and the party political battle plays a useful role in highlighting issues of public concern. The enforcement of accountability to Parliament is not an exact science and it is not possible to set down clear rules for its implementation. The quality of accountability will rely on a number of factors, including the relative size of the parties as Westminster and the level of party discipline, the salience of certain key political issues, the position in the electoral cycle and the strength of the Prime Minister. Although the codification of ministerial responsibility helps to define aspects of accountability, there will still be loopholes. The problems of locating responsibility are likely to continue to bedevil committee inquiries. The Committee on Public Administration in 2000 conducted an inquiry into the maladministration of the State Earnings Related Pension and found that,

> ". . . former ministers explained why there could be no political responsibility, while former officials explained why permanent Secretaries and Accounting Officers were not to be held responsible. Doctrines of accountability and responsibility are central to parliamentary government in Britain, but this case illustrates the gap that can exist between theory and practice."[29]

The parliamentary resolution and ministerial code do not guarantee accountability. As Robin Butler, the head of the home civil service between 1988 and 1998 has commented, "Ministers are accountable to Parliament, not a piece of paper."[30] The importance of the resolution ultimately relies on MPs themselves and their willingness to enforce the code.

---

[28] Appendix 2, Evidence 37
[29] Public Administration Committee, (1999-2000), *Administrative Failure: Inherited SERPS*, HC433, para 29
[30] Lord Butler of Brockwell, 'Foreword' in Baker, A., (2000), *Prime Ministers and the Rule Book*, Politico's: London, p. vii

However, what is most often missing from debates about accountability and responsibility is the role played by public opinion. Parliament holds Government to account on behalf of the public and is strongest where it reflects or mobilises public support. Bernard Crick provides the most succinct and helpful analysis of what scrutiny should achieve, stating that,

> "Government will make decisions . . . in the knowledge that these decisions, sooner or later, will find their way to debate on the Floor of one of the Houses of Parliament. The type of scrutiny they will get will obviously affect, in purely political terms, the type of actions undertaken. And the civil service will administer with the knowledge that it too may be called upon to justify even the most minute actions."

> ". . . So Parliamentary control is not the stop switch, it is the tuning, the tone and the amplifier of a system of communication which tells governments what the electorate want (rightly or wrongly) and what they will stand for (rightly or wrongly)"[31]

In short, effective scrutiny of Government is achieved through the threat of being called to account by Parliament, on behalf of the public. It is the knowledge of a vigilant Parliament that should be a constant in the minds of ministers and civil servants which affects their behaviour. In this respect the resolution and code could provide a useful benchmark by which ministers and their officials will be judged by MPs and, by extension the public, and it may well prove to be a significant influence on their behaviour. Diana Woodhouse, again in written evidence to the Commission, provided a useful perspective,

> "Ultimately the key to motivating a minister to both account and be held to account is fear of the consequences of not doing so. The worst consequence is losing the support of the electorate. If ministers individually believed that their failure to accord with the principles of accountable government could mean being returned to the opposition benches, or not being returned at all, their motivation might increase."[32]

The Commission believes that Parliament is strongest where it engages with and articulates the interests of civil society. "Parliaments are not to be seen as governments, or rivals to governments, but as political communication systems linking governments and electorates."[33] This, however, requires Parliament to adapt and clarify its role in the light of changes to government and society.

---

[31] Crick, B., *op cit*, p.80
[32] Appendix 2, Evidence 37
[33] Crick, B., *op cit*, p.260

Appendix 2

Written evidence submitted to the Commission

Evidence 1:   Age Concern

Evidence 2:   Dr Nicholas Baldwin, Wroxton College

Evidence 3:   Charter88

Evidence 4:   Consumers' Association

Evidence 5:   Ann Cryer MP

Evidence 6:   Equal Opportunities Commission

Evidence 7:   Matthew Flinders, University of Sheffield

Evidence 8:   Sir Christopher Foster

Evidence 9:   Green Party

Evidence 10: Rt Hon Lord Howe of Aberavon

Evidence 11: Lord Howell

Evidence 12: Lord Inglewood MEP

Evidence 13: Institute of Directors

Evidence 14: Rt Hon Michael Jack MP

Evidence 15: Professor George Jones, London School of Economics

Evidence 16: Dr Lynne Jones MP

Evidence 17: Geoffrey Marshall, The Queens College, Oxford

Evidence 18: Des McConaghy

Evidence 19: David Millar

Evidence 20: Rt Hon Lord Naseby

Evidence 21: National Society for Prevention of Cruelty to Children

Evidence 22: Dr Ralph Negrine, University of Leicester

Evidence 23: Elizabeth France, Data Protection Commissioner

Evidence 24: OFTEL, Office of Telecommunications

Evidence 25: OFWAT, Office of Water Services

Evidence 26: Baroness Platt of Whittle

Evidence 27: Andrea Ross-Robertson, University of Dundee

Evidence 28: RADAR, Royal Association of Disability and Rehabilitation

Evidence 29: Professor Michael Rush, University of Exeter

Evidence 30: Michael Ryle

Evidence 31: Thomas Saalfeld, University of Kent

Evidence 32: Lord Tanlaw

Evidence 33: Penelope Tay

Evidence 34: Damien Welfare

Evidence 35: Lord Wolfson of Marylebone

Evidence 36: Womens' National Commission

Evidence 37: Professor Diana Woodhouse, Oxford Brookes University

Appendix 3

Meetings of the Commission

This appendix shows the Parliamentarians and other individuals who attended meetings of the Commission or who made a contribution to the Commission's work. We are very grateful to all those who contributed to the Commission.

I. Parliamentarians:

Westminster:
Douglas Alexander MP
Graham Allen MP
Rt Hon Margaret Beckett MP
Rt Hon Tony Benn MP
Andrew Bennett MP
Rt Hon Peter Brooke MP
Rt Hon Viscount Cranborne
Rt Hon David Davis MP
Ed Davey MP
Gwyneth Dunwoody MP
Rt Hon Frank Field MP
Mark Fisher MP
Lorna Fitzsimons MP
Rt Hon the Lord Howe of Aberavon
Archy Kirkwood MP
Rt Hon Peter Lilley MP
Martin Linton MP
Peter Luff MP
Rt Hon Robert Maclennan MP
Martin O'Neill MP
Professor the Lord Norton of Louth
Giles Radice MP
Nick Raynsford MP
Rt Hon Lord Rodgers of Quarry Bank
Rt Hon Robert Sheldon MP
Rt Hon Gillian Shepherd MP
Rt Hon Baroness Williams of Crosby
Tony Wright MP
Andrew Tyrie MP
Rt Hon Sir George Young MP

Edinburgh:
Margaret Curran MSP
Patricia Ferguson MSP
Andy Kerr MSP
David McLetchie MSP
Mary Mulligan MSP
George Reid MSP
Sir David Steel MSP
John Swinney MSP
Murray Tosh MSP
Mike Watson MSP
Andrew Wilson MSP

2. Other participants in Commission meetings

Richard Blackman, Federal Trust
David Corner, Director of Corporate Policy, National Audit Office
Sir Christopher Foster
Paul Grice, Chief Executive, Scottish Parliament
Andrew Lean, Performance and Innovation Unit, The Cabinet Office
Andrew Likierman, Managing Director of Financial Management, Reporting and Audit, HM Treasury
Michael Lugton, Head of Constitutional Policy and Parliamentary Liaison, Scottish Executive
Joyce MacMillan, Journalist, Member of the Consultative Steering Group on the Scottish Parliament
Caroline Mawhood, Assistant Auditor General, National Audit Office
Professor David McCrone, Governance of Scotland Forum, Edinburgh University
Neil McIntosh, Chairman, Commission on Local Government in Scotland
Sonia Phippard, Director, Central Secretariat, Cabinet Office
Muir Russell, Permanent Secretary, Scottish Executive
Roy Stone, Private Secretary, Chief Whip
Sir Stewart Sutherland, Principal, Edinburgh University
Jonathan Tross, Head of Constitutional Secretariat, Cabinet Office
Bill Thomson, Head of the Chamber Office, Scottish Parliament
Frank Viebert, European Policy Forum
Andrew Whetnall, Director of Local Government, Department of the Environment, Transport and the Regions

In addition we are grateful to the Study of Parliament Group and to the Clerks from the Houses of Commons and Lords.

3. Meetings of the Commission

The full Commission met 11 times between September 1999 and March 2001.

The Commission also met in three sub-groups; on the chamber, select committees and financial scrutiny.

In October 2000, the Commission attended a residential 'away-day' in Hampshire.

In addition the Commission organised consultation and discussion meetings:

- 19 November 1999: Meeting with Members of the House of Commons Liaison Committee.
- 18/19 January 2000: Visit to the Scottish Parliament
- 28 January 2000: Meeting with Clerks of the Houses of Commons and Lords
- 13 March 2000: Meeting with former Ministers
- 18 May 2000: Seminar on Scrutiny of European Issues
- 13 July 2000: Seminar with MPs to discuss select committee reform
- 10 January 2001: Meeting with Senior Civil Servants

Appendix 4

Survey of MPs: The effectiveness of Parliament, parliamentary role and workloads

This poll was conducted as part of the Hansard Society's Commission on Parliamentary Scrutiny chaired by Lord Newton of Braintree. The questionnaire was concerned with MPs' perceptions of their work and the levels of support and training. It was distributed in June 2000. There were 179 responses in total.

1 – General background

1.1 Which party do you represent?

	Frequency	Percent
Conservative	55	30.7
Labour	101	56.4
Liberal Democrat	14	7.8
National	5	2.8
Other	4	2.2
Total	179	100.0

1.2 In which year were you elected?

	Frequency	Percent
No reply	1	.6
1959–1963	1	.6
1964–1965	3	1.7
1966–1969	1	.6
1970–1973	3	1.7
1974–1978	11	6.1
1979–1982	5	2.8
1983–1986	19	10.6
1987–1991	27	15.1
1992–1996	31	17.3
1997–2001	77	43.0
Total	179	100.0

1.3 Do you hold a front bench or back bench position?

	Frequency	Percent
Back bench	114	63.7
Front bench	43	24.0
No reply	21	11.7
Chairman's panel	1	.6
Total	179	100.0

1.4 Do you serve on a select committee?

	Frequency	Percent
No reply	4	2.2
Yes	95	53.1
No	80	44.7
Total	179	100.0

1.5 What sort of constituency do you represent?

	Frequency	Percent
No reply	7	3.9
Inner city	28	15.6
Suburban	43	24.0
Rural	49	27.4
Inner city/suburban	12	6.7
Suburban/rural	40	22.3
Total	179	100.0

1.6 Do you intend to stand at the next election?

	Frequency	Percent
No reply	2	1.1
Yes	158	88.3
No	19	10.6
Total	179	100.0

1.7 Gender

	Frequency	Percent
No reply	2	1.1
Female	33	18.4
Male	144	80.4
Total	179	100.0

2 – The work of Parliament

2.1 How importantly do you regard the following roles of Parliament?
Scrutinising legislation

	Frequency	Percent
No reply	1	.6
Very Important	152	84.9
Quite Important	18	10.1
Neutral response	4	2.2
Of little importance	3	1.7
Not important at all	1	.6
Total	179	100.0

Scrutinising Government departments

	Frequency	Percent
No reply	2	1.1
Very important	132	73.7
Quite important	37	20.7
Neutral response	6	3.4
Of little importance	1	.6
Not important at all	1	.6
Total	179	100.0

Debating issues of national importance

	Frequency	Percent
No reply	2	1.1
Very important	116	64.8
Quite important	43	24.0
Neutral response	16	8.9
Not important at all	2	1.1
Total	179	100.0

Solving constituents' problems

	Frequency	Percent
No reply	1	.6
Very important	101	56.4
Quite important	47	26.3
Neutral response	23	12.8
Of little importance	5	2.8
Not important at all	2	1.1
Total	179	100.0

Supporting party policy

	Frequency	Percent
No reply	5	2.8
Very important	44	24.6
Quite important	65	36.3
Neutral response	50	27.9
Of little importance	10	5.6
Not important at all	5	2.8
Total	179	100.0

2.2 Which of these do you think is the most important role for Parliament?

	Frequency	Percent
No reply	34	20.7
Scrutinising legislation	66	36.9
Scrutinising government departments	28	15.6
Debating issues of national importance	11	6.1
Solving constituents' problems	21	11.7
Supporting party policy	3	1.7
Other	9	5.0
Total	179	100.0

2.3 How effective are the following mechanisms in securing information and explanation from Government?
Departmental question time

	Frequency	Percent
No reply	3	1.7
Very effective	7	3.9
Quite effective	38	21.2
Neutral response	60	33.5
Not effective	54	30.2
Not effective at all	17	9.5
Total	179	100.0

Written questions

	Frequency	Percent
No reply	3	1.7
Very effective	14	7.8
Quite effective	77	43.0
Neutral response	57	31.8
Not effective	18	10.1
Not effective at all	10	5.6
Total	179	100.0

Select committee hearings

	Frequency	Percent
No reply	5	2.8
Very effective	65	36.3
Quite effective	85	47.5
Neutral response	18	10.1
Not effective	5	2.8
Not effective at all	1	.6
Total	179	100.0

Ministerial statements

	Frequency	Percent
No reply	3	1.7
Very effective	12	6.7
Quite effective	69	38.5
Neutral response	59	33.0
Not effective	27	15.1
Not effective at all	9	5.0
Total	179	100.0

Private notice questions

	Frequency	Percent
No reply	4	2.2
Very effective	12	6.7
Quite effective	65	36.3
Neutral response	66	36.9
Not effective	26	14.5
Not effective at all	6	3.4
Total	179	100.0

Prime Minister's Questions

	Frequency	Percent
No reply	4	2.2
Very effective	5	2.8
Quite effective	9	5.0
Neutral response	33	18.4
Not effective	56	31.3
Not effective at all	72	40.2
Total	179	100.0

Opposition Day debates

	Frequency	Percent
No reply	4	2.2
Very effective	7	3.9
Quite Effective	34	19.0
Neutral response	50	27.9
Not effective	51	28.5
Not effective at all	33	18.4
Total	179	100.0

2.4 Which of these is the most effective mechanism?

	Frequency	Percent
No reply	29	16.2
Departmental question time	4	2.2
Written questions	19	10.6
Select committee hearings	103	57.5
Ministerial statements	11	6.1
Private notice questions	8	4.5
Opposition Day debates	3	1.7
Other	2	1.1
Total	179	100.0

2.5 How effective is Parliament in scrutinising government activity in the following areas?

Departmental Policy Making

	Frequency	Percent
No reply	5	2.8
Very effective	4	2.2
Quite effective	42	23.5
Neutral response	61	34.1
Not effective	51	28.5
Not effective at all	16	8.9
Total	179	100.0

Government expenditure

	Frequency	Percent
No reply	5	2.8
Very effective	10	5.6
Quite effective	45	25.1
Neutral response	63	35.2
Not effective	48	26.8
Not effective at all	8	4.5
Total	179	100.0

Executive agencies

	Frequency	Percent
No reply	6	3.4
Very effective	1	.6
Quite effective	13	7.3
Neutral response	45	25.1
Not effective	75	41.9
Not effective at all	39	21.8
Total	179	100.0

Government activity in issues which cut across dept boundaries

	Frequency	Percent
No reply	5	2.8
Very effective	I	.6
Quite effective	6	3.4
Neutral response	50	27.9
Not effective	76	42.5
Not effective at all	41	22.9
Total	179	100.0

European Council of Ministers

	Frequency	Percent
No reply	10	5.6
Quite effective	7	3.9
Neutral response	22	12.3
Not effective	61	34.1
Not effective at all	79	44.1
Total	179	100.0

Central Government and the Cabinet Office

	Frequency	Percent
No reply	5	2.8
Very effective	I	.6
Quite effective	24	13.4
Neutral response	62	34.6
Not effective	58	32.4
Not effective at all	29	16.2
Total	179	100.0

Quangos

	Frequency	Percent
No reply	5	2.8
Quite effective	3	1.7
Neutral response	25	14.0
Not effective	82	45.8
Not effective at all	64	35.8
Total	179	100.0

Utility regulators

	Frequency	Percent
No reply	7	3.9
Very effective	1	.6
Quite effective	10	5.6
Neutral response	31	17.3
Not effective	75	41.9
Not effective at all	55	30.7
Total	179	100.0

Other public services

	Frequency	Percent
No reply	6	3.4
Very effective	3	1.7
Quite effective	41	22.9
Neutral response	66	36.9
Not effective	46	25.7
Not effective at all	17	9.5
Total	179	100.0

2.6 How effective are the following bodies in helping Parliament to hold Government to account?

Parliamentary Commissioner for Standards

	Frequency	Percent
No reply	5	2.8
Very effective	18	10.1
Quite effective	55	30.7
Neutral response	49	27.4
Not effective	24	13.4
Not effective at all	28	15.6
Total	179	100.0

The Ombudsman

	Frequency	Percent
No reply	5	2.8
Very effective	11	6.1
Quite effective	68	38.0
Neutral response	66	36.9
Not effective	21	11.7
Not effective at all	8	4.5
Total	179	100.0

National Audit Office

	Frequency	Percent
No reply	5	2.8
Very effective	44	24.6
Quite effective	99	55.3
Neutral response	28	15.6
Not effective	3	1.7
Total	179	100.0

Audit Commission

	Frequency	Percent
No reply	6	3.4
Very effective	26	14.5
Quite effective	89	49.7
Neutral response	43	24.0
Not effective	14	7.8
Not effective at all	1	.6
Total	179	100.0

Commissioner for Public Appointments

	Frequency	Percent
No reply	7	3.9
Very effective	5	2.8
Quite effective	26	14.5
Neutral response	82	45.8
Not effective	47	26.3
Not effective at all	12	6.7
Total	179	100.0

Public utility regulators

	Frequency	Percent
No reply	6	3.4
Very effective	3	1.7
Quite effective	20	11.2
Neutral response	73	40.8
Not effective	54	30.2
Not effective at all	22	12.3
6.00	1	.6
Total	179	100.0

Parliamentary Commissioner for Standards

	Frequency	Percent
No reply	13	7.3
Yes	26	14.5
No	140	78.2
Total	179	100.0

2.7 Have you referred any cases to the following?
Commissioner for Public Appointments

	Frequency	Percent
No reply	13	7.3
Yes	14	7.8
No	152	84.9
Total	179	100.0

Ombudsman

	Frequency	Percent
No reply	3	1.7
Yes	170	95.0
No	6	3.4
Total	179	100.0

National Audit Office

	Frequency	Percent
No reply	14	7.8
Yes	52	29.1
No	113	63.1
Total	179	100.0

Overall, how effective is Parliament?

	Frequency	Percent
No reply	3	1.7
Very effective	4	2.2
Quite effective	44	24.6
Neutral response	72	40.2
Not effective	46	25.7
Not effective at all	10	5.6
Total	179	100.0

3 – The work of individual Members of Parliament

3.1 MPs are expected to represent a number of different interests in Parliament. How important are the following interests in determining your role as a representative?

My political party

	Frequency	Percent
No reply	4	2.2
Very important	48	26.8
Quite important	80	44.7
Neutral response	38	21.2
Not important	8	4.5
Not important at all	1	.6
Total	179	100.0

My geographical constituency

	Frequency	Percent
No reply	4	2.3
Very important	121	67.6
Quite important	45	25.1
Neutral response	6	3.4
Not important	2	1.1
Not important at all	1	.6
Total	179	100.0

Individual constituents

	Frequency	Percent
No reply	4	2.2
Very important	85	47.5
Quite important	60	33.5
Neutral response	24	13.4
Not important	5	2.8
Not important at all	1	.6
Total	179	100.0

Constituency party

	Frequency	Percent
No reply	5	2.8
Very important	10	5.6
Quite important	49	27.4
Neutral response	62	34.6
Not important	42	23.5
Not important at all	11	6.1
Total	179	100.0

The nation as a whole

	Frequency	Percent
No reply	4	2.2
Very important	104	58.1
Quite important	56	31.3
Neutral response	10	5.6
Not important	4	2.2
Not important at all	1	.6
Total	179	100.0

Sectional interests

	Frequency	Percent
No reply	4	2.2
Very important	15	8.4
Quite important	44	24.6
Neutral response	55	30.7
Not important	41	22.9
Not important at all	20	11.2
Total	179	100.0

A particular cause

	Frequency	Percent
No reply	5	2.8
Very important	26	14.5
Quite important	60	33.5
Neutral response	61	34.1
Not important	18	10.1
Not important at all	9	5.0
Total	179	100.0

3.2 How important are the following roles in your work as an MP?

Holding the Government to account

	Frequency	Percent
No reply	4	2.2
Very important	93	52.0
Quite important	53	29.6
Neutral response	24	13.4
Not important	3	1.7
Not important at all	2	1.1
Total	179	100.0

Examining legislation

	Frequency	Percent
No reply	4	2.2
Very important	72	40.2
Quite important	54	30.2
Neutral response	37	20.7
Not important	9	5.0
Not important at all	3	1.7
Total	179	100.0

Speaking in the chamber

	Frequency	Percent
No reply	3	1.7
Very important	34	19.0
Quite important	55	30.7
Neutral response	55	30.7
Not important	26	14.5
Not important at all	6	3.4
Total	179	100.0

Dealing with constituents' grievances

	Frequency	Percent
No reply	4	2.2
Very important	95	53.1
Quite important	64	35.8
Neutral response	14	7.8
Not important	1	.6
Not important at all	1	.6
Total	179	100.0

Voting with my political party

	Frequency	Percent
No reply	4	2.2
Very important	42	23.5
Quite important	78	43.6
Neutral response	42	23.5
Not important	12	6.7
Not important at all	1	.6
Total	179	100.0

Informing constituents about Government activity

	Frequency	Percent
No reply	4	2.2
Very important	35	19.6
Quite important	75	41.9
Neutral response	36	20.1
Not important	20	11.2
Not important at all	9	5.0
Total	179	100.0

Protecting the interests of the constituency

	Frequency	Percent
No reply	4	2.2
Very important	118	65.9
Quite important	46	25.7
Neutral response	8	4.5
Not important	2	1.1
Not important at all	1	.6
Total	179	100.0

Writing/giving speeches

	Frequency	Percent
No reply	5	2.8
Very important	22	12.3
Quite important	63	35.2
Neutral response	60	33.5
Not important	24	13.4
Not important at all	5	2.8
Total	179	100.0

Working on a departmental select committee

	Frequency	Percent
No reply	25	14.0
Very important	43	24.0
Quite important	53	29.6
Neutral response	29	16.2
Not important	8	4.5
Not important at all	21	11.7
Total	179	100.0

Writing articles for newspapers/magazines

	Frequency	Percent
No reply	6	3.4
Very important	11	6.1
Quite important	38	21.2
Neutral response	53	29.6
Not important	52	29.1
Not important at all	19	10.6
Total	179	100.0

Appearing on radio/television

	Frequency	Percent
No reply	5	2.8
Very important	18	10.1
Quite important	55	30.7
Neutral response	56	31.3
Not important	29	16.2
Not important at all	16	8.9
Total	179	100.0

3.3 Which of these is the most important role?

	Frequency	Percent
No reply	25	14
Holding the government to account	59	33.0
Examining legislation	23	12.8
Speaking in chamber	1	.6
Dealing with constituents' grievances	27	15.1
Voting with political party	4	2.2
Informing constituents about government activity	1	.6
Protecting interests of constituency	33	18.4
Writing/giving speeches	1	.6
Working on departmental select committee	4	2.2
Appearing on TV	1	.6
Total	179	100.0

3.4 Which is second most important?

	Frequency	Percent
No reply	25	14
Holding government to account	23	12.8
Examining legislation	16	8.9
Speaking in chamber	7	3.9
Dealing with constituents' grievances	33	18.4
Voting with political party	13	7.3
Informing constituents about government activity	7	3.9
Protecting interests of constituency	42	23.5
Writing/giving speeches	1	.6
Working on a departmental select committee	8	4.5
Appearing on TV	3	1.7
No reply	1	.6
Total	179	100.0

3.5 Which is the least important?

	Frequency	Percent
No reply	25	14.0
Holding government to account	3	1.7
Examining legislation	9	5.0
Speaking in chamber	8	4.5
Dealing with constituents' grievances	14	7.8
Voting with political party	7	3.9
Informing constituents about government activity	14	7.8
Protecting interests of the constituency	14	7.8
Writing/giving political speeches	17	9.5
Working on a departmental select committee	13	7.3
Writing articles for newspapers/magazines	36	20.1
Appearing on TV	18	10.1
Total	179	100.0

3.6 How many hours do you work in an average week?

	Frequency	Percent
No reply	41	22.9
21–30	1	.6
41–50	8	4.5
51–60	21	11.7
61–70	42	23.5
71–80	44	24.6
81–90	16	8.9
91–100	6	3.4
Total	179	100.0

3.7 How many hours on average do you spend at Westminster each week on the following?

In the chamber

	Frequency	Percent
No reply	14	7.8
Zero	2	1.1
1–2	28	15.6
3–5	69	38.5
6–10	43	24.0
11–15	13	7.3
16–20	7	3.9
21–25	3	1.7
Total	179	100.0

On a standing committee

	Frequency	Percent
No reply	14	7.8
Zero	54	30.2
1–2	46	25.7
3–5	31	17.3
6–10	22	12.3
11–15	9	5.0
16–20	3	1.7
Total	179	100.0

On a departmental select committee

	Frequency	Percent
No reply	15	8.4
Zero	65	36.3
1–2	16	8.9
3–5	41	22.9
6–10	34	19.0
11–15	3	1.7
16–20	4	2.2
21–25	1	.6
Total	179	100.0

On parliamentary party work

	Frequency	Percent
No reply	14	7.8
Zero	22	12.3
1–2	61	34.1
3–5	52	29.1
6–10	23	12.8
11–15	5	2.8
16–20	2	1.1
Total	179	100.0

On All-Party Groups

	Frequency	Percent
No reply	15	8.4
Zero	22	12.3
1–2	70	39.1
3–5	52	29.1
6–10	15	8.4
11–15	5	2.8
Total	179	100.0

Meeting constituents in Parliament

	Frequency	Percent
No reply	14	7.8
Zero	34	19.0
1–2	98	54.7
3–5	26	14.5
6–10	6	3.4
11.00	1	.6
Total	179	100.0

Meeting with others in Parliament

	Frequency	Percent
No reply	14	7.8
Zero	8	4.5
1–2	36	20.1
3–5	56	31.3
6–10	44	24.6
11–15	18	10.1
16–20	3	1.7
Total	179	100.0

Dealing with constituency casework

	Frequency	Percent
No reply	14	7.8
Zero	4	2.2
1–2	3	1.7
3–5	20	11.2
6–10	41	22.9
11–15	36	20.1
16–20	35	19.6
21–25	11	6.1
25 +	15	8.4
Total	179	100.0

Writing/giving speeches outside Parliament

	Frequency	Percent
No reply	14	7.8
Zero	18	10.1
1–2	57	31.8
3–5	56	31.3
6–10	26	14.5
11–15	6	3.4
16–20	1	.6
25 +	1	.6
Total	179	100.0

Writing articles for newspapers or general media work

	Frequency	Percent
No reply	15	8.4
Zero	18	10.1
1–2	79	44.1
3–5	50	27.9
6–10	15	8.4
11–15	1	.6
16–20	1	.6
Total	179	100.0

3.8 How many letters do you receive each week?

	Frequency	Percent
No reply	27	15.1
1–50	6	3.4
51–100	22	12.3
101–150	24	13.4
151–200	25	14.0
201–250	27	15.1
251–300	20	11.2
301–350	10	5.6
351–400	7	3.9
401–450	1	.6
451–500	4	2.2
500 +	6	3.4
Total	179	100.0

3.9 How many letters do you send each week?

	Frequency	Percent
No reply	27	15.1
1–50	3	1.7
51–100	25	14.0
101–150	35	19.6
151–200	23	12.8
201–250	23	12.8
251–300	16	8.9
301–350	8	4.5
351–400	8	4.5
401–450	1	.6
451–500	5	2.8
500 +	5	2.8
Total	179	100.0

3.10 How many hours do you spend in the constituency on the following?
Seeking grants/funds

	Frequency	Percent
No reply	18	10.1
Zero	35	19.6
1–2	94	52.5
3–5	25	14.0
6–10	4	2.2
11–15	3	1.7
Total	179	100.0

Promoting business opportunities

	Frequency	Percent
No reply	18	10.1
Zero	22	12.3
1–2	92	51.4
3–5	35	19.6
6–10	11	6.1
11–15	1	.6
Total	179	100.0

Helping constituents with local council issues

	Frequency	Percent
No reply	18	10.1
Zero	6	3.4
1–2	24	13.4
3–5	65	36.3
6–10	47	26.3
11–15	14	7.8
16–20	3	1.7
21–25	1	.6
25 +	1	.6
Total	179	100.0

Helping constituents with access to welfare

	Frequency	Percent
No reply	18	10.1
Zero	13	7.3
1–2	44	24.6
3–5	57	31.8
6–10	32	17.9
11–15	11	6.1
16–20	2	1.1
21–25	1	.6
25 +	1	.6
Total	179	100.0

Individual child support agency cases

	Frequency	Percent
No reply	18	10.1
Zero	11	6.1
1–2	74	41.3
3–5	54	30.2
6–10	14	7.8
11–15	5	2.8
16–20	2	1.1
21–25	1	.6
Total	179	100.0

Individual immigration cases

	Frequency	Percent
No reply	18	10.1
Zero	25	14.0
1–2	88	49.2
3–5	31	17.3
6–10	10	5.6
11–15	4	2.2
16–20	1	.6
21–25	2	1.1
Total	179	100.0

Individual constituent's policy concerns

	Frequency	Percent
No reply	18	10.1
Zero	10	5.6
1–2	71	39.7
3–5	54	30.2
6–10	19	10.6
11–15	5	2.8
16–20	1	.6
21–25	1	.6
Total	179	100.0

Constituency surgeries

	Frequency	Percent
No reply	19	10.7
1–2	41	22.9
3–5	94	52.5
6–10	19	10.6
11–15	3	1.7
16–20	2	1.1
11.00	1	.6
Total	179	100.0

Informing constituents about Government activity

	Frequency	Percent
No reply	19	10.7
Zero	22	12.3
1–2	85	47.5
3–5	38	21.2
6–10	13	7.3
11–15	2	1.1
Total	179	100.0

Attending local party meetings

	Frequency	Percent
No reply	19	10.7
Zero	4	2.2
1–2	91	50.8
3–5	53	29.6
6–10	10	5.6
16–20	1	.6
25 +	1	.6
Total	179	100.0

Other activities

	Frequency	Percent
No reply	18	10.1
Zero	91	50.8
1–2	11	6.1
3–5	30	16.8
6–10	22	12.3
11–15	4	2.2
16–20	3	1.7
Total	179	100.0

3.11 Individuals go to Westminster with particular goals. Please indicate how important the following are to you.

Serving on a select committee

	Frequency	Percent
No reply	26	14.5
Very important	55	30.7
Quite important	53	29.6
Neutral response	18	10.1
Not important	13	7.3
Not important at all	14	7.8
Total	179	100.0

Serving on a standing committee

	Frequency	Percent
No reply	30	16.8
Very important	12	6.7
Quite important	46	25.7
Neutral response	39	21.8
Not important	28	15.6
Not important at all	24	13.4
Total	179	100.0

Chairing a select committee

	Frequency	Percent
No reply	38	21.2
Very important	28	15.6
Quite important	24	13.4
Neutral response	31	17.3
Not important	22	12.3
Not important at all	36	20.1
Total	179	100.0

Serving as a junior minister

	Frequency	Percent
No reply	36	20.1
Very important	35	19.6
Quite Important	34	19.0
Neutral response	24	13.4
Not important	15	8.4
Not important at all	35	19.6
Total	179	100.0

Serving in Cabinet

	Frequency	Percent
No reply	40	22.4
Very important	43	24.0
Quite important	26	14.5
Neutral response	18	10.1
Not important	13	7.3
Not important at all	39	21.8
Total	179	100.0

Shadow Cabinet portfolio

	Frequency	Percent
No reply	49	27.4
Very important	27	15.1
Quite important	22	12.3
Neutral response	19	10.6
Not important	13	7.3
Not important at all	49	27.4
Total	179	100.0

4 – Support and training

4.1 How well-prepared were you for the tasks demanded of you on becoming an MP?

	Frequency	Percent
No reply	8	4.5
Very well prepared	17	9.5
Quite well prepared	57	31.8
Neutral response	52	29.1
Not very well prepared	25	14.0
Not prepared at all	20	11.2
Total	179	100.0

4.2 Did you receive any training?

	Frequency	Percent
No reply	1	.6
Yes	60	33.5
No	118	65.9
Total	179	100.0

4.3 Who provided this training?

	Frequency	Percent
No reply	134	74.8
Other MPs	13	7.3
Parliament	6	3.4
Party	23	12.8
Other	3	1.6
Total	179	100.0

4.4 How useful was the training?

	Frequency	Percent
No reply	112	62.6
Very useful	8	4.5
Quite useful	12	6.7
Neutral response	24	13.4
Not useful	15	8.4
Not useful at all	8	4.5
Total	179	100.0

4.5 Would you like further training in the following?
Parliamentary procedure

	Frequency	Percent
No reply	36	20.1
Yes	65	36.3
No	78	43.6
Total	179	100.0

Parliamentary resources

	Frequency	Percent
No reply	43	24.0
Yes	47	26.3
No	89	49.7
Total	179	100.0

Parliamentary commissioners

	Frequency	Percent
No reply	42	23.5
Yes	51	28.5
No	86	48.0
Total	179	100.0

Information technology

	Frequency	Percent
No reply	35	19.6
Yes	92	51.4
No	52	29.1
Total	179	100.0

Subject-specific policy areas

	Frequency	Percent
No reply	53	29.6
Yes	55	30.7
No	71	39.7
Total	179	100.0

4.6 How many staff do you have in constituency (total)?

	Frequency	Percent
No reply	1	.6
Zero	17	9.5
1	47	26.3
2	75	41.9
3	29	16.2
4	6	3.4
5	3	1.7
6	1	.6
Total	179	100.0

Full time staff in constituency

	Frequency	Percent
No reply	1	.6
Zero	62	34.6
1	80	44.7
2	34	19.0
3	2	1.1
Total	179	100.0

Part time staff in constituency

	Frequency	Percent
No reply	1	.6
Zero	67	37.4
1	63	35.2
2	36	20.1
3	10	5.6
4	1	.6
6	1	.6
Total	179	100.0

4.7 How many staff do you have in Westminster (total)?

	Frequency	Percent
No reply	2	1.1
Zero	45	25.1
1	83	46.4
2	32	17.9
3	15	8.4
4	2	1.1
Total	179	100.0

Full time staff in Westminster

	Frequency	Percent
No reply	2	1.1
Zero	87	48.6
1	70	39.1
2	19	10.6
3	1	.6
Total	179	100.0

Part time staff in Westminster

	Frequency	Percent
No reply	2	1.1
Zero	108	60.3
1	51	28.5
2	16	8.9
3	2	1.1
Total	179	100.0

4.8 Is this enough staff?

	Frequency	Percent
No reply	5	2.8
Yes	45	25.1
No	129	72.1
Total	179	100.0

Appendix 5

Survey of the subject-matter of House of Commons Select Committee Reports, 1997–98 and 1998–99

Introduction

The object of the survey was to provide an overview of the subject-matter of select committee reports during the first two Sessions of the 1997–2001 Parliament, based on select committee clerks' classification of their own committee's reports.

Method

A questionnaire was sent to the clerk of each departmental select committee, the Environmental Audit Committee and the Public Administration Committee. The questionnaire contained one sheet for each report produced by the committee during the 1997–98 and 1998–99 Sessions of Parliament.

Clerks were invited to indicate, by ticking one or more of 28 boxes, the subject-matter of each report. Since select committee reports rarely confine themselves to a single, narrowly-defined topic, respondents were permitted to tick as many boxes as they felt were appropriate in respect of each report.

It was agreed at the outset that none of the data should be presented in such a way as to allow individuals' responses to be identified. In practice, this means that a breakdown of results by committee is not available, since it would be a simple matter given that data to establish which individuals had produced which responses.

Limitations

The content of select committees' reports is only one measure of their performance and can therefore only tell part of the story. Other important outcomes of select committee work include informing MPs – and through them the broader work of Parliament – about the policy areas covered in the committees' orders of reference (for example by domestic and overseas visits); influencing policy, which may be done indirectly by the threat or possibility of an inquiry; and exposing the Government to public scrutiny, which may be done by taking evidence but need not involve a report.

The concept of "a select committee inquiry" is somewhat elastic, and an inquiry need not result in a report. Multiple evidence sessions may be held on a particular subject without the Committee having any intention of producing a report. On the other hand, a committee may produce a report which is not the result of an inquiry. Sometimes a report may be no more than a vehicle for the publication of some other material: evidence, minutes of informal meetings or notes of overseas visits. Two such reports have been excluded from this analysis. On the other hand, joint reports by two or more select committees have been counted twice (or more) in the analysis. This is both to accommodate the views of the clerks of all the committees concerned and to reflect fairly the fact that the reports were the work of more than one committee. In any Session of Parliament, select committees publish a number of reports which are the result of inquiries begun and largely completed in the previous Session and to undertake a certain amount of work on inquiries which will not result in a report until the next Session. Committees will invariably continue with inquiries which are interrupted by a brief Prorogation, but are less likely, at the beginning of a new Parliament, to pick up the loose ends left by their predecessor committees before a dissolution.

Context

The survey covers two Sessions of Parliament: 1997–98 and 1998–99. The first of these Sessions was long, running from May 1997 to November 1998 and consisting of 241 sitting days. The departmental select committees and the Public Administration Committee were nominated during the week beginning 14 July 1997, so in effect the data for that Session represent 16 months' select committee work, including a three-month Summer recess (a total of 200 sitting days). The 1998–99 Session was a normal Session, the second in the current Parliament. It consisted of 149 sitting days.

Two of the committees included in this survey were set up for the first time in 1997. The International Development Committee followed the establishment of the Department for International Development as an independent Department of State and the Environmental Audit Committee was set up under Standing Order No. 152A as a cross-departmental committee.[1] Most of the committees drew heavily on the new 1997 intake for their membership and many had new chairmen at the beginning of the Parliament.

Finally, the two sessions in question occurred immediately after the first change in Government since the departmental select committee system was established in its present form. There were inevitably a number of major policy initiatives and White Papers, which might have distorted the figures for those kinds of inquiries (see Table 6).

Findings

The complete findings of the survey relating to the subject-matter of reports are set out in the Table at Annex C. This shows the number of reports, and the percentage of the total number of reports, which fell into each category. This information is provided for each of the two sessions, and for the total period.

---

[1] The Standing Order was made on 10 November 1997 and the Committee was nominated two days later.

This section considers the total number of reports, the way in which the questionnaires were completed and the findings of the survey. The classification of reports is considered separately under the three subject areas of expenditure, administration and policy.

The number of reports

A total of 260 select committee reports were published during the two Sessions in question: 117 in 1997–98 and 143 in 1998–99. Two reports from the latter Session have been excluded from this analysis. The Seventh Report of the Foreign Affairs Committee, *Kosovo: Interim Report*, was not a substantive report. It consisted only of terms of reference for future inquiry (which would normally be issued as a press notice), and its primary purpose was the publication of the evidence which was appended to it. The Seventh Report of the Environment, Transport and Regional Affairs Committee, *Meeting with the European Commission Officials to Discuss Air Transport*, was a vehicle for the publication of an informal note of a meeting, and did not constitute a substantive report.

Special reports have not been included in the analysis. The vast majority of special reports are nothing more than a vehicle for the committee to publish a Government response which had been submitted to the committee as a memorandum.[2] The remainder are largely concerned with procedural matters such as the interpretation of the committee's order of reference or the unauthorised disclosure of draft reports.

This analysis is therefore based on a total of 258 reports, 117 from 1997–98 and 141 from 1998–99. A list of all those reports is at Annex B. It should be noted throughout that respondents were permitted to indicate as many different subject areas as they liked for each report. In the tables below, the sum of the number of reports falling into each category is invariably greater than the total number of reports, and the sum of the percentage of reports falling into each category is always greater than 100 per cent.

The mean number of reports per committee was 14.3 over the two sessions – 6.5 in the first session and 7.8 in the second – with the most prolific committee, Environment, Transport and Regional Affairs (ETRA), producing 33 and the least prolific, Scottish Affairs, producing four. ETRA is perhaps a special case, having two sub-committees and more staff than any other select committee,[3] and apart from ETRA, the most prolific committee was Trade and Industry, which produced 26 reports. As has already been noted, the number of reports produced by a committee is only one indicator of its output and should be treated with caution when trying to compare the workload and output of different committees.

---

[2] Government responses may also be published by the Government as a Command Paper. In one case during the period in question, a Government response took the form of a private letter to the Chairman of a committee, and in at least one case, a Government response was delivered in the form of a speech by the relevant Minister in a standing committee meeting.

[3] The Education and Employment Committee is the only other departmental select committee which has the power to appoint two sub-committees, but it has only eight staff whereas ETRA has ten.

Approaches to the questionnaire and the distribution of subject-matter between reports

Unsurprisingly, there was some variation in the number of boxes ticked from one committee to another. Table 1 shows some of the main features of the number of different subject areas indicated for each report. Although the mean number of subject areas per report by each committee ranges from 1.5 to 4.6, this upper limit is exceptional – of the 18 committees surveyed, 13 fell into the range of 1.5 to 2.9 and only two had ticked an average of four or more boxes per report.[*] The greatest number of boxes ticked in respect of any one report was nine, and this was report from the committee which produced the 4.6 average.

Table 1: Number of different subject areas indicated per report

Overall average (mean)		2.55
Lowest average per committee		1.5
Highest average per committee		4.6
No. of committees' responses within the range of:	1.5 to 1.9	6
	2.0 to 2.4	5
	2.5 to 2.9	2
	3.0 to 3.4	0
	3.5 to 3.9	3
	4.0 to 4.4	1
	> 4.5	1

Although this variation in the number of different subject areas indicated for each report undoubtedly reflects different individuals' interpretation of the questionnaire and guidance notes, it probably also reflects the fact that some committees have a tendency to produce short reports which are very narrowly-focused whereas others tend to produce longer reports which are broader in scope.

Expenditure, administration and policy

Table 2 shows the subject-matter of reports only in relation to the three main subject headings, expenditure, administration and policy. Since respondents were allowed to tick more than one box per report, the sum of the percentage columns is greater than 100 per cent and the number of reports in each category for each period is greater than the total number of reports during that period.

Table 2: Subject-matter of reports by three main subject areas

	1997–98		1998–99		Total	
	No.	%	No.	%	No.	%
Expenditure	35	29.9	53	37.6	88	34.1
Administration	61	52.1	92	65.2	153	59.3
Policy	79	67.5	120	85.1	199	77.1
No. reports	117	–	141	–	258	–

[*] When the number of boxes ticked per report was calculated, main categories were not counted if one or more of their sub-categories was counted. For example, if boxes A (Expenditure) A3 (Waste and fraud) and A6 (PFI/PPP) had all been ticked, only A3 and A6 would have been counted. The same applies, *mutatis mutandis*, to the sub-categories of B6 (Machinery of Government) and C6 (Pre-legislative scrutiny).

Although policy is included in the subject-matter of more than three quarters of select committee reports, this is not to the exclusion of expenditure and administration: more than one third of reports included some examination of expenditure and well over a half considered administrative matters. More than one fifth of all reports examined only expenditure and/or administration.

Respondents were asked for information about the scale of the inquiries which led to each report, as well as about the length of the reports themselves. The first of these factors is probably the most significant, reflecting more accurately the amount of time invested by the committee itself, as opposed to the committee secretariat, in a report.

Table 3 shows the distribution of reports on expenditure, administration and policy for reports which resulted from major inquiries and for those which resulted from minor inquiries. The overall figures from Table 2 are included for comparison. There is remarkably little difference in the distribution of subject areas between reports based on major inquiries and those based on minor inquiries, although those based on major inquiries are slightly less likely to consider expenditure and significantly more likely to consider policy. This suggests that there is no strong correlation between the scale of an inquiry and its subject-matter.

Table 3: Distribution of subject areas by scale of inquiry

Scale of inquiry	Expenditure	Administration	Policy	Mean no. of subjects per report
	%	%	%	
Major (n=57)	28.1	57.9	94.7	1.74
Minor (n=69)	33.3	60.9	79.7	1.65
Overall (n=258)	34.1	59.3	77.1	1.71

Expenditure

Table 4 shows the sub-categories which were specified for reports dealing with expenditure. The percentages shown in the second column for each period are of reports relating to expenditure, not of all reports. The main concern of most of them was value for money (45 per cent of all reports on expenditure), and the closely-associated area of waste and fraud (20.4 per cent). This suggests that the main concern for most committees, when they were engaged in inquiries into expenditure, was the efficiency and effectiveness with which the money was spent, rather than what it was spent on, or the mode of expenditure (e.g. public/private partnerships).

Table 4: Subject-matter of reports on expenditure

	1997–98		1998–99		Total	
	No.	%*	No.	%*	No.	%*
Expenditure (no sub-category specified)	14	40.0	11	20.7	25	28.4
Annual Report	7	20.0	9	17.0	16	18.2
Estimates	3	8.6	5	9.4	8	9.1
Waste and fraud	7	20.0	11	20.7	18	20.4
Value for money	14	40.0	26	49.1	40	45.0
Procurement/contracting out	1	2.9	9	17.0	10	11.4
PFI/PPP	4	11.4	5	9.4	9	10.2
No. reports on expenditure	35	–	53	–	88	–

*As a percentage of the number of reports relating to expenditure during the period concerned, not the total number of reports. Rounded to one decimal place.

One of the most striking features of the expenditure reports is the large proportion for which no further sub-category is specified. These account for 28.4 per cent of all reports on expenditure, compared to 6.5 per cent and 3.5 per cent for reports on administration and policy, respectively. A likely explanation for this is that many inquiries focus primarily on a policy area (see Table 2) and consider expenditure in relation to that. The indication of expenditure in the subject-matter of a report without any sub-category may reflect the fact that the expenditure implications of the policy under consideration were discussed in the report, but that expenditure per se was not a major focus of the inquiry.

A number of points which are not apparent from the Table are worth noting. The Committee of Public Accounts, which accounts for a large part of Parliament's scrutiny of Government expenditure, was not included in the survey.[5] Most committees conduct some kind of inquiry each session based on the relevant department's annual report and expenditure plans. These inquiries may be very detailed, involving lengthy memoranda of evidence from the department concerned and oral evidence sessions with senior officials and the Secretary of State, but often do not result in a report.[6]

Ten committees produced reports on their departments' annual reports during the period in question, four of them producing reports in both sessions and two of them producing two reports in 1998–99. Five committees in 1997–98 and four in 1998–99 produced no reports relating to expenditure.

Only two departmental select committees produced no reports relating to expenditure in either session and the greatest proportion of reports relating to expenditure of any committee was 80 per cent. The number of committees giving expenditure as a subject area of 50 per cent or more of their reports was four in 1997–98 and seven in 1998–99. This suggests that, although scrutiny of expenditure might have been weaker in the first session of the new Parliament, it had begun to improve by the second session.

Administration

The subject-matter of administration reports is more evenly-distributed than the expenditure reports and is shown in Table 5. All committees produced at least one report relating to administration in each of the two sessions, with eleven committees giving it as one of the subject areas in 50 per cent or more of their reports in the first session, and seven in the second session.

The number of "confirmation hearing" reports is low-only four committees produced any such reports at all – but this reflects the fact that committees do not necessarily produce a report following confirmation hearings.[7] Only the Treasury Committee has publicly adopted a policy of doing so in respect of members of the Monetary Policy Committee.

---

[5] The PAC produced 110 reports during the period in question, all of which related to expenditure.
[6] See, for example, Memoranda of Evidence submitted to the Home Affairs Committee by the Home Office and the Lord Chancellor's Department (HC 1063, Session 1997–98) and Minutes of Evidence taken before the Social Security Committee on 20 July 1999, *DSS Departmental Report 1999* (HC 749-i, Session 1998–99).
[7] See, for example, Minutes of Evidence taken before the Education and Employment Committee on 15 July 1998, *New Appointments Hearing: The Ofsted Complaints Adjudicator: Ms E Rassaby* (HC 981-i). The phrase, "confirmation hearings" is a convenient shorthand for reports based on evidence sessions with people newly-appointed to public offices, or with people whose appointment to a public office is proposed. See section B4, notes to the questionnaire, Annex A.

A significant proportion of reports were concerned with the performance of executive agencies and non-departmental public bodies: more than half of those reports which were concerned with administration and nearly one third of all reports.

Table 5: Subject-matter of reports on administration

	1997–98		1998–99		Total	
	No.	%*	No.	%*	No.	%*
Administration (no sub-category specified)	3	4.9	7	7.6	10	6.5
Executive agency	15	24.6	19	20.6	34	22.2
NDPB/Quango	17	27.9	28	30.4	45	29.4
Regulator	12	19.7	9	9.8	21	13.7
Confirmation hearing	2	3.3	4	4.3	6	3.9
Quality of public service	22	36.1	36	39.1	58	37.9
Machinery of Government, of which:	20	32.8	35	38.0	55	35.9
Structure/organisation	10	16.4	19	20.6	29	18.9
Access to information	6	9.8	12	13.0	18	11.8
Performance agreement/objectives	3	4.9	4	4.3	7	4.6
No. reports on administration	61	–	92	–	153	–

*As a percentage of the number of reports relating to administration during the period concerned, not the total number of reports. Rounded to one decimal place.

Policy

The majority of reports (77.1 per cent) were concerned with policy. However, this still leaves a significant proportion of reports – more than one fifth – which were concerned only with expenditure and/or administration. Of all the categories, the descriptions of the policy categories are the least self-explanatory and should not be taken literally. More detailed descriptions are contained in the notes at Annex A.

There was considerably more scrutiny of existing policy than of new policy initiatives, and more scrutiny of firm new proposals ("white paper") than of proposals at the consultation stage ("green paper"). This might be because committees prefer not to get involved in examining policy proposals at the same time as public consultation is taking place (and the lobbying organisations which produce so many contributions to select committee inquiries are concentrating on the consultation exercise) and it might be because the external pressure for committees to examine a policy area is greatest when the Government's mind appears to be made up.

Although there was very little pre-legislative scrutiny by departmental select committees, three bills were referred to *ad hoc* select committees or joint committees during the two sessions.[8] Only one bill was referred to a departmental select committee,[9] but half of the 18 committees conducted some form of pre-legislative scrutiny.

---

[8] The draft Bill on the Food Standards Agency was referred to the Select Committee on Food Standards in February 1999. The Financial Services and Markets Bill and the draft Local Government (Organisation and Standards) Bill were referred to joint committees in March 1999 and May 1999, respectively.
[9] Twenty First Report from the Environment, Transport and regional Affairs Committee, Session 1998–99, *Railways Bill*, HC 827.

Table 6: Subject-matter of reports on policy

	1997–98		1998–99		Total	
	No.	%*	No.	%*	No.	%*
Policy (no sub-category specified)	2	2.5	5	4.2	7	3.5
White paper	22	27.8	26	21.7	48	24.1
Green paper	12	15.1	18	15.0	30	15.1
Audit of existing policy	51	64.6	63	52.5	114	57.3
Board of inquiry	12	15.2	17	14.2	29	14.6
Blue sky thinking	11	13.9	15	12.5	26	13.1
Pre-legislative scrutiny, of which:	7	8.9	9	7.5	16	8.0
Bill on committee's initiative	2	2.5	6	5.0	8	4.0
Bill on referral	0	0.0	1	0.8	1	0.5
Secondary legislation	3	3.8	1	0.8	4	2.0
Royal Commission	3	3.8	4	3.3	7	3.5
No. reports	79	–	120	–	199	–

*As a percentage of the number of reports relating to policy during the period concerned, not the total number of reports. Rounded to one decimal place.

Just over 30 per cent of all reports related to policies which were the subject of a consultation exercise or to newly-announced policies. More than 40 per cent of reports contained some attempt to audit existing policies. This suggests that there is some attempt to examine policy developments systematically, but committees are rather more likely to examine a policy once it is established than when it is in its early stages.

The quality of Government responses

In addition to the questions on the subject-matter of reports, respondents were asked to evaluate the quality of Government responses on a scale of 1 to 5, where 3 indicates a response of satisfactory quality, 1 or 2 a good response and 4 or 5 an unsatisfactory response.[10] This question was not intended to elicit information about whether or not the committee's recommendations were accepted – this was the subject of a separate question – but to take into account whether or not the response was delivered on time, whether it dealt with all the committee's recommendations adequately and whether it engaged with the report as a whole, rather than only the summary of conclusions and recommendations. The aggregate answers to this question are shown in Table 7. The difference between the number of reports and the number of responses included in the analysis is largely a consequence of the fact that a number of reports did not receive a response.

Table 7: Evaluation of Government responses

Score	Number of responses	Percentage of total
1	11	4.7
2	80	34.2
3	103	44.0
4	33	14.1
5	7	3.0
TOTAL	234	100.0

[10] This scoring system reflects the one used in the House of Commons annual reporting system and should therefore have been familiar to all respondents.

The vast majority of responses (82.9 per cent) were considered to be satisfactory or better. However, a significant proportion (17.1 per cent) were considered to be unsatisfactory. Where specific complaints were recorded, they included failure to address all the recommendations contained in the report, serious misunderstanding of what the committee meant by its recommendations and failure to produce the response within a reasonable time.

ANNEX A
Sample questionnaire and guidance notes

Education & Employment	First Report	1997–98
Teacher Recruitment: What can be done?		
Scale of inquiry	☐ MAJOR (7+) ☐ MEDIUM (2–6) ☐ MINOR (0–1)	
Length of Report	☐ LONG ☐ MEDIUM ☐ SHORT	

Subject-matter (Please indicate all that are of significant relevance)

A. Expenditure		**B. Administration**		**C. Policy**	
1. Annual Report	☐	1. Executive agency	☐	1. New policy (white paper)	☐
2. Estimates	☐	2. NDPB/QUANGO	☐	2. Consultation (green paper)	☐
3. Waste & fraud	☐	3. Regulator	☐	3. Audit of existing policy	☐
4. Value for money	☐	4. Confirmation hearing	☐	4. "Board of inquiry"	☐
5. Procurement/contracting out	☐	5. Quality of public services	☐	5. Blue sky thinking	☐
6. PFI/PPP	☐	6. Machinery of Government	☐	6. Pre-legislative scrutiny	☐
Government response: Command paper ☐ Special Report ☐ Other ☐		(a) structure/organisation ☐ (b) access to information ☐ (c) APA/objectives ☐		(a) Bill on Cttee's initiative ☐ (b) Bill on referral ☐ (c) Secondary legislation ☐	
Quality of the response (5=low) ☐ 1 ☐ 2 ☐ 3 ☐ 4 ☐ 5				7. "Royal commission" ☐	
Proportion of recommendations accepted ☐ ALL ☐ MOST ☐ SOME ☐ FEW ☐ NONE					
If the inquiry was conducted by a sub-committee, please specify:					
Any other comments?					

HANSARD SOCIETY QUESTIONNAIRE
NOTES

1a There should be one form for each select committee report published during the 1997–98 and 1998–99 sessions. Special Reports are not included.

2a **Scale of Inquiry:** As a general rule, inquiries should be classified as follows: 7 or more evidence sessions = major; 2–6 evidence sessions = medium, fewer than two evidence sessions = minor. However, there may be compelling reasons for placing individual inquiries into different categories. An inquiry which consisted of five or six evidence sessions might be classified as major if an unusually large volume of written evidence was received and the committee devoted a lot of time to the inquiry outside evidence sessions (e.g. visits or numerous deliberative meetings). Likewise, an inquiry which consisted of two evidence sessions might really have been minor if they were very brief or poorly attended. The results will be compared with other factors such as subject matter; they will not be used to make comparisons between committees.

3a **Length of Report:** Relative to the size of report which the committee usually produces. A committee which regularly produces 200-paragraph reports might classify a 50-paragraph report as short. For others, 50 paragraphs might be medium. This is largely a question of individual judgement. As with scale of inquiry, this information will be used to make comparisons between different reports from the same committee.

4a **Type of Report:** This is the key question in the survey. Tick as many of the boxes as you think are appropriate – some reports will focus quite narrowly on one particular subject whereas others will cover a wide range of subjects. The object is to identify those areas which constitute a significant part of each report, for example, those areas in which recommendations are made or which the report considers at some length or in some depth.

A report may fall into one of the major categories without necessarily falling into one of the sub-categories. Ticking one of the there major headings does not necessarily mean that one of the sub-categories should also be ticked.

Many of the categories are self-explanatory. Some of the less obvious ones are explained below:

B4 (Confirmation hearing): Although the Treasury Committee has adopted a policy of holding "confirmation hearings" with new members of the MPC, this category could be read a bit more broadly to include any reports based on evidence from people newly-appointed to public offices, or people whose appointment to a public office is proposed (e.g. regulators, agency chief executives and senior civil servants).

C1 (New policy): In particular, reports based on white papers and announcements of new policy initiatives.

C2 (Consultation): Report on a green paper, consultation paper or a policy which is still at the consultation and development stage.

C4 ("Board of inquiry"): Inquiry into a single, reasonably well-defined event or decision. Examples might include the Defence Committee's inquiry into the Chinook crash, the Culture, Media and Sport Committee's inquiry into the decision to move *News at Ten* or the Trade and Industry Committee's inquiry into Georgian nuclear material at Dounreay.

C5 (Blue sky thinking): Reports which examine policy ideas of the committee's own devising or initiatives proposed by some body other than Government.

C7 ("Royal Commission"): Long inquiries into weighty topics. Closely allied to blue sky thinking, differing more in scale and scope than in substance.

5a Government response: The question on the quality of the response is intended to encompass issues such as the extent to which the response adequately addressed the recommendations contained in the report, whether or not it appeared that the author had read anything more than the summary of conclusions and recommendations and whether the response was delivered on time (in the case of pre-legislative scrutiny, this might be before the legislation is considered in the House, rather than before the customary two-month deadline expires).

A response of satisfactory quality should be indicated by a 3, better than satisfactory 1 or 2, worse 4 or 5.

The question on the proportion of recommendations accepted is intended to give an impression only, hence the use of vague terms like "few" and "most" rather than percentages.

ANNEX B
House of Commons, Departmental select committees: List of select committee reports, 1997–98 and 1998–99

Agriculture Committee

Session 1997–98
First Report	MAFF/Intervention Board Departmental Report 1997
Second Report	CAP Reform: Agenda 2000
Third Report	The UK Beef Industry
Fourth Report	Food Safety
Fifth Report	Vitamin B6
Sixth Report	Flood and Coastal Defence
Seventh Report	Vitamin B6: the Government's Decision

Session 1998–99
First Report	MAFF/Intervention Board Departmental Report 1998 and the Comprehensive Spending Review
Second Report	CAP Reform: Rural Development
Third Report	The UK Pig Industry
Fourth Report	UK Pig Industry: the Government's Response
Fifth Report	Badgers and Bovine Tuberculosis
Sixth Report	Genetically Modified Organisms
Seventh Report	Outcome of the CAP Reform Negotiations
Eighth Report	Sea Fishing
Ninth Report	MAFF/Intervention Board Departmental Report 1999

Culture, Media and Sport Committee

Session 1997–98
First Report	The Royal Opera House
Second Report	The Millennium Dome
Third Report	Preservation of Historic Ships: The Case of HMS Cavalier
Fourth Report	The Multi-Media Revolution
Fifth Report	Objectives and Performance of the Department for Culture, Media and Sport
Sixth Report	Not Only the Dome: The Millennium Celebrations in the United Kingdom
Seventh Report	The Eyre Review and the Royal Opera House
Eighth Report	Report and Accounts of the BBC for 1997–98
Ninth Report	The Future of News at Ten

Session 1998–99
First Report	The Heritage Lottery Fund
Second Report	The Preservation of HMS Cavalier
Third Report	Back to the Dome
Fourth Report	Staging International Sporting Events
Fifth Report	The Performing Right Society and the Abolition of the Classical Music Subsidy
Sixth Report	The DCMs and its Quangos

Defence Committee

Session 1997–98

First Report	Peace Support Operations in Bosnia and Herzegovina
Second Report	Draft Visiting Forces and International Headquarters (Application of Law) (Amendment) Order 1998
Third Report	NATO Enlargement,
Fourth Report	Lessons of the Chinook Crash on the Mull of Kintyre
Fifth Report	The Reserves Call Out Order 1998
Sixth Report	The Defence Evaluation and Research Agency
Seventh Report	Aspects of Defence Procurement and Industrial Policy
Eighth Report	The Strategic Defence Review

Session 1998–99

First Report	The Strategic Defence Review: Territorial Army Restructuring
Second Report	The Appointment of the New Head of Defence Export Services
Third Report	The Future of NATO: the Washington Summit
Fourth Report	The Draft Visiting Forces and International Headquarters (Application of Law) Order 1999 and the Draft International Headquarters and Defence Organisations (Designations and Privileges) (Amendment) Order 1999
Fifth Report	Security of Supply and the Future of Royal Ordnance Factory Bishopton
Sixth Report	The Reserves Call Out Order 1999 and Progress of Territorial Army Restructuring
Seventh Report	The Strategic Defence Review: Defence Medical Services
Eighth Report	Major Procurement Projects Survey: the Common New Generation Frigate Programme
Ninth Report	Defence Research

Education and Employment Committee

Session 1997–98

First Report	Teacher recruitment: what can be done?
Second Report	The New Deal
Third Report	The Dearing Report: some funding issues
Fourth Report	The relationship between TECs and the proposed Regional Development Agencies
Fifth Report	Disaffected Children
Sixth Report	Further Education
Seventh Report	Pathways into Work for Lone Parents
Eighth Report	The New Deal Pathfinders
Ninth Report	The Role of Headteachers

Session 1998–99

First Report	Active Labour Market Policies and their Delivery: Lessons from Australia
Second Report	Part-time Working
Third Report	Highly Able Children
Fourth Report	The Work of OFSTED
Fifth Report	The Role of School Governors
Sixth Report	The One Service Pilots
Seventh Report	The Performance and Future of the Employment Service
Eighth Report	Access for All? A Survey of Post-16 Participation
Ninth Report	Opportunities for Disabled People

Environment, Transport and Regional Affairs Committee

Session 1997–98

First Report	Regional Development Agencies
Second Report	Sewage Treatment and Disposal
Third Report	The Proposed Strategic Rail Authority and Railway Regulation
Fourth Report	Air Traffic Control
Fifth Report	The Future for Allotments
Sixth Report	Sustainable Waste Management

Seventh Report	London Underground
Eighth Report	Regional Air Services
Ninth Report	English Nature
Tenth Report	Housing
Eleventh Report	Implementation of the Best Value Framework
Twelfth Report	The Departmental Annual Report 1998 and Expenditure 1998–99
Thirteenth Report	The Protection of Field Boundaries

Session 1998–99

First Report	Railway Safety
Second Report	Millennium Compliance in the Transport Industry
Third Report	The Future of National Air Traffic Services
Fourth Report	The Countryside Agency
Fifth Report	Regional Eurostar Services
Sixth Report	The Maritime and Coastguard Agency
[Seventh Report	Meeting with the European Commission Officials to Discuss Air Transport][11]
Eighth Report	Local Government Finance
Ninth Report	Integrated Transport White Paper
Tenth Report	Regional Development Agencies
Eleventh Report	Reducing the Environmental Impact of Consumer Products
Twelfth Report	The Future of the UK Shipping Industry
Thirteenth Report	The Operation of the Landfill Tax
Fourteenth Report	Aviation Safety
Fifteenth Report	Departmental Annual Report 1999 and Expenditure Plans 1999–2002
Sixteenth Report	Multilateral Environmental Agreements
Seventeenth Report	Housing: PPG3
Eighteenth Report	Tendered Bus Services
Nineteenth Report	Young and Newly-Qualified Drivers: Standards and Training
Twentieth Report	Town and Country Parks
Twenty First Report	Railways Bill

Foreign Affairs Committee

Session 1997–98

First Report	The Treaty of Amsterdam
Second Report	Dependent Territories Review: Interim Report
Third Report	Hong Kong
Fourth Report	Entry Clearance Operations with Particular Reference to Islamabad and New Delhi

Session 1998–99

First Report	Foreign Policy and Human Rights
Second Report	Sierra Leone
Third Report	European Union Enlargement
Fourth Report	Gibraltar
Fifth Report	Foreign and Commonwealth Office Resources
Sixth Report	South Caucasus and Central Asia
[Seventh Report	Kosovo: Interim Report][12]

Health Committee

Session 1997–98

First Report	Tobacco Advertising and the Proposed EC Directive
Second Report	Children Looked After by Local Authorities
Third Report	The Welfare of Former British Child Migrants

---

[11] This Report was excluded from the analysis. It was not a substantive report, but a vehicle for the publication of an informal note of a meeting with European Commission officials.

[12] This Report was excluded from the analysis. It was not a substantive report, but a vehicle for publishing evidence and announcing terms of reference for further inquiry.

Session 1998–99
First Report   The Relationship between Health and Social Services
Second Report   Primary Care Groups
Third Report   Future NHS Staffing Requirements
Fourth Report   The Long Term Care of the Elderly
Fifth Report   Regulation of Private and Other Independent Healthcare
Sixth Report   Procedures related to Adverse Clinical Incidents and Outcomes in Medical
                     Care

Home Affairs Committee

Session 1997–98
First Report   Police Disciplinary and Complaints Procedure
Second Report   The Confidentiality of Police Settlements of Civil Claims
Third Report   Alternatives to Prison Sentences
Fourth Report   Electoral Law and Administration

Session 1998–99
First Report   The Work of the Criminal Cases Review Commission
Second Report   Freemasonry in Public Life
Third Report   Accountability of the Security Service
Fourth Report   Police Training and Recruitment
Fifth Report   Drugs and Prisons

International Development Committee

Session 1997–98
First Report   Montserrat
Second Report   The Development White Paper
Third Report   Debt Relief
Fourth Report   The Renegotiation of the Lomi Convention
Fifth Report   The Department for International Development: 1998 Departmental Report
Sixth Report   Montserrat – Further Developments
Seventh Report   Sudan
Eighth Report   The Future of the Commonwealth Development Corporation

Session 1998–99
First Report   The Future of the EC Development Budget
Second Report   The Provisions of the Commonwealth Development Corporation Bill *[Lords]*
Third Report   Kosovo: The Humanitarian Crisis
Fourth Report   Debt Relief and the Cologne G8 Summit
Fifth Report   Department for International Development: 1999 Departmental Report
Sixth Report   Conflict Prevention and Post-Conflict Reconstruction
Seventh Report   Women and Development

Northern Ireland Affairs Committee

Session 1997–98
First Report   Northern Ireland Public Expenditure: Current Plans and Priorities
Second Report   Electoral Malpractice in Northern Ireland
Third Report   Composition, Recruitment and Training of the RUC
Fourth Report   Prison Service in Northern Ireland

Session 1998–99
First Report   Public Expenditure in Northern Ireland: Special Educational Needs
Second Report   Electricity Supplies in Northern Ireland: Impact of the 26 December 1998
                     Storm
Third Report   Impact in Northern Ireland of Cross-Border Road Fuel Price Differentials
Fourth Report   The Operation of the Fair Employment (Northern Ireland) Act 1989:
                     Ten Years On

Science and Technology Committee

Session 1997–98

First Report   The Implications of the Dearing Report for the Structure and Funding of
                    University Research
Second Report   The Year 2000-Computer Compliance
Third Report   Glaxo Wellcome and SmithKline Beecham: The Merger Proposals
Fourth Report   The Cloning of Animals from Adult Cells
Fifth Report   British Biotech
Sixth Report   Science and the Comprehensive Spending Review

Session 1998–99

First Report   The Scientific Advisory System: Genetically Modified Foods
Second Report   The National Endowment for Science, Technology and the Arts
Third Report   The Scientific Advisory System: Mobile Phones and Health
Fourth Report   The Regulation of the Biotechnology Industry

Scottish Affairs Committee

Session 1997–98

First Report   Welfare to Work in Scotland: The New Deal
Second Report   The Operation of Multi-Layer Democracy

Session 1998–99

First Report   Inward/Outward Investment in Scotland
Second Report   Tourism in Scotland

Social Security Committee

Session 1997–98

First Report   Tax and Benefits: An Interim Report
Second Report   Social Security Reforms: Lessons from the United States of America
Third Report   Tax and Benefits: Pre-Budget Report
Fourth Report   Disability Living Allowance
Fifth Report   Pension on Divorce

Session 1998–99

First Report   Tax and Benefits: Implementation of Tax Credits
Second Report   Family Credit Fraud
Third Report   Disability Living Allowance
Fourth Report   Child Benefit
Fifth Report   Pension on Divorce: Parts III and IV of the Welfare Reform and Pensions Bill
Sixth Report   War Pensions Agency Business Plan 1999–2000
Seventh Report   The ONE Service Pilots
Eighth Report   The Modernisation of Social Security Appeals
Ninth Report   Social Security Implications of Parental Leave
Tenth Report   The 1999 Child Support White Paper

Trade and Industry Committee

Session 1997–98

First Report   Co-ordination of Inward Investment
Second Report   Progress in the Liberalisation of the Gas Market
Third Report   The Post Office
Fourth Report   Coal
Fifth Report   Energy Policy
Sixth Report   Small and Medium Sized Enterprises
Seventh Report   Reform of European Structural Funds
Eighth Report   Aspects of Defence Procurement and Industrial Policy
Ninth Report   Georgian Nuclear Material at Dounreay
Tenth Report   Developments in the Liberalisation of the Domestic Electricity Market
Eleventh Report   Industrial and Trade Relations with Japan
Twelfth Report   Industrial and Trade Relations with Central Europe

Session 1998–99

First Report	Vehicle Pricing
Second Report	Strategic Export Controls
Third Report	Multilateral Agreement on Investment
Fourth Report	Draft Limited Liability Partnership Bill
Fifth Report	Telephone Numbering
Sixth Report	Ethical Trading
Seventh Report	"Building Confidence in Electronic Commerce": The Government's Proposals
Eighth Report	Trade Marks, Fakes and Consumers
Ninth Report	The Impact on Industry of the Proposed Climate Change Levy
Tenth Report	Electronic Commerce
Eleventh Report	The Horizon Project for Automated Payment of Benefits through Post Offices
Twelfth Report	The 1999 Post Office White Paper
Thirteenth Report	Small Businesses and Enterprise
Fourteenth Report	Electronic Commerce Bill

Treasury Committee

Session 1997–98

First Report	Accountability of the Bank of England
Second Report	The Barnett Formula
Third Report	Confirmation Hearings
Fourth Report	The 1998 Budget
Fifth Report	The UK and Preparations for Stage Three of Economic and Monetary Union
Sixth Report	The Monetary Policy Committee of the Bank of England: Confirmation Hearings
Seventh Report	Bank of England: Operation of Accountability – One Year On
Eighth Report	The New Fiscal Framework and the Comprehensive Spending Review
Ninth Report	The Mis-Selling of Personal Pensions

Session 1998–99

First Report	Office for National Statistics
Second Report	The World Economy and the Pre-Budget Report
Third Report	Financial Services Regulation
Fourth Report	The 1999 Budget
Fifth Report	The Monetary Policy Committee of the Bank of England: Confirmation Hearings
Sixth Report	Inland Revenue
Seventh Report	Public Service Agreements
Eighth Report	The Monetary Policy Committee – Two years on
Ninth Report	Demutualisation
Tenth Report	Valuation Office Agency

Welsh Affairs Committee

Session 1997–98

First Report	The Impact of the Government's Devolution Proposals on Economic Development and Local Government in Wales
Second Report	The Present Crisis in the Welsh Livestock Industry
Third Report	Welsh Office Departmental Report 1998
Fourth Report	Investment in Industry in Wales

Session 1998–99

First Report	The Closure of the Welsh Industrial and Maritime Museum
Second Report	Broadcasting in Wales and the National Assembly
Third Report	Childcare in Wales
Fourth Report	Health Issues in Wales
Fifth Report	Paediatric Cardiac Services in Wales
Sixth Report	Denbighshire County Council's Funding Legacy

Public Administration Committee

Session 1997–98

First Report	Commissioner for Public Appointments
Second Report	Report of the Health Service Ombudsman
Third Report	Your Right to Know the Government's Proposals for a Freedom of Information Act
Fourth Report	Ministerial Accountability and Parliamentary Questions
Fifth Report	Report of the Northern Ireland Ombudsman for 1997
Sixth Report	The Government Information and Communication Service

Session 1998–99

First Report	Report of the Parliamentary Ombudsman for 1997–98
Second Report	Annual Report of the Health Service Ombudsman for 1997–98
Third Report	Freedom of Information Draft Bill
Fourth Report	Ministerial Accountability and Parliamentary Questions
Fifth Report	Freedom of Information Draft Bill: The Committee's Response to the Home Office Reply
Sixth Report	Quangos

Environmental Audit Committee

Session 1997–98

First Report	'Pre-Budget Report
Second Report	The Greening Government Initiative
Third Report	The Pre-Budget Report: Government Response and Follow-up
Fourth Report	Climate Change: UK Emission Reduction Targets and Audit Arrangements

Session 1998–99

First Report	The Multilateral Agreement on Investment
Second Report	Climate Change: Government Response and Follow-up
Third Report	The Comprehensive Spending Review and Public Service Agreements
Fourth Report	The Pre-Budget Report 1998
Fifth Report	Genetically Modified Organisms and the Environment: Co-ordination of Government Policy
Sixth Report	The Greening Government Initiative 1999
Seventh Report	Energy Efficiency
Eighth Report	The Budget 1999: Environmental Implications

ANNEX C
Subject-matter of select committee reports, 1997–98 and 1998–99

	1997–98		1998–99		Total	
	No.	%*	No.	%*	No.	%*
TOTAL	117	–	141	–	258	–
Expenditure, of which:	**35**	**29.9**	**53**	**37.6**	**88**	**34.1**
No further sub-category specified	14	12.0	11	7.8	25	9.7
Annual Report	7	6.0	9	6.4	16	6.2
Estimates	3	2.6	5	3.5	8	3.1
Waste and fraud	7	6.0	11	7.8	18	7.0
Value for money	14	12.0	26	18.4	40	15.5
Procurement/contracting out	1	0.9	9	6.4	10	3.9
PFI/PPP	4	3.4	5	3.5	9	3.5
Administration, of which:	**61**	**52.1**	**92**	**65.2**	**153**	**59.3**
No further sub-category specified	3	2.6	7	5.0	10	3.9
Executive agency	15	12.8	19	13.5	34	13.2
NDPB/Quango	17	14.5	28	19.9	45	17.4
Regulator	12	10.3	9	6.4	21	8.1
Confirmation hearing	2	1.7	4	2.8	6	2.3
Quality of public service	22	18.8	36	25.5	58	22.5
Machinery of Government, of which:	20	17.1	35	24.8	55	21.3
Structure/organisation	10	8.5	19	13.5	29	11.2
Access to information	6	5.1	12	8.5	18	7.0
Performance agreements/objectives	3	2.6	4	2.8	7	2.7
Policy, of which:	**79**	**67.5**	**120**	**85.1**	**199**	**77.1**
No further sub-category specified	2	1.7	5	3.5	7	2.7
White paper	22	18.8	26	18.4	48	18.6
Green paper	12	10.3	18	12.8	30	11.6
Audit of existing policy	51	43.6	63	44.7	114	44.2
Board of inquiry	12	10.3	17	12.1	29	11.2
Blue sky thinking	11	9.4	15	10.6	26	10.1
Pre-legislative scrutiny, of which:	7	6.0	9	6.4	16	6.2
Bill on committee's initiative	2	1.7	6	4.3	8	3.1
Bill on referral	0	0.0	1	0.7	1	0.4
Secondary legislation	3	2.6	1	0.7	4	1.6
Royal Commission	3	2.6	4	2.8	7	2.7

*As a percentage of the total number of reports. Rounded to one decimal place.

Appendix 6

Financial Procedures

(i) Control of supply

The control of supply, by which Parliament votes specific sums of money for spending on particular services, is the basis of parliamentary control and accountability. Standing Order No. 48 provides that the Crown must recommend proposals for expenditure. Before the Government presents specific proposals to Parliament however, there is an extensive planning process within government. Inside the Treasury, the Budget and Public Finances Directorate set the agenda between the differing departmental demands for money. A Cabinet Committee on Expenditure chaired by the Chancellor of the Exchequer with the Chief Secretary as a member provides a more formal mechanism of control than in the past. Treasury participation in this process is a key element of control. The pre-eminence afforded to Treasury control though PES is complementary to the overall role of the Treasury in managing and controlling public expenditure. The past decade has seen growing codification of the internal rules and procedures of Treasury control. These may be found in guides such as *Government Accounting* or in the *Treasury Handbook: Supply and other Financial Procedures of the House of Commons*. *The Code of Fiscal Stability* contains the foundation for future development in this area. Three principles for 'parliamentary control of the purse' (a phrase adopted since Gladstone's reforms) were adopted in *Government Accounting 1989*:

- The constitutional protection afforded by the principle of statutory authorisation of the expenditure of public funds and for the raising of finance through taxation;
- The principles of propriety and regularity that requires parliamentary approval for departmental activities and services;
- The principle of delegation of considerable authority to the Treasury to approve departmental expenditure, subject to ultimate parliamentary authority.

The responsibilities of departmental Accounting Officers include applying for funds for the purposes authorised by Parliament; being the principal witness on behalf of the Department before the Committee of Public Accounts; and in exercising authority over internal control systems. They are directly responsible to Parliament. In practical terms the effectiveness of the Comptroller and Auditor General depends on his obtaining the co-operation of Accounting Officers and the Government Departments which is crucial to the Treasury system of internal audit.

(ii) The Budget and forward spending plans

At the centre of the system of scrutiny is the need for accurate information. There have been a number of changes in recent years:

- From November 1993, under the previous Conservative Government, until 1997, there was a unified budget containing both taxation and spending proposals. The new Labour Government reverted to the previous practice of a spring budget.

- In July 1997 the new Chancellor introduced a special budget followed in November 1997 with the publication of a Pre-Budget Report (also known as a Green Budget). The Pre-Budget Report contained details of government spending plans alongside the aims and objectives of the government's economic policy.
- The Spring Budget sets out the annual tax burden containing details found in the Treasury's Red Book[1]. Precise details of the national accounts may be found in information published by the Office for National Statistics. The accounts set out in much greater detail the measures of the tax burden accompanied by statistical data.[2] Major changes are planned for the nature of accounts; from the existing cash based system to an accruals basis. It is widely claimed that the introduction of resource accounting and budgeting by 2002 is likely to lead to improvements in the provision of information and in the scrutiny of the Government.
- Substantial improvements in the form of information provided since 1991 in Departmental Reports. These are laid before Parliament each year in February and March;
- Improvements in financial information from the Treasury about government spending plans as a statistical supplement to the Financial Statement and Budget Report;
- There is a statutory requirement for the Treasury to provide Parliament with economic forecasts of government spending at least twice per year (currently contained in the Pre-Budget Report and the Budget). In addition detailed information is provided to select committees, and in the financial memoranda which are attached to Bills;
- Information about government spending and policy are also to be found in the documents received by the National Audit Office and the Public Accounts Committee.

(iii) Departmental spending plans

Until the 1997 General Election, the amount of money a department was intending to spend in any particular financial year was announced in the previous year, usually (since 1991) in the departmental Annual Report, published in the spring. These reports (about twenty each year, one for each major department) contained figures for the following three years, of which the later years were intended to be provisional and subject to change before the next year's annual report. The figures were the culmination of an annual Public Expenditure Survey, which involved negotiations between the department and the Treasury on the amount which was necessary, or could be afforded, for the services that the department was expecting to provide.

The incoming Labour government announced that it would undertake a Comprehensive Spending Review, intended to examine departmental spending "from a zero base", i.e. with no existing spending taken for granted. The results of this review were published in two stages in the summer of 1998, firstly in the *Economic and Fiscal Strategy Report*,[3] which announced overall totals and the general procedure, and then in the *Comprehensive Spending*

---

[1] HM Treasury, *Budget 1999*, HC 298, 1998–99, also: Terrence Daintith and Alan Page, *The Executive in the Constitution Oxford*, Oxford University Press, 1999)
[2] See Robert Twigger, *The Burden of Taxation* House of Commons Research Paper, 99/67 (25th June 1999).
[3] Cm 3978, June 1998. Further issues of the EFSR have been published in the same volumes as the 1999 and 2000 Budget Reports.

Review itself,[4] which gave more details for each department. A fundamental change in this system is that, for most types of expenditure, the figures are fixed for three years. The *Departmental Expenditure Limits* (DELs) were further divided into capital and current spending. Limits are placed on the amounts which can be transferred from capital to current spending.[5] Some expenditure cannot reasonably be forecast for three years forward and is designated *Annually Managed Expenditure* (AME). The main components are cyclical social security benefits (unemployment benefit etc.), debt interest and local authority expenditure. Altogether there are only about ten categories of AME but which between them they account for about half of government expenditure. The scrutiny of this form of expenditure is therefore disproportionately significant.

At the time of the 1998 Review it was announced that the next one would be in 2000, again with a three year timespan (2001–02 to 2003–04), overlapping by a year with the 1998 review. This review has now been called the *Spending Review 2000*, dropping the description "comprehensive", as it is not intended to be zero-based. It is planned that successive reviews will continue to occur at two-year intervals, each covering a three-year period overlapping the previous one by a year. It is too early to assess the full effects of this system although announcements made in the 2000 Budget involved significant expenditure increases for 2000–01 and 2001–02, somewhat negating the concept of fixed three-year totals. The figures in the 1998 Comprehensive Spending Review were announced without any previous public consultation, and Parliament was not invited to approve them. A similar procedure appears to be happening in 2000.[6]

(iv) Estimates; departmental spending

Parliament has an important role to play in scrutinising levels of departmental spending. There are a number of different stages in the process and scrutiny can consist of anything from a fairly mechanical examination of a particular set of figures to the examination of a policy and its outcomes. The parliamentary oversight of this process varies in quality. The occasion when Parliament is asked to approve levels of government spending is on the presentation of Estimates, which cover a particular financial year (April–March) and are presented to the House of Commons at about the beginning of that year.[7] Further ("supplementary") Estimates are presented during the course of the year when necessary. The main Estimates are not usually approved until July, and in the mean time Government expenditure is authorised by "Votes on Account", which are preliminary estimates generally based on 40 per cent of the previous year's figures (usually approved in March). This system is intended to allow government activity to continue without prejudice to later decisions

---

[4] Cm 4011, July 1998.

[5] Amounts unspent in one financial year can be carried forward to the next. This "end-year flexibility" is intended to relieve the pressure on departments to spend before the end of a financial year on pain of losing the relevant funding. Unexpected expenditure can be financed through a (small) "DEL margin", corresponding to the previous Contingencies Reserve, although departments are expected to establish their own margins within their DEL total.

[6] An exception has been made with the health budget, where the overall figures for the next three years were announced in the 2000 Budget and the Prime Minister announced a process of consultation to decide how the money should be spent.

[7] On the comparatively rare occasions when the amount spent during a year is found to have exceeded the amount voted by Parliament, an "Excess Vote" is approved retrospectively following a report by the Committee of Public Accounts.

on the main Estimates. Not all Government spending is subjected to the Estimates process; the main kinds excluded are:

- Consolidated Fund Standing Services, where an Act of Parliament has stipulated that expenditure is to be charged direct to the Consolidated Fund rather than to "money provided by Parliament";[8]
- Spending from the National Insurance Fund on pensions and sickness benefit;
- Local Government self-financed expenditure, raised (mainly) through Council Tax.

Each Estimate consists of an "ambit", describing what the money is to be spent on, a figure for the amount to be granted by Parliament and a figure for "appropriations in aid", where associated income is available which can be spent on the service concerned.[9] There are 85 estimates for 2000–01 (the number varies slightly each year), grouped for convenience into 21 classes.[10] An individual Estimate is also called a Vote, because it is the level at which Parliament can grant ("vote") the money. The figures in each Estimate are disaggregated into subheads, but Parliament is not invited to approve the expenditure at subhead level, and departments can transfer ("vire") expenditure from one subhead to another without Parliamentary approval, although such "virement" sometimes requires the approval of the Treasury.[11] Parliament can reduce an estimate (or refuse it altogether) but may not increase it.

(v) Estimates; Procedures

The procedure on each of these kinds of Estimate is basically the same;
- It is open to the House of Commons to approve individual Estimates but in practice the vast majority are approved en bloc about three times in each year, usually without any debate or division;
- A bill – the Consolidated Fund Bill – is then brought in to approve the totals, which have been granted;
- Once a year, in July, the Bill also lists the ambits of the Estimates and lists the total amounts voted for each since the last such Bill. This process, called "appropriation", provides the legal authority for spending the money on particular services,[12] and this Bill is therefore called the Consolidated Fund (Appropriation) Bill and becomes the Appropriation Act. Consolidated Fund Bills are usually passed without debate in either House; in the Commons this procedure is laid down by Standing Order.

---

[8] The main types are interest payments on the national debt, most payments to the European Union, the salaries of judges, MEPs, Speaker of the House of Commons, the Comptroller and Auditor General and various other office holders where annual control by Parliament is thought to imply the danger of political control.

[9] Income which is of a kind not approved for Appropriations in Aid, or which exceeds the figure mentioned in the Estimates, is paid to the Consolidated Fund at the end of the financial year ("Consolidated Fund Extra Receipts"). Each Estimate contains a forecast of the income which is likely to be received in this way.

[10] Supply Estimates 2000–01, HC (1999–2000) 377.

[11] If the change is particularly significant, the Treasury will present a Supplementary Estimate for a token amount (£1,000) to obtain parliamentary approval for the change.

[12] The expenditure will also usually have been authorised in general terms (i.e. without amounts being specified) in some other Act of Parliament, but it is possible for the Government to spend money solely on the authority of an Estimate and the resulting Appropriation Act; money to be authorised in this way is marked with a solid square in the Estimates.

- Day by day issuing of the money is authorised by the Comptroller and Auditor General and at the end of the year Appropriation Accounts are produced, showing how much of the money granted by Parliament was actually spent. These contain an audit certificate by the Comptroller and Auditor General. Appropriation Accounts can be scrutinised by the Committee of Public Accounts, although it usually does so only for those accounts where the C&AG's audit certificate is qualified in some way.

(vi) Resource Accounting and Budgeting

The main change, compared with the current system, is a move to accruals accounting similar to that used in commercial organisations, where expenditure is recognised when the service concerned is provided or received, rather than when the money changes hands. In particular, this means that capital equipment is charged over the useful life of the asset, rather than all at once at the time of purchase. In addition, a balance sheet recognises the value of the assets held as well as cash balances. Departments will also be charged 6 per cent each year on the value of their assets, to recognise that such holdings increase the national debt. The effect on the Estimates system is that each year Parliament will be asked not only to approve a cash total (the amount authorised to be spent in that year), but also resource totals for the amount to be used. There will be one cash total for each of about 58 departments [13] and one or more resource totals (a "request for resources" or RfR). Many departments (44 of the 58) will have only one RfR, but some have up to five; the total number of RfRs planned is currently 84.[14] Each will have its own ambit, and RfRs therefore correspond fairly closely to the existing Votes.[15] The object of the move to RAB is to allow decisions to be taken on a basis, which reduces distortions between capital and current expenditure and recognises the value of assets.

---

[13] including six pension funds
[14] These figures are from Annex C of a Treasury Memorandum of 17 May 2000 published as Appendix 1 to the Liaison Committee, Third Report, Session 1999–2000, *Resource Accounting and Budgeting*, HC 841.
[15] Parliament will also approve a figure for Appropriations in Aid corresponding to each RfR and also one figure for each department of "non-operating Appropriations in Aid", where income arises in cash but not resource terms (e.g. the sale of an asset).

Bibliography

Publications and Articles

Adonis, A., (1994) *Parliament Today*, Manchester University Press: Manchester

Arter, D., (2000), *The Model for Parliaments in the Future? The Case of the Finnish Committee for the Future*, Paper presented to the Fourth Workshop of Parliamentary Scholars and Parliamentarians, Wroxton College, August

Ashley, J., (2000), *I Spy Strangers: Improving Access to Parliament*, Hansard Society: London

Bach, S., (1999), 'The office of the Speaker in Comparative Perspective', in *The Uneasy Relationships Between Parliamentary Members and Leaders, Special Issue of the Journal of Legislative Studies*, Vol. 5., Nos. 3/4

Baker, A., (2000), *Prime Ministers and the Rule Book*, Politicos: London

Bailey, S. D., (1954), *The Future of the House of Lords*, Hansard Society: London

Banham., J., (1995), *The Anatomy of Change: Blueprint for a new era*, Weidenfeld & Nicholson: London

Beattie, A., (1995), 'Ministerial Responsibility and the Theory of the British State', in Rhodes, R.A.W. and Dunleavy, P. (eds) in *The Prime Minister, Cabinet and the Core Executive*, Macmillan: London

Bergman, T., & Damgaard, E., (eds), *Delegation and Accountability in European Integration, Special edition of the Journal of Legislative Studies*, Vol. 6, No. 1

Beyme, K. von, (2000), *Parliamentary Democracy: Democratization, Destabilization, Reconsolidation 17891–1999*, Macmillan: Basingstoke

Black, R. W., (2000), *Supporting Democratic Scrutiny by Public Audit*, Public Management and Policy Association: London

Bogdanor, V., (1997), *Power and the People*, Gollancz: London

Bogdanor, V., (1997), 'Ministerial Accountability', *Under the Scott Light British Government seem through the Scott Report – Special Edition of Parliamentary Affairs*, Vol. 50, No. 1

Brazier, A., (2000), *Parliament and the Public Purse: Improving Financial Scrutiny*, Hansard Society Commission Discussion Paper 3, Hansard Society: London

Brazier, A., (2000), *Systematic Scrutiny: Reforming the Select Committees*, Hansard Society Scrutiny Commission, Discussion Paper 1, Hansard Society: London

Brazier, R., (1997), *Ministers of the Crown*, Clarendon: Oxford

Burnham, J., & Jones, G., (2000), *Accounting to Parliament by British Prime Ministers: Trends and Discontinuities; Illusions and Realities*, Paper presented to the PSA 50th Annual Conference, 10–13 April 2000

Lord Butler of Brockwell, 'Foreword' in Baker, A., (2000), *Prime Ministers and the Rule Book*, Politico's: London

Butler, D., Adonis, A., & Travers, T., (1994), *Failure in British Government: The Politics of the Poll Tax*, Oxford University Press: Oxford

Butler, D., & Butler, G., (2000), *Twentieth Century British Political Facts*, Macmillan: London

Cocker, P., (1994), *Modern British Politics and Government*, Hodder and Stoughton (Publishers) Ltd: London

Coleman, S., (1999), *Electronic Media, Parliament and the People*, Hansard Society: London

Coleman, S., (ed), (1999), *Parliament in the Age of the Internet*, Oxford University Press in association with the Hansard Society: Oxford

Coleman, S., (2000), *A Review of the National Discussion on the Reform of the Second Chamber*, Hansard Society: London

Coleman, S., (2000), *Sounding out the Public: A Review of the National Discussion on the Reform of the Second Chamber*, Hansard Society: London

Coleman, S. and Normann, E., (2000), *New Media and Social Inclusion*, Hansard Society: London

Commission to Strengthen Parliament, (2000), *Strengthening Parliament*, chaired by Lord Norton of Louth, Conservative Party

Constitution Unit, (1996), *Delivering Constitutional Reform*, Constitution Unit, London

Corder, H., *et al*, (2000), *Report on Parliamentary Oversight and Accountability*, Report presented to the South African Parliament

Cowley, P., (1997), *Unbridled Passions? Free votes, issues of conscience, and the accountability of Members of Parliament*, Paper presented to the Second Workshop of Parliamentary Scholars and Parliamentarians, Wroxton College, August

Cowley, P., (ed), (1998), *Conscience and Parliament*, Frank Cass: London

Cowley, P., & Norton, P., (1998), *Rebelliousness in the British House of Commons*, Paper presented to the Third Workshop of Parliamentary Scholars and Parliamentarians, Wroxton College, August

Cowley, P., (2000), *Can sheep bark? British Labour MPs and the modification of Government policy*, Paper presented to the Fourth Workshop of Parliamentary Scholars and Parliamentarians, Wroxton College, August

Crick, B., (1970), *The Reform of Parliament*, Weidenfeld and Nicholson: London

Dainith, T and Page A., (2000), *The Executive in the Constitution*, Oxford University Press: Oxford

Drewry, G., (ed) (1989) *The New Select Committees: A study of the 1979 Reforms*, Clarendon Press: Oxford

Dunleavy, P., (1995), *Re-inventing Parliament: Making The Commons More Effective*, Charter 88/Democratic Audit: London

Erskine May, (1997) *Parliamentary Practice*, 22nd Edition, Butterworths: London

Evans, P., (1999), *Handbook of House of Commons Procedure*, Vacher Dod: London

Fabian Society, *Paying for Progress: Commission on Taxation and Citizenship*, Fabian Society: London

Fatchett, D., (1994), *Reforming the Commons*, Fabian Society: London

Finer, S. E., (1956), 'The Individual Responsibility of Ministers', *Public Administration*, Vol. 34

Flinders, M., (2000), 'The politics of accountability: A case study of Freedom of Information Legislation in the United Kingdom', *Political Quarterly*, Vol. 71, No. 4

Flinders, M., (2000), 'The Enduring Centrality of Individual Ministerial Responsibility Within the British Constitution', *Journal of Legislative Studies*, Vol.6, No. 3

Flinders, M., (2001), 'Mechanisms of Judicial Accountability in British Central Government', *Parliamentary Affairs*, Vol. 54, No. 1

Flinders, M., (2000), *Shifting the Balance? Parliament, the Executive and the British Constitution*, Paper submitted to the Commission

Foster, C. D., (2000), *Two Concepts of Accountability: Is a bridge between them possible?*, Public Management and Policy Association: London

Garrett, J., (1992), *Westminster: Does Parliament Work?*, Victor Gollancz: London

Giddings, P., (1994) 'Select committees and Parliament Scrutiny: Plus Ca Change', *Parliamentary Affairs*, Vol. 47, No.4

Giddings, P., (1997), 'Parliament and the Executive', *Under the Scott Light: British Government seem through the Scott Report – Special Edition of Parliamentary Affairs*, Vol. 50, No. 1

Giddings, P., (1998), 'The Parliamentary Ombudsman: a successful alternative?', in Oliver, D., & Drewry, G., (eds for the Study of Parliament Group), *The Law and Parliament*, Butterworths: London

Griffith, J.A.G. & Ryle, M., (1988), *Parliament: Functions, Practice and Procedure*, Sweet & Maxwell: London

Hadfield, B (ed) (1995) *Judicial Review: A Thematic Approach*, Gill and Macmillan: Dublin

Hansard Society, (1992), *Making the Law: Report of the Hansard Society Commission on the Legislative Process*, Hansard Society: London

Hansard Society, (1996) *The Report of the Commission on the Regulation of Privatised Utilities*, Chaired by John Flemming FBA, Hansard Society/European Policy Forum: London

Hanson, AH; Crick, B (eds), (1970), *The Commons in Transition*, Collins Clear-Type Press: London and Glasgow

Hayward, J., (ed), (1995), *The Crisis of Representation in Europe*, Frank Cass: London

Hazell, R., (1999), *Constitutional Futures: A History of the Next Ten Years*, Oxford University Press: Oxford

Hennessy, P., (1995), *The Hidden Wiring, Unearthing the British Constitution*, Indigo: London

Hennessy, P., (1996), *Muddling Through: Power, Politics and the Quality of Government in Postwar Britain*, Indigo: London

Hennessy, P., (1999), *The Blair Centre: A question of command and control?*, Public Management Foundation: London

Hennessy, P., 'Why Mr Blair's premiership will end in tears', *Independent*, 20 May 2000

Hunt, T., 'Time for Labour to have the courage of its convictions', *Times*, 16 December 2000

Jones, G., (2000), *The Political Behaviour of Australian MPs on Parliamentary Committees: A 'New Institutional' Perspective*, Paper delivered to the Fourth Workshop of Parliamentary Scholars and Parliamentarians at Wroxton College, August

Joseph Rowntree Reform Trust, (2000), *State of the Nation Poll October 2000*, conducted by ICM

Judge, D., (1993), *The Parliamentary State*, Sage: London

Kavanagh, D., & Seldon, A., (1999), *The Powers Behind the Prime Minister*, Harper Collins: London,

King, A., (1976), "Modes of Executive-Legislative Relations: Great Britain, France and West Germany", *Legislative Studies Quarterly*, Vol. 1, No. 1

Laundy, P., *Parliament and the People: The reality and the public perception*, Ashgate: Aldershot

Leigh, D., & Vulliamy, E., (1997), *Sleaze: The Corruption of Parliament*, 4th Estate: London

Longley, L. D., & Davidson, R. H., (1998), *The New Roles of Parliamentary Committees*, Frank Cass: London

McDonald, O., (1989), *Parliament at Work*, Methuen: London

McKie, David., (1999), *Media Coverage of Parliament*, Hansard Society: London

Mancuso, M., (1995), *The Ethical World of British MPs*, McGill-Queen's University Press

Marquand, D., (1988), *The Unprincipled Society*, Fontana: London

Marr, A., (1995), *Ruling Britannia: The Failure and Future of British Democracy*, Michael Joseph: London

Marshall, G., (ed), (1989), *Ministerial Responsibility*, Oxford University Press: Oxford

Milburn, A., (3 March 1999), *Speech to the Trades Union Congress*

Mill, J. S., (1972), *Utilitarianism, Liberty, Representative Government: Selections from Auguste Comte and Positivism*, Everyman's Library: London

Muller, W. C., & Saalfeld, T., (eds), (1997), *Members of Parliament in Western Europe: Roles and Behaviour*, Frank Cass: London

Negrine, R., (1998), *Parliament and the Media: A study of Britain, Germany and France*, RIIA: London

Negrine, R., (1996), *The Communication of Politics*, Sage: London

Nicholson, I.F., 'Another view of Crichel Down, in Marshall, G., Ed., (1989), *Ministerial Responsibility*, Oxford University Press: Oxford,

Norton, P., (1981), 'The House of Commons and the Constitution: The challenges of the 1970s', *Parliamentary Affairs*, Vol. 34

Norton, P., (1991), *The British Polity*, Second Edition, Longman Publishing Group: New York

Norton, P., (1992), 'From overlooked to overworked', in B. Jones & L. Robins, *Two Decades in British Politics*, Manchester University Press: Manchester

Norton, P., (1993), *Does Parliament Matter?*, Harvester Wheatsheaf: London

Norton, P., (ed), (1998), *National Parliaments and the European Union*, Frank Cass: London

Norton, P., (1997), 'UK: Restoring Confidence?' in *Parliaments and Publics – Special Edition of Parliamentary Affairs*, Vol. 50, No. 3

Norton, P. (1998), *Parliaments and Governments in Western Europe*, Frank Cass: London

Norton, P., (1998), *The Consequences of Devolution*, King-Hall Paper No 6, Hansard Society: London

Norton, P., & Wood, D., (1994), *Back from Westminster*, Kentucky University Press

Power, G., (1996), *Reinventing Westminster: The MP's role and reform of the House of Commons*, Charter88: London

Power, G., (1998), *Representatives of the People? MPs and their constituents*, Fabian Society: London

Power, G., (2000), *Creating a Working Parliament: Reform of the Commons Chamber*, Hansard Society: London

Power, G., (2000), *Parliamentary Scrutiny of Draft Bills*, Constitution Unit/Hansard Society: London.

Power, G., (ed), (2000), *Under Pressure: Are we getting the most from our MPs?*, Hansard Society: London

Radice, L., Vallance, E., & Willis, V., (1987), *Member of Parliament: The job of a backbencher*, Macmillan: Basingstoke

Rhodes, R.A.W., & Dunleavy, P., (eds), (1995) *Prime Minister, Cabinet and the Core Executive*, Macmillan: London

Rhodes, R.A.W., (2000), *The Governance Narrative: Key Findings and Lessons from the ESRC's Whitehall Programme*, Public Management and Policy Association: London

Rhodes, R.A.W., (2000), 'New Labour's Civil Service: Summing-up joining-up', *Political Quarterly*, Vol. 71, No. 2

Richard, I., & Welfare, D., (1999), *Unfinished Business: Reforming the House of Lords*, Vintage: London

Riddell, P., (1993), *Honest Opportunism: The rise of the career politician*, Hamish Hamilton: London

Riddell, P., (1998), *Parliament Under Pressure*, Victor Gollancz: London

Ridley, F. & Rush, M., (1994), *British Government and Politics since 1945: Changes in Perspective: Special Edition of Parliamentary Affairs*, Vol. 47, No. 4

Rush, M., (1981), *Parliamentary Government in Britain*, Pitman: London

Russell, M., (2000), *Reforming the House of Lords: Lessons from Overseas*, Oxford University Press: London

Ryle, M, & Richards, P.G., (1988), *The Commons under Scrutiny*, Routledge: London

Ryle, M., (1997), 'Introduction: An Investigation into Select Committees', *Contemporary British History*, Vol. 11, No. 3

Saalfield, T., (2000), 'Members of Parliament and Governments in Western Europe: Agency relations and problems of oversight', *European Journal of Political Research*, 37: 353–376

Searing, D., (1994), *Westminster's World: Understanding Political Roles*, Harvard University Press: Cambridge, Mass.

Shell, D., (1998), *Bi-cameralism Reconsidered*, Paper presented to the Third Workshop of Parliamentary Scholars and Parliamentarians, Wroxton College, August

Shell, D., & Giddings, P.,(1999), *The Future of Parliament – Reform of the Second Chamber*, King Hall Paper 8, Hansard Society: London

Skelcher, C., Weir, S., & Wilson, L., (2000), *Advance of the Quango State*, Local Government Information Unit: London

Silk, P and Walters, R., (1999), *How Parliament Works*, Longman: London

St. John Stevas, N., (ed) (1965) *Bagehot's Historical Essays*, Doubleday: London

Taylor, E., (1963), *The House of Commons at Work*, Pelican: Aylesbury

Theakston, K., (1995), *The Civil Service since 1945*, Blackwell: Oxford

Tyrie, A., (2000), *Mr Blair's Poodle: An Agenda for Reviving the House of Commons*, Centre for Policy Studies: London

Walkland, S. A., (1979), *The House of Commons in the Twentieth Century*, Clarendon Press: Oxford

Walkland and Ryle., (1977), *The Commons in the Seventies*, Fontana: London

Weir, S. & Beetham, D., (1999), *Political Power and Democratic Control in Britain*, Routledge: London,

Weir, S., & Wright, T., (1996), *Power to the Back Benches? Restoring the Balance between Parliament and Government*, Democratic Audit: London

Wintour, P., 'MPs look into Blair's secret department', *Guardian*, 24 June 2000

Wober, J.M., (2000), *Watching Parliament on TV – The Views from Scotland, England, Wales and Northern Ireland*, The Scottish Parliament Programme

Woodhouse, D., (1994), *Ministers and Parliament*, OUP: Oxford

Woodhouse, D., (1997), 'Ministerial Responsibility: Something Old, Something New', *Public Law*, Summer

Wright, T., (1994), *Citizens and Subjects: An essay on British Politics*, Routledge: London

Wright, T. & Marquand, D., (1996), 'Commentary: Reinventing Parliament', *Political Quarterly*, Vol. 67, No. 2

Wright, T., (Ed), (2000), *The British Political Process*, Routledge: London

Government and Parliamentary Publications

Cabinet Office,(1988), *Improving Management in Government: the Next Steps'*.

Cabinet Office, (1992), *Questions of Procedure for Ministers*, HMSO

Cabinet Office, (1993), *Open Government*, Cm 2290, HMSO

Cabinet Office, (1997), Ministerial Code: *A code of Conduct and Guidance on Proceedings of Ministers*

Cabinet Office/OPS (1997), *Departmental Evidence and Response to Select Committees*, (Machinery of Government and Standards Group)

Cabinet Office, (2000), *Review of the Public Sector Ombudsman in England*

Cabinet Office/Performance and Innovation Unit, (2000), *Wiring It Up, Whitehall's management of Cross-Cutting Policies and Services*

Committee of Public Accounts, (1993–94), *The Proper Conduct of Public Business*, HC 154

Committee of Public Accounts, (1993–94), *Looking after the Financial Affairs of People with Mental Incapacity*

Committee of Public Accounts, (1997–98), *HM Treasury: Resource Accounting and Resource-Based Supply*, HC 731

Committee of Public Accounts, (1998–99), thirty-fifth report: *Public Trust Office: Protecting the Financial Welfare of People with Mental Incapacity*

Committee of Public Accounts, (1999–2000), twenty-fourth report: *The Passport Delays of Summer 1999*

Education and Employment Select Committee, (1998–9), *The Work of Ofsted*, HC 884

Environment Transport and Regional Affairs Select Committee, Session 1999–2000, *Audit Commission*, HC174-I.

HM Government (1999), *The Government's Annual Report 98/99*, The Stationery Office Limited, London

HM Treasury (1997), *Output and Performance Analysis: Official Guidance*

HM Treasury (1998), *Code for Fiscal Stability*

HM Treasury (2000), *Resource Accounting Manual*

House of Commons, (2000), *Standing Orders of the House of Commons: Public Business*, HC 518

House of Commons Library Research Paper, (1996), *Special Standing Committees in both Houses*, 96/14

House of Commons Library Research Paper, (1996), *Forms of Investigatory Inquiry & the Scott Inquiry*, 96/22

House of Commons Library Research Paper, (1996), *The Collective Responsibility of Ministers: An Outline of the Issues*, 96/55

House of Commons Library Research Paper, (1997), *The Accountability Debate: Next Steps Agencies*, 97/4

House of Commons Library Research Paper, (1997), *Aspects of Parliamentary Reform*, 97/64

House of Commons Library Research Paper, (1997), *Parliamentary Reform: the Commons 'Modernisation' Programme*, 97/107

House of Commons Library Research Paper, (1998), *The Scotland Bill: Devolution and Scotland's Parliament*, 98/1

House of Commons Library Research Paper, (1998), *The Scotland Bill: Some Operational Aspects of Scottish Devolution*, 98/2

House of Commons Library Research Paper, (1998), *The Scotland Bill: Some Constitutional and Representational Aspects*, 98/3

House of Commons Library Research Paper, (1998), *Lords Reform: The Legislative Role of the House of Lords*, 98/103

House of Commons Library Research Paper, (1999), *The House of Lords Bill: Options for 'Stage Two'*, 99/6

House of Commons Library Research Paper, (2000), *Lords Reform: Major developments since the House of Lords Act 1999*, 00/60

House of Commons Library Research Paper, (2000), *Lords Reform: The Interim House – background statistics*, 00/61

House of Commons Library Research Paper, (2000), *Shifting Control? Aspects of the executive-parliamentary relationship*, 00/92

Liaison Committee, (1982–83), *The Select Committee System*, HC 92

Liaison Committee, (1996–97), *The Work of Select Committees, Volume 1*, HC 323-1

Liaison Committee, (1999–2000), *Shifting the Balance: Select committees and the Executive*, HC 300

Liaison Committee, (1999–2000), *Independence or Control?*, HC 748

Lord Chief Justice Scott, Chairman, (1995–6) *Report of the Inquiry into the Export of Defence Equipment and Dual-Use Goods to Iraq and Related Prosecutions*, HC 115

National Audit Office : *Looking after the Financial Affairs of People with Mental Incapacity*, London HC 258, 4 March 1994

National Audit Office: *Protecting the Financial Welfare of People with Mental Incapacity*, Session 1998–99, HC 206, 12 February 1999.

National Audit Office: *Resource Accounting and Budgeting in Government*, Report by the Comptroller and Auditor General, Session 1994–95, HC 123, 1995

Public Service Committee, (1995–96), *Ministerial Accountability and Responsibility*, HC 313-I

Public Service Committee, (1995–96), *First special report: Government Response to the Second Report from the Committee on Ministerial Accountability and Responsibility*, HC 67

Public Service Committee (1996–97), *Ministerial Accountability and Responsibility*, HC 234

Procedure Committee, (1984–85), *Public Bill Procedure*, HC 49-1

Procedure Committee, (1977–98), First Report HC 588-1

Procedure Committee, (1989–90), *The Working of the Select Committee system*, HC 19-I

Procedure Committee, (1994–95), *Prime Minister's Questions*, HC 555

Procedure Committee, (1998–99), *The Procedural Consequences of Devolution*, HC 185

Procedure Committee, (1998–99), *The Procedural Consequences of Devolution: Government Response to the Fourth Report from the Committee*, HC 814

Procedure Committee, (1998–99), *The Procedure for Debate on the Government's Expenditure Plans*, HC 295

Procedure Committee, (1999–2000), *Deadlines for Tabling of Oral Questions*, HC 735

Procedure Committee, (1999–2000), *Delegated Legislation*, HC 48

Procedure Committee, (1999–2000), *Letters sent by Ministers following undertakings in Debates*, HC 734

Procedure Committee, (1999–2000), *Programming of Legislation and Timing of Votes*, HC 589

Procedure Committee, First Special Report, (1999–2000), *Government Response to the Sixth Report of Session 1998–99: Procedure for Debate on the Government's Expenditure Plans*, HC 388

Review Body on Senior Salaries, (2001), *Report No. 47: Review of parliamentary pension scheme*, Cm 4996

Review Body on Senior Salaries, (2001), *Report No. 48: Review of parliamentary pay and allowances, Vol. 1: Report*, Cm 4997-I

Review Body on Senior Salaries, (2001), *Report No. 48: Review of parliamentary pay and allowances, Vol. 2: Independent Study of pay and allowances*, Cm 4997-II

Review of Management and Services: Report to the House of Commons Commission by a team led by Mr Michael Braithwaite, July 1999, HC 745

Royal Commission on the Reform of the House of Lords, (2000), *A House for the Future*, Chaired by Rt. Hon Lord Wakeham, Cm 4534

Scottish Office, *Shaping Scotland's Parliament, A Summary of the Report of the Consultative Steering Group on the Scottish Parliament*

Select Committee on the Modernisation of the House of Commons, (1997–98), *The Legislative Process*, HC 190

Select Committee on the Modernisation of the House of Commons, (1997–98), *Explanatory Material for Bills*, HC 389

Select Committee on the Modernisation of the House of Commons, (1997–98), *Carry-Over of Public Bills*, HC 543

Select Committee on the Modernisation of the House of Commons, (1998–99), First Report, *The Parliamentary Calendar: Initial proposals*, HC 60

Select Committee on the Modernisation of the House of Commons, (1998–99), Second Report, *Sittings of the House in Westminster Hall*, HC 194

Select Committee on the Modernisation of the House of Commons, (1999–2000), First Report, *Programming of Legislation and Timing of Votes*, HC 589

Select Committee on the Modernisation of the House of Commons, (1999–2000), Fourth Report, *Sittings in Westminster Hall*, HC 906

Select Committee on the Modernisation of the House of Commons, (1999–2000), Third Report, *Thursday Sittings*, HC 954

Select Committee for the Parliamentary Commissioner for Administration, (1994–95), *The Child Support Agency*, HC 199.

Select Committee for the Parliamentary Commissioner for Administration, (1994–1995), HC 135

Select Committee on Public Administration, (1997–98), *Ministerial Accountability and Parliamentary Questions*, Fourth Report, HC 820

Select Committee on Public Administration, (1997–98), *Your Right to Know: the Government's Proposals for a Freedom of Information Act*, HC 398-II

Select Committee on Public Administration, (1998–99), *Quangos* HC 209-I

Select Committee on Public Administration, (1999–2000), *Report of the Parliamentary Ombudsman for 1998–9*, HC 106

Select Committee on Public Administration, (1999–2000) *Administrative Failure: Inherited SERPS*, HC 433

Select Committee on Public Administration, (1999–2000), *Review of Public Sector Ombudsmen in England*, HC 612

Select Committee on Sittings of the House, (1991–92), *Select Committee on Sittings of the House*, HC 20-I

Social Security Select Committee (1995–96), *The Performance and Operation of the Child Support Agency*, HC 50

Social Security Select Committee (1998–99), *The 1999 Child Support White Paper*, HC 798

Treasury and Civil Service Committee (1985–86), *Civil servants and ministers*, HC 92

Treasury and Civil Service Committee (1989–90), *Progress in the Next Steps Initiative*, HC 496

Treasury and Civil Service Committee (1990–91), *The Next Steps Initiative*, HC 481

Treasury and Civil Service Committee (1996–97), *Resource Accounting and Budgeting*, HC 186

Treasury and Civil Service Committee (1993–94), *The Role of the Civil Service*, HC 27-I

Index

Numbers in *italics* refer to Figures

Accommodation, Commons Select Committee 21
accountability
    defining 1-2
    enforcing 43-4
Accounting Officers 174
accruals accounting 178
adjournment debates 50, 51, 55, 56, 94
Adonis, A. 32
Age Concern 22, 39, 41, 81, 123
Agriculture, Commons Select Committee reports
    166
Alexander, Douglas, MP 125
All-Party Parliamentary Group on Domestic
    Violence 85
Allen, Graham, MP 125
ambits 177
Animals in Scientific Procedures, Lords *ad hoc*
    Committee 73, 75, 77, 111
annual reports 86, 88, 113
Annually Managed Expenditure (AME) 176
appropriation 177
Appropriation Accounts 178
Appropriation Act 177
"appropriations in aid" 177
Audit Commission 67, 69, 101, 111
audit inquiries 66, 69, 110
backbenchers
    pursuit of issues 115
    and questions 52, 54
    structure of debate in the chamber 49
Badawi, Zeinab ix
Bagehot, Walter: *The English Constitution* 114
Baker, Kenneth 118
Baldwin, Dr Nicholas 14, 33, 123
BBC Parliament 81, 84
Beckett, Rt Hon Margaret, MP vii, 13n, 98, *98*, 125
Beith, Rt Hon Alan, MP ix
Benefit Agency (BA) *74*
Benn, Rt Hon Tony, MP 82, 125
Bennett, Andrew, MP 125
Blackman, Richard 126
Blair, Rt Hon Tony, MP 6
Blunkett, David, MP *105*
Boothroyd, Rt Hon Betty, MP viii, 47, 58, 80
Brazier, Alex ix
Bridges, Sir Edward 116
British Social Attitudes Survey 9
Brittan, Leon 117
Brixton Prison 118
Broadcasting, Commons Select Committee 21
Brooke, Rt Hon Peter, MP 125
Brown, Professor Alice ix
Budget 174-5
Budget Report 175
Budget (Scotland) Bill (2001) 64
Burnham, J. 6
Burns, Lord, GCB ix, *103*
business plans 35, 44
Butler, D. 32
Butler, Robin (Lord Butler of Brockwell) 121

Byatt, Sir Ian 7, 29, 37-8
Byers, Stephen, MP 80
Cabinet
    Committee on Expenditure 174
    and MPs' ambitions 18
Cabinet Office 6, 57, 119
Centre for Management and Policy Studies 5
chamber, the (House of Commons)
    in decline 46
    failure to adapt 47-9
    the importance of 58
    improving questions and answers 56-8
        oral questions 57-8
        Prime Minister's Questions (PMQs) 56-7
        written questions 58
    mechanisms for accountability in 50-53
        debates 50-51
        questions and statements 51-3
    one day each week for committee activity 54, 59,
        109
    plenary session of the Parliament 53, 59, 109
    recommendations 59
    reform 53-6
        debates on committee reports 56
        more statements, fewer debates 54-5
        public interest debates 55
        shortening hours 54, 83
        time limits and order of speakers 56
    role of the chamber – the importance of party
        politics 46-7
    should remain central to accountability xii, 46-59
    sitting days/hours 47-8, *48*, 79
Chancellor of the Exchequer 174, 175
Charter88 123
'Chatham House rule' vii
Chester, Norman 51
Chief Secretary 174
Child Support Agency (CSA) 55, 89, 94-7, 101
'Citizen Audit' 9
Citizen's Charter 1, 9
citizens' juries 1
civil service 2, 90
Civil Service Code 120
Clark, David, MP 58
Code of Fiscal Stability, The 174
Code of Practice on Access to Government
    Information 120
Code of Practice on Open Government (1994) 58,
    59, 104, 110
Coleman, Dr Stephen 79
Commission on Parliamentary Scrutiny
    discussion papers viii
    established (September 1999) vii
    meetings of the Commission 125-7
    membership ix
    method of inquiry and research vii-viii
    seven principles for reform x-xiii, 107-13
        Principle 1: Parliament at the apex xi, 11-12,
            13, 89-106, 107
        Principle 2: Parliament must develop a culture
            of scrutiny xi, 14-28, 107

Principle 3: committees should play a more
    influential role within Parliament xi, 19,
    29-45, 107-9
Principle 4: the chamber should remain central
    to accountability xii, 46-59
Principle 5: financial scrutiny should be central
    to accountability xii, 60-69, 110-11
Principle 6: the House of Lords should
    complement the Commons xii, 70-77, 111-12
Principle 7: Parliament must communicate
    more effectively with the public xiii, 78-88,
    112-13
sub-groups vii, viii
survey of MPs' attitudes to Parliament viii, x,
    10-11, *11*, 16-17, 23, 43, 50, 80, 128-55
vision of parliamentary accountability 121-2
written evidence submitted to the Commission
    123-4
*Parliament and the Public Purse: Improving Financial
    Scrutiny* (discussion paper) viii
commissioners 101
commissions 1, 102-4
Commonwealth Parliamentary Association viii
Comprehensive Spending Review 175-6
Comptroller and Auditor General (C&AG) 68, 100,
    174, 178
Conservative Government: budget 174
Consolidated Fund (Appropriation) Bill 177
Consolidated Fund Bills 177
Consolidated Fund Standing Services 177
constituencies
    interests of 17
    MPs' role 17, 18, 55
constituency Fridays 54
constitution 1
Constitution, Lords Select Committee 73
constitutional legislation (1997-2000) *3*
constitutional reform 3-4, 6
Consultative Steering Group: Financial Issues
    Advisory Group 63
Consumers' Association 29, 123
Coote, Anna ix
Corner, David 126
Council of Ministers (EU) 4, 5, 75
Council Tax 177
Council Tax Benefit *74*
Court of Protection 91, 93
courts: challenging Government decisions 1, 9, 105
Cranborne, Rt Hon Viscount 125
*Creating a Working Parliament: Reforming the
    Commons Chamber* (Commission on Parliamentary
    Scrutiny discussion paper) viii
Crichel Down, Dorset case (1950-54) 116-17
Crick, Bernard 115, 122
crime 9
cross-cutting 73, 74, *74*
cross-party activity xi, xii, 20, 25, 32, 55, 59, 71, 110,
    115
Cryer, Ann, MP 123
Culture, Media and Sport, Commons Select
    Committee reports 166
Curran, Margaret, MSP 126
Currie, Edwina 117
Data Protection Act (1998) 104

Data Protection Commission (DPC) 7, 12
Data Protection Commissioner 7, 33, 103, 104
Davey, Ed, MP 125
Davies, Howard *103*
Davis, Rt Hon David, MP 67, 92, 125
debates 50-51, 54-5, 78, 79
    adjournment 50, 51, 55, 56, 94, 100
    committee reports 34, 56
    emergency 54
    and the introduction of Westminster Hall 48
    Opposition Day Debates 50, 51, 54, 55, 59
    order of speakers 56
    party political 47
    and the Prime Minister 6
    public interest xii, 55, 59, 110
    short 54, 55, 59, 109
    structure in the chamber 49
    timing 15, 56
    topical 10
Defence, Commons Select Committee 37
    reports 167
democracy
    direct 1
    parliamentary 1, 116
departmental allocations 66, 69, 110
departmental budgets 61, 110
Departmental Expenditure Limits (DELs) 176
departmental reports 35, 44
devolution 3, 4, 73
dissemination 80
dual-purposes committees 41, 45, 109
Dugdale, Thomas 117
Dunwoody, Gwyneth, MP 125
Early Day Motions 55
ECHR *see* European Convention on Human Rights
Economic Affairs, Lords Select Committee 73
Economic and Fiscal Strategy Report 175
Economic and Social Research Council (ESRC) 9
Edmonds, David 8, 103
Education and Employment, Commons Select
    Committee 7, 22, 74
    reports 167
Education and Employment, Department for
    (DFEE) *74*
emergency debates 54
Employment Service (ES) *74*
Environment, Transport and Regional Affairs,
    Commons Select Committee (ETRA) 31, 37, 67,
    100, 158
    reports 167-8
    *Meeting with the European Commission Officials to
        Discuss Air Transport* 158
Environment, Transport and the Regions,
    Department of 22, *100*
Environmental Audit, Commons Select Committee
    33, 157
    reports 156, 172
Equal Opportunities Commission 85, 123
Erskine May 52
ESRC *see* Economic and Social Research Council
Estimates 60-63, 66, 68, 69, 110
    departmental spending 176-7
    procedures 177-8
Estimates Days 60

European Communities, Lords Select Committee 75
European Convention on Human Rights (ECHR) 3, 4
European Economic Community (EEC) 75
European Scrutiny, Commons Select Committee 75
European Scrutiny Reserve 75
European Union
    Council of Ministers 4, 5
    and the House of Commons 5, 75, 77, 112
    scrutiny by the House of Lords 5, 75, 77, 112
European Union, Lords Select Committee 73, 75
executive agencies xi, 1, 2-3, 35, 44, 89, 90-101, 105
executive/legislature distinction 16
Falconer of Thoroton, Lord 72
Ferguson, Patricia, MSP 126
Field, Rt Hon Frank, MP 125
Finance and Audit Sub-Committees 66, 69
Financial Issues Advisory Group (FIAG) 63
financial procedures 174-8
    the Budget and forward spending plans 174-5
    control of supply 174
    departmental spending plans 175-6
    Estimates; departmental spending 176-7
    Estimates; Procedures 177-8
    Resource Accounting and Budgeting 178
financial scrutiny xii, 60-69
    authorising Government spending 60-63, *64*
        Estimates and select committees 61-2
        reforming the Estimates 61
        Resource Accounting and Budgeting 62-3
        Scottish Parliament budget procedures 63, *64*
    financial audit and accountability of Government
        expenditure 65-8
        an alternative approach: Finance and Audit
            Sub-Committee 66
        Parliament and the Audit Commission 67
        the Public Accounts Committee and the
            National Audit Office 65
        resources for financial scrutiny 66-7
        the Sharman Report: holding to account 68
Financial Services and Markets Act (2000) *103*
Financial Services Authority (FSA) 103, *103*
Financial Statement 175
Finer, Professor Samuel 117
Fisher, Mark, MP 125
Fitzsimons, Lorna, MP 125
Flinders, Matthew 123
focus groups 1
Foreign Affairs, Commons Select Committee
    reports 168
    Kosovo: Interim Report 158
Foster, Sir Christopher 123, 126
France, Elizabeth 7, 33, 103, 104, 123
freedom of information
    and the Information Commissioner 7
    legislation 3, *36*
Freedom of Information Act (2000) 33, 58, 59, 104, 110
Giddings, Philip 9
Gladstone, William Ewart 174
Government
    announcements 83
    Annual Report 57, 59, 86, 110
    the changing structure of 2-6

the 'agencification' of Government 2-3
    centre of Government 5-6
    constitutional reform 3-4
    Europe 4-5
decisions challenged 1
declining trust in 9
dismissal of 116
expansion of 1
financial scrutiny of *see* financial scrutiny
and the House of Lords 70
influence of Parliament 30
Parliament holds to account xi, 1, 6, 11, 17, 89, 106, 107, 115-16, 122
and Parliament's scrutiny xi, 6, 11, 16, 17, 27, 28, 89, 106, 115
party political battle 16
political appointees 5
the public face of Parliament 46
publications 81
response standards 40, 108, 163-4
scrutiny and accountability 54
Government Accounting 174
Greater London Authority 3
Green Budget 175
Green Party 10, 123
Grice, Paul 126
Griffith, J.A.G. 115
Haldane Committee (1918) 116
Hansard Society
    Commission on Parliamentary Scrutiny
        established vii
    commissions set up in recent years vii
    Hansard and the internet 81
    *Making the Law: Report of the Hansard Society
        Commission on the Legislative Process* vii, 25, 114
    New Media and Social Inclusion 85
    *The Report of the Commission on the Regulation of
        Privatised Utilities* 102
Hazell, Professor Robert ix
Health, Commons Select Committee 67
    reports 168-9
Health Services Ombudsman 32
Heath, Sir Edward 5, 6
Hennessy, Professor Peter 5
Home Affairs, Commons Select Committee 33, 67, 93, *98*, 99, 104
    reports 169
Home Office 97, 98, 99
Home Secretary 99, 118
House of Commons
    annual report 86, 88, 113
    the chamber *see* chamber, the
    clerks' department 42, 43, 45, 109
    culture of 19, 21, 24
    decline in Prime Ministerial attendance 6
    effectiveness 76, 112
    and Estimates 177
    ethos 13-16, 27
    European Union 5, 75, 77, 112
    financial scrutiny by *see* financial scrutiny
    House of Lords should complement xii, 70-77, 111
    institutional structure and parliamentary roles 15-19

lack of trust in 9
legal services 42
Library 42, 66
list of organisations obliged to report to
    Parliament 35, 44, 101, 108
and the media 10, 83, 112
Petitions Committee (proposed) xiii, 87, 88, 113
publications 81
and rapporteur system 38, 108
reform 14, 19, 70
Resolutions 102
and select committees 19, 40-41
Sessional Returns 86
TV broadcasting 78
House of Lords
    ad hoc committees 73, 75, 77, 111
    annual report 86, 88, 113
    clerks' department 42, 43, 45, 109
    complementary and co-ordinated scrutiny 76
    cross-departmental issues 74, 111
    debates 56
    effectiveness 76, 112
    European Union scrutiny 5, 75, 77, 112
    Grand Committee 72, 76
    holding the Government to account 70
    'joined-up' issues 74, 111
    legal services 42
    list of organisations obliged to report to
        Parliament 35, 44, 101, 108
    Lords Committees: existing good practice 73-5
    Norton committee 4
    recommendations 76-7
    reform 3, 4
    role of 70, 111
    scrutiny role 71-3
    should complement the Commons xii, 70-77, 111
    starred questions 40, 71
    unstarred questions 54
housing 9
Housing Benefit *74*
Housing Corporation *100*
Howard, Michael 118
Howe of Aberavon, Rt Hon Lord 123, 125
Howell, Lord 123
human rights (proposed joint committee) 73
Human Rights Act (1998) 33
Hurd, Douglas 104
immigration 9
India: pre-budget inquiries 63
Information, Commons Select Committee 21
Information Commissioner 7
Inglewood, Lord, MEP 123
Insolvency Bill 82
inspectorates/inspectors 1, 30, 33, 89, 101
Institute of Directors 20, 123
Inter-Parliamentary Union viii
International Development, Commons Select
    Committee 157
    reports 169
International Development, Department for 157
internet 81, 84, 85, 88, 112, 113
interpellation 54
Jack, Rt Hon Michael, MP 24, 32, 123
Jackson, Robert, MP ix

Jenkins, Kate ix
Jones, Professor George 6, 123
Jones, Dr Lynne, MP 41, 123
judicial inquiries 30
judicial review 9, 104-5
Justice and Home Affairs Committee (Scottish
    Parliament) 41
Kerr, Andy, MSP 126
King, Professor Anthony 20
Kirkwood, Archy, MP 125
Labour Government
    Comprehensive Spending Review 175
    constitutional reform programme 3
    emphasis on 'joining-up' government 74
    'Modernisation Committee' established 12
    ONE established 74, *74*
    and parliamentary business 16
    spring budget 174
    subject specific committees established 30
Leader of the House of Commons 16
Lean, Andrew 126
legislation
    constitutional (1997-2000) *3*
    scrutiny of 16, 34, 40, 41, 45, 109
    timing 15
Legislative Process, The (HC190) 12
Liable Relatives Unit 97
Liaison, Commons Select Committee vii, xiii, 23, 26
    and committee reports 39, 40
    concordats with select committees 35, *36*
    and dual-purpose committees 41, 45, 109
    and Estimates Days 60
    on ministerial office 22
    monitoring progress over the Parliament 35, 108
    potential of 27
    and press activity 81
    proposed renaming and restructuring 25-8
    and rapporteur system 38
    reports 13, 26, 29
    and select committees' core duties 35, 44
    selection of subjects 31
    Independence or Control? 26
    *Shifting the Balance: Select Committees and the
        Executive* 20, 26, 29, 67, 85
    Shifting the Balance: Unfinished Business 26
Likierman, Andrew 126
Lilley, Rt Hon Peter, MP 125
Linton, Mark, MP 125
local authorities *74*
Local Government self-financed expenditure 177
Lord Chancellor's Department 92, 93
Luff, Peter, MP 125
Lugton, Michael 126
McConaghy, Des 123
McCrone, Professor David 126
Macdonald of Tradeston, Lord 72
McIntosh, Neil 126
Maclennan, Rt Hon Robert, MP vii, 125
McLetchie, David, MSP 126
MacMillan, Joyce 126
Major, John 6, 52, 57
Marshall, Geoffrey 123
Martin, Speaker Michael 52
Mawhood, Caroline 126

Maze Prison 118
media *see* Parliament: the media
Millar, David 5, 39, 123
Millennium Dome 72
ministerial accountability 1-2, 12, 13, 43, 46, 54, 89, 104, 114, 117, 118, 119
Ministerial Code 80
ministerial responsibility doctrine 116-18
    changes to 118-20
ministers
    activity in the Council of Ministers 4
    announcements 80, 83
    and committee reports 40
    daily question time 51
    and executive agencies 3
    and MPs' training 24
    number of 21
    and Opposition Days 55
    questioning 30, 53, 58, 71, 72, 73, 76, 111, 112
    'Questions of Procedure for Ministers' 119
    resignation of 117-18, 120, 121
    statements xii, 52, 55, 83, 87, 112
Modernisation Committee 12, 13
Monetary Policy, Commons Select Committee 161
Moran, Margaret, MP ix
morning sittings 54, 83
Morris, Estelle, MP *105*
MPs
    career paths 16, 21, 28, 107
    Commission's survey viii, ix, 10-11, *11*, 16-17, 23, 43, 50, 80, 128-55
    conflicting pressures on 70
    constituency role 17, 18, 55
    enhancing understanding of parliamentary roles 23-4
    importance of parliamentary roles to 18, *19*
    Opposition 17
    party role 14, 16, 17, 19, 107, 115
    and PMQs 50, 56
    and Private Notice Questions 55
    promotion 16
    scrutiny role xi, 2, 14, 16, 17, 18, *18*, 28, 107
    select committees xi, 18-24, 31, 32, 38, 40, 43, 44, 48, 56, 107
    training 23, 24, 107
    working conditions 13
MSPs viii, 25, 87
Mulligan, Mary, MSP 126
NAO *see* National Audit Office
Naseby, Rt Hon Lord 21, 123
National Audit Office (NAO) x, 32, 42, 60, 65-9, 91, 92, 93, *98*, 99, *100*, 101, 102, 106, 111, 175
national debt 178
National Health Service (NHS) 67, 69
National Insurance Fund 177
National Society for the Prevention of Cruelty to Children 123
National Union of Teachers *105*
NDPBs *see* non-departmental public bodies
Negrine, Dr Ralph 79, 123
New Contract for Welfare: Children's Rights and Parents' Responsibilities, A (Government White Paper) 96
New Zealand: pre-budget inquiries 63

Newton of Braintree, Rt Hon Lord ix, 128
Next Steps agencies 2, 90, 120
No 10 Policy Unit 57
Nolan, Lord 90
non-departmental public bodies (NDPBs) 68, 100, 101, 105
non-governmental organisations (NGOs) 1, 10
Nordic countries 5
Northern Ireland: devolution 3
Northern Ireland Affairs, Commons Select Committee reports 169
Northern Ireland Ombudsman 32
Norton Commission 4, 25, 54, 57
Norton of Louth, Professor the Lord (Philip) 4, 49, 125
O'Brien, Mike, MP *98*
ODPC *see* Office of the Data Protection Commissioner
Office for National Statistics 68, 101, 175
Office of the Data Protection Commissioner (ODPC) 33, 103, 104
Official Solicitor's Office 92
Ofgem (Office of Gas and Electricity Regulation) *102*
OFREG (Office for the Regulation of Electricity and Gas) (Northern Ireland) *102*
Ofsted (Office for Standards in Education) 7, 102
Oftel (Office of Telecommunications) 8, *102*, 123
Ofwat (Office of Water Services) 7, 9-10, 29, 78, *102*, 123
Ombudsman, the *see* Parliamentary Commissioner for Administration
ombudsmen 1, 8-9, *8*, 32, 89
ONE 74, *74*
O'Neill, Martin, MP 80, 125
Opposition Day Debates 50, 51, 54, 55, 59, 94, *98*, 99
Opposition parties
    negotiation with 15
    party political battle 16
    and questions 52, 53
    trading Opposition Days 55, 109
oral questions 51-2
Order of Questions 52
ORR (Office of the Rail Regulator) *102*
outcomes 66, 69, 110
PAC *see* Public Accounts, Commons Select Committee
Parliament
    at the apex of the system of scrutiny xi, 11-12, 13, 89-113
    and the Council of Ministers 5
    defining accountability 1-2
    and dismissal of the Government 116
    dominance of the executive 15
    effectiveness 13, 43
    ethos 18, 21, 23
    and the executive agencies 90-101
        Child Support Agency case history 94-7
        Housing Corporation case history *100*
        Passport Agency case history 97-100
        Public Trust Office case history 91-3
        quangos and non-departmental public bodies 100-101

extra-parliamentary scrutiny 101-5
  the growth of judicial review 104-5
  regulators and inspectorates 102-4
financial scrutiny by *see* financial scrutiny
influence on Government 30
internet 81
leadership and co-ordination in 25
  a parliamentary executive 26-7
  parliamentary steering committee 25-6
list of organisations obliged to report to 35
the media xiii, 10, 78, 79-81, 87, 112
  ministerial announcements 80
  publicity and dissemination 80-81
must develop a culture of scrutiny xi, 28
new forms of accountability and redress 6-9
the parliamentary perspective on accountability
  10-11
petitions 86-7
power of 105
press office (proposed) xiii, 84, 88, 112
and the public xiii, 9-10, 30, 47, 78-88, 107
the public face of 46
publications 81, 85, 88
publicising 84-6
  a designated press office 84
  greater use of the internet 84
  layout of reports 85
  publication of an annual report 86
  systematic consultation 85
recall of 86, 88, 113
reform of 12-13, 27, 47, 56, 106
resourcing of 42, 45, 109
role of 1, 6, 11, 13, 16-19, 27, 89, 106, 107, 110,
  114-15, 116, 122
select committees' role xi, 19
steering committee 19, 25-6, 28, 107
updating parliamentary proceedings 83-4
website 84, 88, 112
*Parliament and the Public Purse: Improving Financial
  Scrutiny* (Commission on Parliamentary Scrutiny
  discussion paper) viii
Parliamentary Commissioner for Administration
  (PCA or Ombudsman) x, 8, 12, 32, 95, *95*, 96,
  100, 101, 106
'parliamentary control of the purse' 174
parliamentary democracy 1, 116
Parliamentary Finance Office (PFO) (proposed) 66,
  69, 111
Parliamentary Office of Science and Technology 42
parliamentary private secretaries (PPSs) 21, 22, 23,
  52, 107
party politics, role of 27, 47
Passport Agency 55, 82, 89, 97-100
payroll vote 21, 22, 28, 107
PCA *see* Parliamentary Commissioner for
  Administration
Performance and Innovation Unit 5
performance indicators 35, 37, 44, 66, 69, 108, 110
Pergau Dam case 104
PES *see* Public Expenditure Survey
petitions 86-7, 113
Petitions Committee (proposed) xiii, 87, 88
petrol crisis (2000) 86
Phippard, Sonia 126

Platt of Whittle, Baroness 123
PMQs *see* Prime Minister's Questions
PNQs *see* Private Notice Questions
police 67, 69
policy announcements 84, 112
political parties
  MPs' role 14, 16, 17
  and organisation of business in the chamber
    15-16, 47
poll tax 32
Power, Greg ix
PPSs *see* parliamentary private secretaries
Pre-Budget Report (Green Budget) 175
press office, Parliament (proposed) xiii, 84, 88, 112
pressure groups 1, 10, 30
Prime Minister
  appearance before a select committee 57, 59
  appoints Ofsted's Chief Inspector 7
  decline in attendance in the Commons 6
  growing influence 6
  the strength of 121
Prime Minister's Office
  and accountability of the Prime Minister 6
  power of 1, 5
Prime Minister's Questions (PMQs) 6, 50, 52, 58,
  59, 78, 79, 110
Prior, James 118
Private Notice Questions (PNQs) xii, 52, 55, 59, 84,
  86, 87, 99, 110, 112
privatisation 7
Privy Councillors 55
Procedure, Commons Select Committee 29, 30, 38,
  54, 63
  The Procedural Consequences of Devolution 4
  *The Procedure for Debate on the Government's
    Expenditure Plans* 61
Project Management Groups 74
PSAs *see* public service agreements
public, the
  declining trust in Government 9
  and Parliament xiii, 9-10, 30, 47, 78-88, 107
  and select committees 44
Public Accounts, Commons Select Committee
  (PAC) 20, 60, 65-9, 91, *95*, 96, 99, *100*, 101, 111,
  161, 174, 175
  'The Passport Delays of Summer 1999' *98*
Public Administration, Commons Select Committee
  5, 13, 157
  and the Cabinet Office 6, 57
  NDPBs 100
  PMQs 52
  reports 32, 172
  State Earnings Related Pension inquiry (2000)
    121
  survey of reports 156
  turnover of membership 22
  written questions 52-3, 58
Public Expenditure Survey (PES) 174, 175
Public Finance and Accountability (Scotland) Act
  (2000) 63
Public Guardianship Office (PGO) 93
public interest debates xii, 59, 455
Public Petitions Committee (Scottish Parliament) 87
Public Service Agreements (PSA) 38, 66, 69, 110

public service charters 9
Public Service Committee 12, 58, 90, 119, 120
Public Trust Office 89, 91-3, 94
publications 81
publicity 80-81
qualified majority voting 4
quangos xi, 1, 35, 44, 100
Question Time 51-2, 57-8, 59, 83, 110
questions 109
  open-ended 56, 59, 110
  oral 51-2, 57-8, 59, 71, 110
  Order of Questions 52
  Prime Minister's Questions (PMQs) 6, 50, 52,
    56-7, 78, 79, 110
  Private Notice Questions (PNQs) xii, 52, 55, 59,
    84, 86, 87, 99, 110
  Scott Report and 53
  starred 40, 71
  topical 71
  unstarred 54
  written 52-3, 58, 59, 71, 110
Quinlan, Sir Michael 53
RAB see Resource Accounting and Budgeting
RADAR (Royal Association of Disability and
  Rehabilitation) 85, 123
Radice, Giles, MP 125
rapporteurs xi, 38, 45, 101, 108
Raynsford, Nick, MP 125
Rebuilding Trust (HL Paper 97) 75
recall of Parliament 86, 88, 113
receiverships 91
Registered Social Landlords (RSLs) 100
regulators xi, 1, 7, 12, 30, 32, 33, 35, 44, 89, 101-5,
  108
Reid, George, MSP 126
request for resources (RfR) 178
research assistants 42
Resource Accounting and Budgeting (RAB) 62-3,
  178
Review Body on Senior Salaries 49
RfR see request for resources
Richards, Steve ix
Riddell, Peter ix
Rippon of Hexham, Lord vii, 114
Robinson, Dr Ann ix
Rodgers of Quarry Bank, Rt Hon Lord 125
Ross-Robertson, Andrea 37, 123
Rossi, Sir Hugh 32
Rossi doctrine 32
Royal Commission on the Reform of the House of
  Lords: A House for the Future 4, 70
Rush, Professor Michael 14, 18, 123
Russell, Muir 126
Rutter, Jill ix
Ryle, Michael 14, 30, 115, 124
Saalfeld, Professor Thomas 15, 124
Sawyer, Lord ix
School Teachers Review Body 105
Science and Technology, Commons Select
  Committee reports 170
Science and Technology, Lords Select Committee
  73, 74
  Air Travel and Health 73
  Complementary and Alternative Medicine 73

Scotland: devolution 3
Scotland Office 4
Scott Report 53, 119, 120
Scottish Affairs, Commons Select Committee 31
  reports 170
Scottish Executive viii, 87
Scottish Parliament viii, 4, 41
  annual report 86
  budget procedures 63, 64
  Bureau 25
  Finance Committee 63, 64
  Public Petitions Committee 87, 88, 113
  Investing in You (expenditure report) 64
  Making a Difference for Scotland (spending plans)
    64
Searing, Donald 15
Second Radcliffe Lecture (1996) 90
select committees xiii, 102
  appointment to 20, 26, 101
  benefits of 30
  chairing 18, 22, 23, 26, 28, 31, 32, 39, 42, 62, 107
  concordat with Liaison Committee 35, 36
  core duties 35, 44, 108, 109
  dual-purpose committees 41, 45, 109
  effectiveness 19, 25, 29, 30, 34, 37, 39, 44, 50, 108
  enhancing 19-23
    committees as an alternative career path 21-3
    committees as forums for parliamentary activity
      20
  ensuring accountability – improving impact 39-40
  and Estimates 61-2
  and executive agencies 3
  Finance and Audit Sub-Committees 66, 69, 110
  and financial scrutiny 31, 32, 61-2, 66
  and government accountability 19
  improving scrutiny 34-5, 36, 37
  internet use 85, 112
  introduced (1979) xi, 13, 19, 20, 29, 49
  and judicial decisions 105
  lack of standardisation 30-31
  list of organisations obliged to report to
    Parliament 35, 44, 108
  making committees relevant to Parliament 40-41
  membership 22, 23, 28, 38, 39, 40
  and MPs 18-24, 31, 32, 38, 40, 43, 44, 48, 56, 115
  and payrole vote 21, 22, 28
  performance indicators 37, 108
  periodic reviews 39, 45, 108
  post-mortem enquiries 32
  powers 39
  and the Prime Minister 57, 59
  and rapporteurs 38, 45, 108
  recommendations
    core duties and performance indicators 44
    developing new methods of work 44-5
    improving impact 45
    integrating committee work into parliamentary
      activity 45
    staffing and support 45
  recording oral evidence sessions on video 84, 87,
    112
  reforms to 19, 29-45
  and regulators 7, 30
  relationship with the Commons chamber 19

reports *31*, 32, 39-42, 44, 45, 56, 81, 85, 88, 108
resources 38, 39, 41-2, 45, 109
role of xi, 19, 29, 30, 35, 44
and scrutiny of legislation 34, 40, 41, 45, 109
staffing 23, 30, 38, 42, 43, 45, 67, 109
strengths of 20, 43
sub-committees xi, 37, 41, 44, 66, 69, 101, 108,
    110
subjects 31
survey of reports 156-73
    approaches to the questionnaire and the
        distribution of subject-matter between
        reports 159
    context 157
    expenditure, administration and policy 159-63
    findings 157-8
    limitations 156-7
    list of reports 166-72
    method 156
    the number of reports 158
    the quality of Government responses 163-4
    questionnaire notes 165-6
    subject-matter of reports 173
systemising scrutiny – improving the coverage of
    select committees 37-8
training 24
the work of the 30-34
    autonomy of committees 31-2
    engagement with external scrutiny bodies 32-3
    impact of committee work 34
Seymour-Ure, Professor Colin ix
Sharman of Redlynch, Lord : *Holding to Account,*
    The Review of Audit and Accountability for Central
    Government report 65, 68, 101
Sheldon, Rt Hon Robert, MP 20, 62, 85, 125
Shepherd, Rt Hon Gillian, MP 125
short debate 54, 55, 59, 109
Social Exclusion Unit 5
Social Security, Commons Select Committee 22, 74,
    85, 94, *95*, 96, 97, 101
    reports 170
Social Security, Department of (DSS) *74*, 97
Speaker, the
    and devolved matters 4
    and Private Notice Questions 52, 55, 59, 84, 87,
        112
    and recall of Parliament 86, 88
Speaker's Office 49
special advisers 42
spending plans 61, 68, 110, 175-6
Spending Review 2000 176
Spring Budget 174, 175
standing committees 5, 15, 41, 48
Standing Orders 177
    No.14 15
    No.24 54, 55
    No.48 174
    No.152A 157
State Earnings Related Pension inquiry (2000) 121
statements xii, 52, 55, 83, 87, 109, 112
Stationery Office 86, 88, 113
Statistics Commission 68, 101
Steel, Sir David, MSP 126

Stem Cell Research, Lords *ad hoc* Committee 73, 75,
    77, 111
Stone, Roy 126
Straw, Jack, MP *98*
Study of Parliament Group 18, 126
Supply Days 60
Sutherland, Sir Stewart 126
Swinney, John, MSP 126
Systematic Scrutiny: Reforming the Select Committees
    (Commission on Parliamentary Scrutiny
    discussion paper) viii
Tanlaw, Lord 124
Tay, Penelope 124
Teachers' Pay Award case 105, *105*
Thatcher, Margaret, Baroness 2
Thomson, Bill 126
Today programme 83
Tosh, Murray, MSP 126
Trade and Industry, Commons Select Committee
    158
    reports 170-71
Travers, T. 32
Treasury *103*, 175, 177
    Budget and Public Finances Directorate 174
Treasury, Commons Select Committee 22, *103*, 161
    reports 171
Treasury Handbook: Supply and other Financial
    Procedures of the House of Commons 174
Treasury and Civil Service, Commons Select
    Committee (TCSC) 117-20
Tross, Jonathan 126
Tyrie, Andrew, MP 125
'usual suspects' 85, 112
utilities, privatised 1, 7, 89, 102
value-for-money inquiries 66, 69, 110
Vibert, Frank 126
virement 177
Votes 177, 178
"Votes on Account" 176
Wakeham, Lord 4, 22
Wakeham Commission 4, 22, 70, 71, 73, 75, 76
Wales: devolution 3
Wales Office 4
Ward, Claire, MP 79
Watson, Mike, MSP 126
Welfare, Damien 124
Welsh Affairs, Commons Select Committee, reports
    171
Welsh Assembly *105*
Westminster Hall 34, 40, 47, 48, 51, 73, 76, 82,
    111
Whetnall, Andrew 126
whips 16, 23, 26, 27, 52, 55
Whitemoor Prison 118
Williams of Crosby, Rt Hon Baroness 125
Wilson, Andrew, MSP 126
Wilson, Sir Harold, Baron 6
Wolfson of Marylebone, Lord 124
Women's National Commission 124
Woodhouse, Professor Diana 117, 121, 122, 124
Wright, Tony, MP 125
written questions 52-3, 58, 59, 71, 110
Young, Rt Hon Sir George, MP vii, 125